Complexity and Social M

Chesters and Welsh are exemplary of a new breed of scholar-activists [...] crossing the traditions and methods of the social sciences with the knowledges and concepts developed in the movements to create wonderful new hybrids.

Michael Hardt, co-author of
Empire and Multitude

This book fuses two key concerns of contemporary sociology: globalisation and its discontents with the 'complexity turn' in social theory.

The authors utilise complexity theory to analyse the shifting constellation of social movement networks that constitute opposition to neo-liberal globalisation. They explore how seemingly chaotic and highly differentiated social actors interacting globally through computer-mediated communications, face to face gatherings and protests constitute a 'multitude' not easily grasped through established models of social and political change.

Drawing upon extensive empirical research and utilising concepts drawn from the natural and social sciences, this book suggests a framework for understanding mobilisation, identity formation and information flows in global social movements operating within complex societies. It suggests that this 'movement of movements' exhibits an emergent order on the edge of chaos, a turbulence that is recasting political agency in the twenty-first century.

Both topical and timely, this unique book will appeal to students and researchers across the social sciences, humanities and the discipline of cultural studies with an interest in the complexity of global movements and social change.

Graeme Chesters is based in the Department of Peace Studies at the University of Bradford. His research looks at the theories and practices of transformative movements, including work on anti-capitalism, global civil society and global complexity, social movement networks, frame analysis, identities and difference. He has also worked with a variety of social movements, NGOs and campaign groups.

Ian Welsh is based in the School of Social Sciences at the University of Cardiff. His current research examines global social movements, globalisation and risk, and socio-environmental change. His other research interests include the social acceptability and public understanding of science in the areas of nuclear power and biotechnology.

International Library of Sociology
Founded by Karl Mannheim
Editor: John Urry
Lancaster University

Recent publications in this series include:

Risk and Technological Culture
Towards a sociology of virulence
Joost Van Loon

**Reconnecting Culture, Technology
and Nature**
Mike Michael

Adorno on Popular Culture
Robert R. Witkin

Consuming the Caribbean
From Arwaks to Zombies
Mimi Sheller

**Crime and Punishment in
Contemporary Culture**
Clarie Valier

States of Knowledge
The co-production of social
science and social order
Shelia Jasanoff

After Method
Mess in social science research
John Law

Brands
Logos of the globol economy
Celia Lury

The Culture of Exception
Sociology facing the camp
*Bulent Diken and
Carsten Bagge Lausten*

Visual Worlds
*John Hall, Blake Stimson and
Lisa Tamiris Becker*

Time, Innovation and Mobilities
Travel in technological cultures
Peter Frank Peters

Complexity and Social Movements
Multitudes at the edge of chaos
Graeme Chesters and Ian Welsh

Complexity and Social Movements
Multitudes at the edge of chaos

Graeme Chesters and Ian Welsh

 Routledge
Taylor & Francis Group

LONDON AND NEW YORK

First published 2006
by Routledge
2 Park Square, Milton Park, Abingdon, Oxon OX14 4RN

Simultaneously published in the USA and Canada
by Routledge
270 Madison Ave, New York, NY 10016

*Routledge is an imprint of the Taylor & Francis Group,
an informa business*

Transferred to Digital Printing 2007

© 2006 Graeme Chesters and Ian Welsh

Typeset in Sabon by
Newgen Imaging Systems (P) Ltd, Chennai, India

British Library Cataloguing in Publication Data
A catalogue record for this book is available from
the British Library

Library of Congress Cataloging in Publication Data
A catalog record for this book has been requested

ISBN10: 0–415–34414–X (hbk)
ISBN10: 0–415–43974–4 (pbk)

ISBN13: 978–0–415–34414–2 (hbk)
ISBN13: 978–0–415–43974–9 (pbk)

Publisher's Note
The publisher has gone to great lengths to ensure the quality of this
reprint but points out that some imperfections in the original
may be apparent

Printed and bound by CPI Antony Rowe, Eastbourne

Contents

Figures

Acknowledgements

With thanks to *all* those who took time from producing the global movement milieu to engage with our research. Without this generosity what we have written would not have been possible – the work is our interpretation and we hope that it resonates with both respondents' and participants' sense of global movement in the twenty-first century. Thanks to our partners, families and friends who have lived with and supported us through this project and the related periods of absence. Without these relationships, we would have had neither the momentum nor the inspiration to finish this work.

This research was supported by the Leverhulme Trust, through the award of a Special Research Fellowship, which provided crucial space in which to re-think the relationship between complexity, social movements and civil society. The empirical research presented was also underpinned by research grants from the ESRC (R000223486) and the British Academy (LRG-33561).

A period of study leave from the Cardiff School of Social Sciences was an invaluable contribution in producing a working draft. Thanks to Jackie Swift for her assistance in preparing the manuscript for submission and Constance Sutherland at Taylor & Francis for her enthusiasm, patience and insistence upon a 'final' date for submission.

Ian Welsh

To Gwyneth, Dylan and Joel, thank you for reminding me of the other worlds that are possible and the need to struggle for them. To Molly and Jess, as I promised your names are in the book.

Graeme Chesters

Preface

This is a work of theory engaging with the increasing relevance of complexity for the social sciences in the context of neo-liberal globalisation. This theoretical work arises from decades of joint experience of, participation in and commentary on grassroots movements and activism. It is thus also a 'non-manifesto' addressing what we see as the emergent dynamics of social change in the early twenty-first century. We offer the book simultaneously to an academic and activist audience as an invitation to recognise in the present a sets of stakes which have been repeatedly declared throughout history, the emergent properties associated with contemporary global dynamics and the reconfiguration of these as social forces with the transformative potential to realise the 'other worlds' that are not only possible but irresistible. If there is to be a social science of complexity worthy of the name then appreciating such long-cycle iterations in increasingly open natural and social systems is crucial. Such work is vital if future orientations are to transcend the cyclical repetitions of boom–bust/war–peace/in group–out group which characterised the long twentieth century and which rapidly re-emerged following the hollow claims of a 'new world order' – an order which quickly degenerated into disorder. We clearly prefer order on the edge of chaos to this sad repetition of 'my/our civilisation is better than yours' bloodshed of the innocent.

As a 'non-manifesto' there is no blueprint here, though there are many ideas for other forms of 'order' associated with minoritarian thinkers. The arguments advanced point towards ways of relating which realise human potential, prioritise the social and end the rule of economics as a discipline by subordinating it to 'democratically' co-ordinated social forces. As this is a 'non-manifesto' it is open to dialogical engagement rather than being a 'you are either for this or against it' statement. We anticipate *not* being read in this manner but declare a willingness to respond in kind if this is necessary and has creative potential.

We write as critically engaged actors in a style aimed at accessibility, whilst aiming to avoid violence to sophistication and nuance. In doing so, we hope a respect for academic detail is balanced by respect for the theoretical significance of the day-to-day understandings of countless activists and engaged citizens. In an attempt to be faithful to both, we use a combination of key extracts from activist discourses, detailed endnotes and the URLs of significant online resources. In these ways we offer the reader access to many of the sources underlying our take, which is offered in full recognition of our own limits and fallibility as humans confronted by the unfolding of complex systems.

If we contribute to the quest for viable meta-narratives fit for a post-enlightenment world where no centre can hold because there is no centre then that is more than enough.

Graeme Chesters, Bradford, 2005
Ian Welsh, Cardiff, 2005

1 Introducing global movements

This book argues that the Globalisation Movement operates as a strange attractor reconfiguring public opposition to global neo-liberalism whilst simultaneously creating 'spaces' where Alternative Globalisation pathways are fused through the multiplicity of engaged actors. This is not an anti-movement, this is not a movement that can be subordinated to national analytical frameworks, this is not a movement that is going to go away. Sociologically this is not a movement that can be engaged with using the standard tool box. This is a network movement actor – or more precisely a network of networks. This is a movement promoting 'the commons' and 'commoners' in North and South through a cumulative process of capacity building that attaches social force to issues normally marginalised in western societies. This movement is a historical iteration of similar forces and concerns that have surfaced periodically for centuries.

This time the movement is millions strong and has mobilised the biggest demonstrations ever witnessed within 'representative' (*sic*) democracies. This is a movement founded in the jungles of Chiapas on principles of inclusion and dialogue, not Jihad as a political strategy, yet it is portrayed as a terrorist front. The movement of movements is portrayed like this as an act of desperation by those who recognise its emergent properties and potential to systematically perturbate dominant discourses and ideologies of neo-liberalism.

Less starkly, this is a movement that prefigures social forms, social processes and social forces which will become normalised as mobility and the information age redistribute the affinities historically associated with space and place. An anatomy of social forms articulating 'interests' which exceed the capacity of 'the system' is discernible within the apparent chaos of the summit sieges best known through the place names Washington, Seattle, Prague, Melbourne, Genoa and Gleneagles.

It is an anatomy even more clearly apparent within the less well-known World Social Forum movement. Combined, these legitimation stripping and proactive capacity-building forces declare the 'other world that *is* possible' and which at times lies surprisingly close to the surface in terms of potentiality. This is a movement pursuing a new cultural politics not a new political culture, recognising that political offices shape people when divorced from cultural accountability. This is a movement of and from the margins operating in and for itself, rendering tangible a 'planetary action system' by declaring collective stakes obscured by the chimera of individual free choice.

This is the movement that can not only constrain the juggernaut of modernity but reconfigure it and reorientate it – this is the on-going expression of the 'green post-modernism' evoked in the mind of Scot Lash (1990) by events in Leipzig in 1989. To green have been added red, black, pink, orange, and purple as social justice, radical flank, tactical frivolity and populist rejections of 'rigged' elections assert their rights via street presence.

This then is going to be a 'big' book within a 'normal' word limit. It is a book of empirically informed theory or theoretically informed empirical enquiry depending upon one's predilections. Between us we have almost five decades accumulated experience of engagement within, and commentary upon social movements utilising forms of direct action. As privileged participant observers we are more alert to the emergent anatomy we perceive and we would hope therefore, to be better able to discern strengths *and* weaknesses.

As academics, we are profoundly aware that many of the key analytical and conceptual approaches applied to social movement studies are incapable of addressing complex global movement dynamics. We have found the terms 'reflexive framing', 'plateau', 'ecology of action' and 'parallelogram of forces' useful devices through which to understand this emergent, at times bewildering and counter-intuitive, movement milieu and it's relations with 'mainstream' institutions. There is no panacea on offer here, just an opening out onto an immanence fuelled by a widely distributed intensity of feeling sedimented in the daily life of millions of human subjects confronted by 'life in fragments' (Bauman 1995). Portraying how these diverse intensities become mobilised as a common cause, how subjects become actors whilst recognising and respecting difference lies at the heart of our project. We draw on the work of known minoritarian thinkers Gregory Bateson, Alberto Melucci, Gilles Deleuze and Felix Guattari and the countless 'unknown' minoritarians encountered through web-lists, social forum events, formal research projects and the social events that constitute the 'movement'.

Whilst this is a terrain littered with complex terms and languages, we endeavour to remain transparent without doing violence to the underlying intellectual and academic stakes. We make no claims to being cognoscenti but regard ourselves as intelligent users attempting to render tangible the processes underlying complex concepts revealing their relevance in a world constituted by tradition, breach and bifurcation.

This is not a definitive account of the actions of the movement (see *Notes from Nowhere* 2003) but an analytical account of the process of emergence, consolidation and extension of a network movement. Our account draws on cases where we are data rich enabling us to delineate processes which typify the global movement milieu. In effect, we offer a qualitative sociology of the philosophical postulates of *Empire* and *Multitude* advanced by Hardt and Negri (2000, 2004) rendering tangible the agency and constitutive processes immanent within their works. We turn now to outline the key terms and concepts developed substantively in subsequent chapters.

This movement has divided the social movement studies community with major commentators asserting the continued primacy of the nation state as an analytical focus over the less clearly defined global domain. We stand resolutely with the latter trend emphasising the ascendancy of a global institutional nexus exercising a legislative 'trickle down effect' with direct impacts upon the degrees of legislative freedom left open to national polities. Notions of a global hegemony capable of orchestrating this global domain to resonate with its national political and economic interests underestimate the dependency of the sole standing super power upon active alliances (Lawson 2005). Whilst the global nexus remained uncontested, traditional power broker moves remained viable but the contestation of the global institutional domain dating from the 1990s began to render the associated stakes visible to increasingly diverse publics. The degrees of freedom evident at the level of global summitry from the 1980s onwards received their first challenges and checks within the public sphere.

The credibility of global institutions dating from the mid-twentieth century including the United Nations, World Bank, and International Monetary Fund have all been challenged by unfolding events and the application of social force. Throughout this work we argue that the accretion of social force around these global stakes represents the consolidation of a global civil society/sphere. We render this apparently inchoate process accessible by identifying a nested set of network actors linking together elements of national civil societies from more than one hundred nations within a bottom-up, collectively accountable process of aesthetic expression, interest representation, conflict and collaboration. Together these social forces constitute an 'alternative globalisation movement' with both proactive policy relevant agendas and a processual form consistent with the material conditions characterised by notions of network societies.

This is a landscape inhabited by little-known actors with Peoples Global Action (PGA) and The World Social Forum movement (WSF) being two of the more important network hubs, from and around which cluster geo-regional and city Social Forum movements. This network of networks has the capacity to generate focussed 'plateau events' which simultaneously fuse significant numbers of people around a common aim in single or multiple locations. Whilst mobilisations against the Iraq 'war', various 'trade rounds' and international summits are prominent examples, the pro-active endeavours of the WSF represent a deeper and longer running up-welling of grass roots sensibilities confronted by the retrenchment in social programmes central to the international order. This is a conflict structured around the meaning of the human species as a zoonpoliticon coming to terms with the fact that human kind has indeed become a force of nature directly influencing the ecological integrity of the planet. Slogans such as 'Kill Capitalism Before It Kills the Planet' are rhetorical expressions of the first 'planetary action system' to assume a tangible social form capable of declaring globally collective stakes whilst asserting the right to 'think local and act global'. The residual and emergent local commons can only be secured at the global level as the misguided decade of thinking global and acting local reveals.

Theoretically we base our stance upon the work of Gregory Bateson, Gilles Deleuze and Felix Guattari, and Alberto Melucci, minoritarian writers we regard as social complexity theorists (Chesters and Welsh 2005). Deleuze and Guattari, in particular, deploy a lexicon of terms and concepts which are often counter-intuitive and subject to 'conceptual drift or refinement' as their usage develops. We are not concerned here with delineating specific views on precise meanings, interpretations or usages but with rendering tangible some of the key relationships and concepts identified by these writers as material processes. In doing so we trace key terms, such as plateau and framing, back to the work of Bateson and foreground his influence. We in effect argue that globalisation renders the work of Bateson and Deleuze and Guattari more tangible as the importance of material, symbolic, cultural, social and economic flows leave their marks on national societies. What were once thought of as discrete nations are increasingly recognised as 'open systems' in terms of complexity theory just as the 'closed' eco-systems of planet earth are now recognised as 'open systems' by the natural sciences.

The fundamental problematic confronting all social theory involves coming to terms with the global ascendancy of the neo-liberal capitalist axiomatic established in the aftermath of Soviet Communism. The promised end of history (Fukyama 1989) ushering in a coherent unfolding of liberal ascendancy and orthodoxy based on rational market actors has clearly stalled as capital recognises its autonomy from state forms. Deleuze and Guattari's notion of the state being confronted by an exterior 'war-machine' becomes more tangible as specific states are required to conform to structural adjustment packages, states become powerless over the images broadcast into their space and when confronted by an increasingly nomadic science which secure atomic weapons for 'rogue states' amidst rationally secure safeguard regimes.

At much more mundane levels the role of the nomad central to Deleuze and Guattari and Melucci (1989) also appears as a tangible emergent social force. Leaving aside deeper theoretical stakes and adopting a more pragmatic stance, these terms *appear* more tangible in 'turbo-capitalisms' neo-liberal phase. As Urry (2000) demonstrates, life has become far more mobile, a mobility constitutive of diasporas of meaning impacting on behavioural patterns. Part of the social complexity of globalisation arises from the operation of these increasingly nomadic trends as the life-long link between individual/place/country begins to be attenuated: overseas retirement; migration to economies where affordable child support can secure career continuity; educational mobility and web-cam prompted migrations are signs which, should they become trends, will significantly transform the social and the political. Such 'life style' nomadism occurs alongside 'work force' nomadism associated with global labour markets (Obando-Rojas *et al.* 2004) as the mobility of things, people and images intensifies constituting increasingly complex open systems out of once 'closed' national systems (of signification).

Just as national media constituted the nations we all imagined (Anderson 1989) we were part of, global media increasingly constitute the global we imagine we are part of. The *production* of globalisation has both economic and sign value (Lash and Urry 1994) but both are produced through working human agents embodying both the conscious and unconscious mind. The meanings attached to the material products of this process are constituted in multiple competing interpretations. An important part of our argument is that the Alternative Globalisation Movement (AGM) represents the first social expression of a global interpretation from 'below', a social force recognised as potentially 'counter hegemonic' by advocates of 'turbo-capitalism' (see Chapter 3). The multiplicity of actors within the AGM, the explicit attempt to forge a global civil society, the 'North–South' aspirations, and increasing sophistication as a global network agent transcend labour internationalism drawing diverse masses onto the streets far in excess of anything that might result from work place politics short of general strikes. Issues of scale apart we also argue that the AGM both constitutes and taps into an immaterial form of withdrawal (see Chapter 2).

Deterritorialisation

The mobility underpinning these emergent trends reflects the opening up of physical borders through the imperative of deregulation central to the prevailing capitalist axiomatic. This places states in a contradictory location in terms of traditional notions of interest representation. States simultaneously advance the globalisation agenda as the only game in town whilst pledging to pursue the interests of their rapidly changing and diversifying civil societies. The resultant tensions multiply the demands made upon citizens who are increasingly urged to accept the responsibilities and challenges by adopting increasingly flexible and reflexive repertoires of self involving the discerning exercise of increasing choice. The potential coalitions of interests multiply as the once firm boundaries constituting social groups and actors are subject to increasing rapid perturbation as 'All that is solid melts into air'. Under such conditions the notion of planes of immanence introduced by Deleuze and Guatarri assume tangible forms as states and global institutions combine to define globally extensive sets of rule-bound domains establishing the primacy of the prevailing capitalist axiomatic over local customs, traditions and rules.

Historically this process has been in train since at least the 1980s when Touraine argued that the scientific technocracy once dependent upon the state had become independent of it (Touraine 1983). The nuclear domain was in effect one of the first in which global regulatory reach (Welsh 2000) *had* to be established if the peaceful uses of atomic energy were to be extended to the developing world with the promise of no proliferation of nuclear weapons. The anatomy of global regimes establishing what had to be achieved whilst leaving some variability in how this was to be done within particular countries has subsequently spread to other areas including financial and economic domains. The originating global nexus is constituted by large organisations composed of discrete divisions, which collectively express the potential immanent within each institution. This involves managing sets of social relations: within institutions; between institutions; between governments; finance; banking; media and representatives of national and global civil societies.

Ultimately, the projected potentiality of this global institutional nexus is carefully honed through external relations and marketing divisions to present a positive immanence within the public sphere. This is a process of deterritorialisation which seeks to establish the universal benefits of the prevailing axiomatic removing barriers to its implementation, effectively rendering space a 'smooth' obstacle-free surface. At the meta level deterritorialisation establishes this positive potential as dominant discourses such as 'progress' and 'modernisation'. These discursive surfaces conceal attempts to reassert a degree of control over the process by particular divisions within an institution or efforts of other corporate players to reassert influence by reterritorialising, redefining the associated institutional stakes and identifying new external terrains requiring 'smoothing' by deterritorialisation. The potential emphasised is the win–win face of globalisation as freedom, prosperity, choice and affluence.

Reterritorialisation

Against this deterritorialisation have to be set the roles of pressure groups, consumer societies, unions, social movement organisations (SMOs) social movements and network actors engaged in national and global civil society initiatives. Here, it is perhaps useful to think of the schizophrenia invoked by Deleuze and Guatarri in relation to capitalism in terms of the multiple and conflicting citizenship roles (Turner 2001) expected of individuals under the prevailing axiomatic. The worker, soldier, parent, carer, lover, consumer or homemaker becomes in effect the singularity where these multiple demands and expectations become rendered material in a life. The social and cultural negotiation of the meanings associated with those lives becomes more complex as the amount of time available for such sense making declines. Confronted by the smooth pace of deterritorialised global regimes of scientific risk regulation and free market accumulation strategies, there are multiple attempts to draw lines in the sand in order to re-establish boundaries, both figurative and literal. The notion of reterritorialisation applies to such attempts to re-appropriate both meaning and influence over the prevailing axiomatic.

As such, deterritorialisation and reterritorialisation are radical variants of the liberal notions of dis- and re-embedding advanced by Giddens (1990, 1991). Unlike the process of re-embedding, which as Bauman (1993) notes can never completely reinstate that which was dis-embedded, reterritorialisation is not tied to operate within the prevailing axiomatic but is part of a 'war machine' exterior to and antipathetic toward it. It is in this sense that we adopt the language of Deleuze and Guattari to denote a process of emergence operating through and around the AGM as a strange attractor with the potential to reconfigure the prevailing capitalist axiomatic, by constituting a counter-hegemonic social force consolidating bottom-up experience of the fragmentary life imposed by global flows. There are some complex processes of translation involved here which stray far into the fields of discourse, discursive construction, contestation and the formulation of viable collective stakes counterposed to individual free choice models.

It is useful to think of this process of reterritorialisation operating through a range of actors ranging from classically conceived pressure groups, SMOs, to social movements and networks actors such as PGA undertaking 'free acts' (Eve *et al.* 1977). The key process of translation within this linked chain of interest representation involves the rendering of particular interest as general interest through the identification of a 'common enemy' (Castells 1997) and declaration of transcendent symbolic stakes (Melucci 1989, 1996a,b) sufficiently coherent to constitute collective actors from multiple identities. This immediately surpasses social movement theorisations dependent upon the existence of a collective identity – criteria substantively questioned since the 1970s (Stallings 1973).

Whilst pressure groups and SMOs predominantly pursue single issue campaigns, social movement (Welsh 2000, 2002) and network actors (Chesters 2003a, Welsh 2004) not only locate single issues within issue clusters but also situate (territorialise) them in relation to the systematic operation of the prevailing axiomatic. Thus, whilst 'anti-nuclear' movements were incorporated into the political interest representations of developed nations as movements expressing concerns over risks, other concerns over (post)colonial exploitation of uranium, native peoples rights, human rights, civil liberties and a range of gender issues were substantively ignored (Welsh 2001). An important part of our argument here is that network actors such as PGA operate within the intertices of established networks through a rhizomatic constellation of 'actors' whom we term internationals or free radicals.

These critically reflexive individuals follow principles designed to promote non-hierarchical social interaction and negotiation of shared meanings between diverse constituencies. As we argue subsequently, this gives the contemporary AGM more depth and breadth than the 'new left' or 'counter culture' associated with the 1960s as North and South are iteratively networked through recurrent events. In this sense we are arguing that the movement milieu is overcoming the limitations arising from the failure to sediment its aspirations within a viable culture (Lash and Urry 1994). The AGM is predicated upon both virtual and face-work interaction which when combined constitute global flows through the agency of multiple actors. The laminar nature of these flows reflects the growing sophistication and complexity of global movement phenomenon.

Complexity theory

Following the emergence of chaos and complexity theory within the natural science (Chesters 2004b) there has been a steady accumulation of social scientific engagement. This has moved through relevance to quantitative empirical social science (Eve *et al.* 1997, Byrne 1998); metaphorical extension for theory building (Thrift 1999); recognition of emergent social complexity (Urry 2004, Chesters and Welsh 2005) and complexity impacts upon humankind via genomic science (Wynne 2005). This is far from a definitive list but underlying it are a number of points worth elaborating in relation to our earlier remarks about our minoritarian theorists of social complexity.

First, it becomes increasingly clear that the initial conditions of a process or event are 'irrecoverable' but shape subsequent paths and expressive forms. In terms of social theory there are then no founding moments which can be known, but can only be established post-hoc and are always contested. In Deleuzian terms they are particular moments of becoming ossified in time by the attribution of meanings, values and so on. Put another way, founding moments are myths.

Second, as in quantum mechanics, the observer and the observed cannot be detached from one another rendering observation and knowing an *ontological* event. Freedom and free acts become usable terms for science and philosophy. In Deleuzian terms: 'ontology first'.

Third, feedback, particularly iterative forms, enabling a system (social or otherwise) to fold over on itself permits the exhibition of emergent properties and *new* forms of organisation. Some regard the turbulence of feedback as primary and the material and abstract laws of science as secondary reflections. In Deluzian terms 'nomad science' maintains a commitment to becoming whilst 'royal science' ossifies becoming in disciplinary laws.

Fourth, that the appearance of order on the edge of chaos is not confined to natural systems such as tectonic plates storing latent energy which is released cataclysmically but applies equally to the perpetuation of established notions of social order through systemic institutional dominance. In Deluzian terms then, social movements are rendered as a nomadic war machine of renewal.

Fifth and finally, qualitative sociology has always argued that society is the product of an almost infinite myriad of individual interactions. Given this, micro changes in the rules and conventions shaping social interaction can have enormous amplitude. In Deluzian (2004) terms difference is determinate in the final instance. (After Eve *et al.* 1997: xi–xxvii, 269–280.)

The interactionist insight mentioned in the final point is *not* an adequate explanatory device in terms of the systemic, collective syncopation of the myriad individual micro changes evoked, however. This involves processes of conscious rational strategy, subjective sensibilities and unconscious aspirations which we address in subsequent chapters through a conceptual cluster of 'reflexive framing', 'plateau' and 'ecology of action' developed since 2000 (Chesters and Welsh 2002, 2004, 2005, Chesters 2003a, Donson *et al.* 2004, Welsh 2004).

Reflexive framing

Reflexive framing refers to the sense-making practices of actors necessary to situate themselves in relation to a domain. In face-work situations this is a complex process utilising all the human senses to process multiple signals in the context of the observers' pre-established knowledge(s), predispositions and prevailing subjective state. The advent of Computer Mediated Communications (CMC) significantly alters the framing capacities of actors (individual and collective) and academic researchers. The capacity to record, review, re-sequence, retrieve, time shift and 're-perform' events marks, we argue, a significant shift in the representational sophistication of the movement milieu, the degree of 'connectivity' possible between movement actors and some erosion of the historic disparity in surveillance between the security state and activists (see Chapter 3).

Reflexive framing is a means of analytically addressing actors' increasing engagement with the global in the context of emergent 'planetary action systems' (Melucci 1996a) – a process distinct from national frame alignment within established political opportunity structures. Reflexive framing also marks a departure from dominant sociological uses of 'reflexivity' and 'reflexive' associated with Beck, Giddens and Lash (1994) which in different ways, operationalise the term in relation to 'knowledge' and knowledge processing practices (Welsh 2000: 20–26). Whilst Lash recognises the importance of aesthetic registers in the mimetic process constituting critical reflection this is a 'second moment', which leaves cognitive processes in a position of primacy (McKechnie and Welsh 2002). Reflexive framing addresses the ontological nature of cognition by recognising the importance of aesthetic primacy. Beyond this, aesthetic registers are expressions of 'identity' or 'self' communicative competences which become vital in contexts lacking a common language (Chapter 3).

Methodologically 'images' of such interaction raise issues of interpretation and analysis which the extension of the term 'text', common within media and cultural studies, to visual media belies. In intellectual terms Derrida's assertion that nothing exists outside of text begins to be attenuated by the capacity to produce multi-media recordings evocative of a range of responses independent of a reader's capacity to engage with text as grammar, syntax and so on. There is a spectral immediacy and audible amplification of context in digital video capture (through off picture sound, for example) which it is difficult to reduce to text (Chesters 2000).

The availability and portability of CMC also democratises genres which have tended to be the preserve of the 'great and the good'. The 'bi-opic' mixture of personal narrative, life experience and reflection upon events and issues is no longer the preserve of senior political figures but a mode of expression widely available. Political minders and press officers are well aware of the impact that media portrayals have upon the sense of 'self' of their charges. Reflexive framing recognises the individual and collective significance of a range of media portrayals within the movement milieu. Compared to the mainstream political milieu where media promi-nence reinforces the 'me, my, I' ego-certainty of politicians, we argue that the movement media milieu militates against this through careful attention to process and the availability of sanctions consistent with underlying principles (Chapter 6). As such reflexive framing is a necessary condition for the constitution of plateaux of resistance, creative expression of the emergent parallelograms of forces (Chapter 7) and the praxis associ-ated with the ecology of action while founding a 'planetary action system' (Chapter 8).

These claims are explored in subsequent chapters but their theoretical antecedents are addressed here for the theoretically inclined. This involves an outline account of the relationship between British social-anthropologist Gregory Bateson, US interactionist Ervin Goffman, and the Italian social movement theorist Alberto Melucci, and opens out to the relevance of Deleuze and Guatarri (Chesters and Welsh 2005).

Bateson: applying frames at home

Bateson (1973/78) was one of the first anthropologists to recognise the analytical importance of culture, cultural codes, practices and customs 'at home' in order to render visible the embedded 'habits of mind' (Bateson's term for a paradigm) blunting social, political and policy 'flexibility' in the face of change. This move reflected his sensitivity to the initial 'modern' formalisation of environmental concerns including climate change and his lifelong engagement with systemic processes of change rather than replication. Bateson identified the dominance of: us *against* the environment; other people the primacy of the sub-global actors (e.g. me, my firm, my nation etc); control over the environment; perpetual belief in the frontier mentality; economic determinism and reliance on technology as key elements of the habit of mind to be avoided (Bateson 1973/78: 468).[1] This dominant habit of mind was so dangerous as to threaten the future of human civilisation.

Against this Bateson advocated an 'ecological habit of mind' based in the acceptance of a universal human subject interacting with both social and natural realms,[2] arguing 'that we should trust no policy decisions which emanate from persons who do not yet have that habit' (1973/78: 437). Bateson's postulated Ecology of Mind is complex and this has no doubt contributed to the paucity of commentary upon his thinking within the social movement literature. Another factor here is that many of the emergent processes addressed by Bateson have taken decades to assume recognisable material forms and expressions, a process significantly enhanced by the post-cold war re-deployment of technical monitoring techniques from military to environmental 'targets'.

Bateson builds a model of human behaviour far more complex than rational actor models by melding cognitive capacities and process within the affective domain that is emotion. In so doing he argues that the signs and symbols associated with formal rationality are cultural criteria selected on the basis of affective aesthetic preferences. He thus warns against accepting the formal logic of any culture or civilisation as expressed in 'hard laws', noting that such laws ossify past frames and preferences as strengths masking their transformation into weakness under changed material circumstances. To Bateson such transitions, or phase shifts, tend to be obscured by behavioural science's pre-occupation with establishing universal constants and laws equivalent to units of measurements such as mass and length within the physical sciences.

Against this, he argues for a model within which energy plays a central part in determining human behaviour. Energy is used in a variety of senses by Bateson from notions of metabolism (1973/78: 28) to more emotional states of being that become patterned through culture representing 'the emotional setting of all the details of behaviour'. The affective domain is thus perceived as central to 'satisfaction and dissatisfaction of the individuals' in a group (1973/78: 39).[3] Collectively this gives rise to an ethos 'a culturally standardized system of organization of the instincts and emotions of the individuals' (1973/78: 81).[4]

Bateson argued that 'a sense of individual autonomy, a habit of mind somehow related to what I have called *free will*, is an essential of democracy' (1973/78: 138).[5] This corresponds closely with the sociological importance subsequently attributed to 'free acts' within complexity theory (Eve *et al.* 1997). For Bateson individual 'free will' becomes aggregated into collective cultural forms through acts of communication constituting shared meaning and solidarity. Bateson emphasises the increasing sophistication of human communication that subordinates responses to hard-wired, chemical messengers (such a pheromones) to the socially selected 'mood signs of another' (such as perfume). Individuals become aware of such communicative signs as a signal 'which can be trusted, distrusted, falsified, denied, amplified, corrected and so forth' (1973/78: 151). Bateson thus lays the foundations for Goffman's subsequent notions of 'natural' and 'social' frames and the process of keying and re-keying frames within a 'strip of activity' (Goffman 1974/86). Bateson's notion of communication is central to our use of reflexive framing and it is to this we now turn.

Bateson: communication as multi-layered activity

Bateson emphasises the range of communicative means at human disposal, the variability within each and the limits of both textual forms and linguistic structures. Communication is regarded as a multi-layered activity containing both substantive rational meaning and effect. Tone of voice, pace of delivery, rhythm, accompanying facial expression and so on are vital components of the communicative process shaping behavioural responses by stimulating energy. Word and text apart he recognised that 'our iconic communication serves functions totally different from those of language and, indeed, performs functions which verbal language is unsuited to perform', commenting that 'The logician's dream that men should communicate only by unambiguous digital signals has not come true and is not likely to' (1973/78: 388). Given the centrality of communication to individual framing and group cohesion it thus follows that *an adequate theory and empirical means of investigating social movement framing cannot rely on textual sources alone[6] and must endeavour to engage with the multi-layered nature of the framing process as it occurs in specific sites and across time.*

The importance of this approach to framing is extended by Bateson, via Kant, to argue that the primary 'aesthetic act is the selection of a fact' (1973/78: 456) which he combines with Jungian insights to argue that the recognition of 'difference', vital to the identification of fact, 'is an idea' (1973/78: 457). The maintenance of healthy homeostatic systems thus become crucially linked to difference, the ability to communicate difference, to recognise and respond to difference for Bateson.[7] Bateson's pre-occupation with this complex terrain arises from his scepticism of political, administrative and economic elites with immensely powerful technologies and techniques at their disposal to recognise and optimise systemic collective interests due to their pre-occupation with entrenched 'facts' (e.g. the primacy of economic growth) selected on the basis of entrenched 'habits of mind'. Bateson underlined this point via the deeply sedimented Darwinian notion of the survival of the fittest, complete with its implicit separation between organism and eco-system. Against this he posited the obvious wisdom that 'The unit of survival is *organism* plus *environment*. We are learning by bitter experience that the organism which destroys its environment destroys itself' (1973/78: 459).[8]

Bateson's take on framing then, is a wide-ranging and systemic one that relates to both individual processes of psychological framing and the collective consequences of these frames in selecting certain differences as categories of fact that structure human activity on the basis of both cognitive and affective processes. His commitment to anthropology at home led him to identify the importance of groups with distinct (sub)cultural identities as bearers of 'an ecology of mind' capable of recognising and reconnecting feedback loops necessary to break the negative impacts of the 'habits of mind' dominant within the prevailing political opportunity structures.

His limited prescriptive thoughts in this area included holistic philosophies eschewing the dualism between 'man' and nature and mobilisations against the Vietnam War. Areas where Bateson is substantially silent include the question of how groups communicating important messages promoting flexibility can be recognised and their 'signal' differentiated from the background noise. It is in this sense that we seek to develop an 'ecology of action' to compliment Bateson's 'ecology of mind'. For our present purposes we use Bateson's work as recounted here to concentrate upon a frame as:

1 An individual sense-making activity establishing a level of abstraction that leaves them ontologically comfortable and able to be an actor in a given situation.
2 A sense-making device that can be communicated through a variety of human expressive media.
3 That can only be *fully* comprehended by exposure to the relevant range of communicative signals.
4 The basis of forms of social solidarity.

We now turn to explore the implications of our reading of Bateson for Goffman's development of frame analysis and its application within the field of social movement studies.

Goffman, frame analysis and movements

Goffman's *Frame Analysis* (1974/86) is the subject of a formidable secondary literature. After acknowledging Bateson, Goffman denotes frame as 'definitions of a situation' being built up 'in accordance with principles of organization – at least social ones – and our subjective involvement in them'; applying the term frame to refer to such of these basic elements 'as I am able to identify' (1974/86: 10–11). Frame analysis is 'a slogan to refer to the examination in these terms of the organization of experience' but was 'too removed from fieldwork' (1974/86: 13). It is worth dwelling on what is subsumed under the words 'as I am able to identify' as a way of making some general points.

Frame Analysis draws on a wide range of forms of interaction including press articles, personal interactions and 'out of frame' events. As such it is part of a US-based formalisation of issues and stakes addressed through French 'high theory' and modern forms of discourse and conversational analysis.[9] Compared to Bateson's pre-occupation with systemic social processes of framework Goffman focuses upon individual sense making, noting the importance of sight as a form of 'quick framing' subordinating other senses (1973/78: 146). When events are rendered in terms of established frames Goffman notes that 'time often seems to drop out or collapse' when compared to the frames of those engrossed in a realm of activity where 'events unfold over time' leading to 'an outcome' (1973/78: 46). Despite his primary concern with individual sense making, Goffman's text is littered with unspecified collectivities, with 'we' and 'our society' being prominent forms, who have to choose between multiple framings of particular 'strips of activity'. These are choices between competing meanings involving 'keying' and 're-keying' which can include 'replicative records of events' (1973/78: 68), with audio and video recording having 'expanded the use of documentation' (69).

Video capture enters Goffman's schema as a new and relatively limited form of documentation akin to 'news reel footage' and documentary television output – not a ubiquitous, mundane technology. In this context Goffman's frequent invocation of visual examples from film, theatre and stage as indicators of power relations expressed in terms of both spatial designations of status (e.g. actor/audience) and attributed meaning *requires* extension. The recognition given to the potential for play and playfulness (1973/78: 45–55) and theatrical performance (1973/78: 124 et. seq.) as means of 're-keying' a set of established frames or meanings is another important area. Towards the end of *Frame Analysis*, Goffman reflects that every definition of a situation presupposes and banks upon an 'array of motivational forces' which through 'extreme measures...seems to be disruptable'. To be able to alter this balance sharply at will is to exercise power (Goffman 1974/86: 447).

Our strong case is that the AGM has exercised such power against the institutions of global neo-liberalism through an effective siege of the signs utilising play, theatrical performance and the mundane presence of CMC constitutive of plateaux of resistance maintained through an ecology of action which introduces, amongst other things, an iterative element to the framing process. We thus depart decisively from established uses of frame and framing within the social movement literature by melding Bateson and Goffman in an entirely novel manner. It is important to clarify this meld before formally addressing our substantive difference with established framing approaches.

Goffmans' appropriation of Bateson departs from his formulation in several important respects. Whilst Bateson prioritised the systemic social and cultural importance of framing, Goffman's emphasis remained limited to the individual and experiential. Whilst Goffman emphasised the importance of an 'outcome', Bateson prioritises the suspension of outcome prioritising the maintenance of intensity through 'process' (central to our use of plateau). Whilst Goffman's term 'strip of activity', and many of his examples, imply a short *duree* we define reflexive framing as an iterative collective process extending over at least a decade. While Goffman notes the importance of recording techniques for the negotiation of 'factual' accounts defining situations, we will engage with digital recording media as means of perturbating established habits of mind associated with prevailing political opportunity structures – the exercise of grass roots power by 'normal run of the mill folk' acting collectively but not in unison.

Re-framing framing: or life after master frames

This section rehearses our key points of departure from a substantive literature. As such, this is a truncated account for the purposes of clarity of exposition rather than a detailed engagement. Zirakzadeh (2000) emphasises the marked disparity between social movement analysts' uses of frame and those of Goffman emphasising Goffman's insistence on the ubiquitous nature of frames, framing processes and the capacity of all citizens to frame events. The issue of substance here is that the attribution of frame generation to special categories such as 'movement intellectuals' overlooks the framework of 'ordinary participants', a view shared by numerous commentators (e.g. Fischer 1997, Tesh 2000, Kenney 2002, Chesters and Welsh 2004). We also share Fischer's view that the framing literature lacks any clear agreement about what a frame is, how a frame is identified, recognised or used (Fischer 1997: 2), that the boundary between frames and other elements of discourse has become blurred (1997: 5), and that key scholars do not make plain how they analytically identify frames (1997: 6). Subsequent attempts to clarify the relationship between frame, ideology and discourse remain inconclusive and contradictory (see Chapter 3).

Academically we would identify the attempt to meld various competing schools of social movement thought through a unitary definition (Diani 1992) as particularly significant here. Frame analysis was initially applied to social movements by Snow *et al.* (1986) in a seminal paper addressing US SMOs. The dominance of pluralist models of interest representation and inclusion within the United States are significant features of all established US approaches. These have orientated resources and frame-work towards a prevailing national political opportunity structure. An important point of departure here is that *our work deals with network actors* (Castells 1996, Jordan 1998, Wall 1999) *intervening at the global level not social movement organisations intervening at a national level.*

Second, the development of frame analysis proceeded by identifying types of frame conducive to movement efficacy. Here the notions of 'master' and 'grievance' frames were central in setting SMOs on the path towards realisable ends within a *national polity*. Movement goals are thus addressed in terms such as 'frame alignment', 'frame resonance', 'amplification' and so on. These developments argued explicitly *against* adopting abstract master frames such as capitalist inequality on the grounds that these could not be transformed in credible grievance frames capable of resonance and amplification. Empirically, we are arguing here that the AGM has prioritised a neo-liberal capitalist axiomatic as its 'master frame' and successfully mobilised millions of people in hundreds of countries on this basis. Theoretically we are arguing that the global level of contestation has become key and cannot simply be dismissed by the reassertion of national primacy (Tarrow 2004).

Third, political opportunity structure approaches emphasise action through existing 'strong channels' neglecting the significance of Granovetter's (1973) seminal paper *'The Strength of Weak Ties'*. Summarised somewhat brutally, this paper argues that the diffusion of information across a society occurs most effectively through 'weak ties... between *different* small groups' (Granovetter 1973: 1376), that networked word of mouth is central in moving people to act upon issues reported in mainstream media and in the attribution of trust to individuals in positions of leadership (1973: 1374).[10] Understood in this way apparently marginal actors assume a position of considerable transformatory potential within and beyond networked societies via CMC (see also Castells 1996).

Fourth, that in a global world of more or less real time media coverage the 'symbolic multipliers' generated through such weak ties raise problems of legitimacy for both political leaders and global institutions. The 'compulsory visibility' and the 'new and distinctive fragility' of political leaders noted by Thompson (1995: 141) have been intensified by the exercise of movement re-framing 'power' in Goffman's sense (see also Chapter 3). These are all points implicit in the work of Melucci to whom we now turn to develop this anatomy of reflexive framing further.

Melucci and planetary action systems

The late Alberto Melucci (1989) represented the last significant European movement theorist explicitly challenging the established American schools outlined earlier on several grounds. Whilst his later work attempted to find some common ground (Melucci 1996a,b) one of us has argued elsewhere that this was ultimately incommensurable with his wider objectives (Welsh 2000). Here it is worth underlining the reductive impact of both master and grievance frames within national systems of political interest representation and their related inability to extend to global levels of analyses. Melucci's invocation of 'planetary action systems' raises important issues for movement engagement at a global level. Underlying Melucci's criticisms of established approaches are a range of factors which can be usefully addressed through the notion of immaterial interests.

This is an area attracting increasing attention from diverse perspectives' including concerns with immaterial labour (Hardt and Negri 2000, 2004) and more abstract philosophical formulations such as those of Lyotard (2004). It is our contention that Melucci, alone amongst social movement theorists, developed an analytical and interpretive schema with the sophistication and flexibility to combine these diverse concerns. Notions of immaterial labour revolve around the necessity of formalising one's personal attributes in terms of emergent labour market conditions requiring collaborative team working characteristics, networking and presentational skills in the production of 'immaterial' goods. The emergence of the information society and knowledge economy create a new subjectivity incorporating work(non)place skills within the private sphere constituting both a generalised intellect and disciplinary fear structured through flexible labour markets (Gorz 1999). To Hardt and Negri the techniques of self associated with immaterial labour are simultaneously the tools of radical transformation which 'the multitude' can now target directly at the global institutional nexus constituting 'Empire' (Hardt and Negri 2004).

Lyotard's concerns are much broader relating to the integrity of the planet upon which all life is dependent and which has become a global laboratory for scientific appropriation and economic utilisation. Orientations towards a future holding the long-term prospect of planetary extinction when the sun loses its integrity becomes a significant question for Lyotard. This philosophical concern can be rendered more tangible by addressing issues of inter-generational equity made increasingly prominent through environmentalist's interventions. The unborn are immaterial beings yet there are interests centrally important to these nascent humans with clean air, water, food and viable cultures being obvious examples. Those alive can attempt to address such immaterial needs, though doing so means abandoning certain habits of mind. Whilst more tangible, such issues remain complex and lead back to fundamental questions related to the meaning of life and human beingness. The prospect of genetic selection and human enhancement raised by genomic science intensify and extend these concerns which are in the process of being rendered as material choices within a neo-liberal eugenic axiomatic (Habermas 2003). The increasing attention to post-human, cyborg futures reflect the early material cultural capacities constituting the immaterial (Haraway 1999).

In Melucci's terms, person and planet are increasingly rendered as information through self-organising systems understood in terms of cybernetics but which simultaneously code symbolic stakes. Central here are certain stakes which *require* collective reflection as the neo-liberal axiomatic of individual choice embeds asymmetrical power relations, effectively sequestering choice and allocating it to profit orientated market forces. For Melucci these collective stakes are declared by movements acting as 'prophets' (McKechnie and Welsh 2002).

'Social movements act as signals to remind us that both the external planet, the Earth as our homeland, and the internal planet, our "nature" as human beings, are undergoing radical transformations' (Melucci 1996a: 7).

For Melucci a pre-occupation with the impact of movements upon prevailing political systems and policies diverts attention away from their role in the 'production of cultural codes' which 'is the principle activity of the hidden networks of contemporary movements' (1996a: 6). This process constitutes a cultural politics rather than a political culture signifying a transformation of both the form and content of political life pursued by 'man' (*sic*) as Marx's ultimate 'zoon politicon' – or political animal. The established dualisms 'producer/consumer', 'capitalist/worker', which structured political institutions and systems are 'breached', as the systemic effects of conflicts organised around these cultural codes produce no outright winners, offering a future of longer working hours and an extended working life.

The stresses and strains associated with the increasingly visible connections between material affluence, environmental degradation and self-betterment are rendered tangible via sensitised individuals whom Melucci encountered as a practising therapist. Like Goffman and framing, much of Melucci's writing was rather removed from field work and an important element of this work is to redress this imbalance by demonstrating the kinds of reflexive framing encountered within the AGM. Here, we find reflexive actors recognising the inescapable presence of difference transcending the old binary opposites underpinning the liberal social democratic polity and pursuing ways of achieving unity in diversity. Their success in rendering visible previously immaterial issues is underpinned by Melucci's recognition of movement as media (1996a: 36) a point developed by Atton (2002). This leads naturally into a consideration of the use of CMC and the virtual domain as a field of co-operation and conflict through which network actors engage with a global power nexus.

Movement as media

The idea that movement are media is important for our notion of reflexive framing on a number of grounds. Goffman insists that bystanders become 'deeply involved' (1974/86: 36) by events they witness. This involvement is particularly complex in the context of theatrical performance where 'multi-channel effects' (1974/86: 146) encode multiple layers of meaning *initially* appropriated by visual fast framing. Melucci's recognition of movement as media opens up the potential for movement to directly channel meaning through lifestyle encoding (social frames and prompts) and by staged acts of intervention. This is a very different sense of media relations to that developed within POS approaches where movement impact is assessed primarily through representation within mainstream media channels, leading Gamson to portray movement activists as 'media junkies' (1995: 85).

Whilst an orientation towards established media forms is one *part* of AGM strategy it is no longer an adequate representation of the totality of movement media activities. CMC have enabled 'autonomous' vehicles such as Indymedia with permanent and dialogical web presence accessible via the World Wide Web. This 'upper-echelon' enables the mounting of images and text from movement events around the world. These images and reports become discursive surfaces which are then dialogically engaged within on-going chatrooms and e-mail lists. This is a process of actively negotiated meaning constitutive of affinity, belonging and community through which multiple individual sensitivities to emergent stakes are consolidated into shared meanings between multiple identities. This virtual domain is widely portrayed as 'democratic' and presented as a metaphorical descriptor of network structures and the 'smooth space' enabling activists to strike directly at the heart of 'Empire' (Hardt and Negri 2004).

The representation of the virtual domain as inherently democratic smooth space is an over-extension ignoring not only issues of network access but also the constraints imposed via system architecture through search, access and surveillance protocols embedded in 'the machine'. The idea that the virtual domain transcends and renders irrelevant national borders is both true and false at one and the same time. Halivais's (2000) survey of the geographical locations of domain names and hyperlink connections to sites outside the national borders of the host domain revealed that the United States hosts almost 70% of domain names and the lowest proportion of hyperlinks to domains outside national borders (9%) (see also Castells 1996: 345–358). Whilst the tendency for hyperlinks to remain within host nations' boundaries is replicated in other countries, links to US domains represent the majority of extra-territorial traffic. Thus whilst the web represents a rhizomatic network structure the 'social borders have their own cartographies' (Harvey 1996: 282).

Halvais concludes by noting Simmel's (1955) point that groups based on shared interests would tend to replace groups based on physical proximity whilst emphasising that the web is relatively young. This is consistent with work on small world networks and we approach the AGM as a diverse interest group whose use of the web represents an exemplar of the kinds of intended and targeted impacts achievable by distributed network actors. As we show in Chapters 3 and 4, the role of social networks constituted and consolidated via mobility, by internationals or free radical within the AGM, do play a significant role here. These roles do not however simply replicate the dominance of frame-work by movement intellectuals but, through adherence to underlying principles originating in the geographical 'South', focus on maintaining an open process – a defining feature of multitude (see Hardt and Negri 2004: 99–105). From the 1990s onwards hacktivism and access denial protests have featured prominently within the activist milieu with many interventions supporting 'Southern' causes.

These points are important for reflexive framing because the multiple acts of laminated communication undertaken by the AGM as a media form are acts of de- and re-territorialisation of both the virtual and physical realms at both global and national levels. The World Wide Web and inter-networking are in their infancy and will undoubtedly develop in surprising and counter-intuitive ways. We are suggesting that the AGM illustrates and pre-figures part of that potential, introducing the possibility of decentralisation and forms of choice which initial US dominance appears to preclude. For present purposes, the role of CMC and reflexive framing in constituting such multi-layered decisional fora is pursued through the notion of plateau used in this work.

Plateaux, ecology of action and parallelogram of forces

> A plateau is always in the middle [*milieu*], not at the beginning or the end. A rhizome is made of plateaus... We call a 'plateau' any multiplicity connected to other multiplicities by superficial underground stems in such a way as to form or extend a rhizome.[11]
>
> (Deleuze and Guatarri 2002: 21–23)

The notion of rhizome advanced here is at once redolent of the contemporary use of network society (Castells 1996) and the embodiment within this term of a number of previous terms such as social network analyses and actor network theory/ies (Latour 1996, 1999, 2004, Law and Hassard 1999). All are descriptors for sets of relations involving agency between the mechanical/artifactual and the social. There are some important caveats to this analogy, however. Network has a connotation of fixed lines of communication or connection bounded in closed conduits. Network analyses typically represent findings diagrammatically depicting linkages and frequencies of interactions between identified and known parties. The rhizomatic differs in that it 'operates by variation, expansion conquest, capture, offshoots' (Deleuze and Guattari 2002: 21) it is this malleability and innovative potential that suggest the importance of the 'strength of weak ties' (Granovetter 1973). Part of our argument is that the AGM is a rhizomatic social form constituting a multitude as a proactive mass movement through the active recognition of difference and singularities capable of constituting plateaux.

Deleuze and Guatarri's use of plateau is derived from Gregory Bateson (1973) where it denotes a sustained plane of intensity not intended to result in any form of climactic outcome or pre-ordained conscious dénouement. Our use of the term plateau is consistent with this despite the presence of declared objectives associated with plateaux such as 'summit sieges' (Chesters 2004a, Chesters and Welsh 2004). To be absolutely clear on this point we distinguish between these acts of 'declaratory posture' and the deeper underlying commitment to specific processes within the AGM. This processual approach is *our* elaboration of 'genealogical method' prioritised by Deleuze and Guattari. Methodologically we thus engage with social movement plateaux not as single time point events associated with mobilisation cycles but as iterative stabilisations of rhizomatic forces in which a fluid, nomadic social force engages with both state forms and global institutions. In terms of engagement with these exterior forces, this is both defensive, in the sense of protecting preferred 'life-worlds', and offensive in prioritising 'other life-worlds'. In terms of internal dynamics, there is both co-operation and conflictual contestation.

Collectively reflexive framing, CMC, face-work exchanges and the iterative refinements produced through plateaux constitute an ecology of action which translates the combination of aesthetic preferences, interests and their attendant symbolic stakes and cultural codes into a planetary action system. We argue that this constitutive process operates as a parallelogram of forces aligning multiple lines of f(l)ight through which *multitudes* engage not only directly with the global institutional nexus of *Empire* but also at the multiplicity of institutional locations – *empires* if you will – constituting the axiomatic. These are themes we return to in Chapters 7 and 8. The network of networks underpinning this argument did not just emerge pre-formed on the streets of Seattle in 1999 but consolidated throughout the decade. Some sense of the precursors and prefigurative events is important in understanding the resultant meld of 'South' and 'North' and it is to this that we now turn.

2 Prefiguration and emergence

Introduction

In this chapter we document examples of the process of emergence through the AGM in terms of both mainstream and movement milieus. The treatment offered here reinforces the importance of 'retrodictive' sense making in relation to complexity events advanced by Eve *et al.* (1997). We argue this is methodologically consistent with the genealogical approach adopted by Deleuze. What emerges as important here is a systematic eye for detail and repetition over an extended period of time. Here, we argue that such repetitions evidence the multiple folding of social, economic and political systems critical to the detection of emergent phenomena (see Chapter 1).

The chapter divides this kind of evidential approach towards the immaterial into three main categories for the purposes of presentational and analytic clarity. We remind the reader that the degrees of separation imposed by us belie the growing connectivity typifying the domains we identify as important. To remain consistent with our relational model of framing we concentrate on meta-, meso- and micro-levels which for the purposes of this chapter can be thought of as relating to the geo-political, national, and global network domains. We address issues of connectivity in the concluding sections which open out onto our empirically informed interrogation of complexity and global movement.

The geo-political – 1986–1994

The end of bio-polar global politics is often regarded as a decisive founding moment and qualifies as one of the most influential myths hampering contemporary social and political science. Far from a clean break and decisive shift to an endless liberal future, the actual transition process has been extended, contested, diverse and far from 'complete'. One of us has addressed these issues in relation to the transition states of Eastern and Central Europe (Tickle and Welsh 1998, Baker and Welsh 2000, Welsh 2004) in ways which inform subsequent chapters. For present purposes however what is important is the comparatively neglected area (in terms of social theory) of development.

Throughout the 1970s and into the 1980s development programmes were an extension of the competing super-power ideologies seeking to promote societal development though centrally planned and free market variants. These efforts were aligned with the pursuit of political influence and strategic advantage within the prevailing system of International Relations. The defeat of Soviet Communism following attempts to match aggressive US arms expenditure programmes resulted in systemic collapse of Soviet overseas aid programmes. In a Deleuzian sense the global became smoother with the axiomatic of capitalist neo-liberal development prevailing. The notable exception to this was China where communism entered crisis, as indicated by events in Tiananmen Square in 1987, but preserved sufficient coherence to reject International Monetary fund (IMF)/World Bank (WB) formulas for restructuring. China effectively rejected key 'loan conditions' refusing to adopt suggested interest rate and repayment structures, factors which have underpinned the country's emergence as the dynamo of the world economy. Similar moves were subsequently made by Brazil and Argentina as the developing world became more confident in challenging IMF and WB strictures.

The humbling of the former Soviet Union massively reduced its standing and negotiating strength within executive elements of the global institutional nexus, particularly the UN. Just as the transition societies of East and Central Europe clamoured to join the EU, Russia's priority was admission to the hallowed ground of global capitalist interest representation. Admission to the G7, rendering it the G8, was a major objective of Soviet foreign policy partially achieved in 1994. Significantly, the G7 continues to meet to exercise certain key functions relating to fiscal matters. Russia's pursuit of membership of the domains of global governance was influential in limiting any residual ambitions to maintain a 'peoples' model of development in African countries, where collective agrarian and land reform approaches had been pursued throughout the 1970s. These self same ambitions ensured that diplomatic linkage inhibited the use of veto powers within the UN.

The high profile bi-lateral summits between Ronald Reagan and Mikhail Gorbachev which dominated the mid 1980s alarmed US officials not only in the Pentagon but across the Washington landscape. Militarily, there were real fears that the two presidents would autonomously announce the satellite verified deconstruction of submarine fleets which would be assembled in designated ports and cut up, live on spy-cam. Neo-conservatives within the Washington administration desperately needed to reassert business as usual by reasserting system imperatives – the pursuit of negotiation through teams of professionals acculturated by the appropriate systems. In this context speculation about Ronald Reagan's faculties probably owed as much to such right wing positioning as attempts by the left to discredit a Republican leader.

Russian quietude provides an overlooked but important backdrop to the consolidation of economic global reach in train via the General Agreement on Tariffs and Trade (GATT) by establishing the World Trade Organisation (WTO) described by some as a 'GATT with teeth' (Purdue 2000). The alignment of the American scientific, commercial, industrial, agricultural and financial economies with foreign policy is a defining feature of the Imperium that is the United States (Welsh 2005). During the 1980s this alignment began to take on more material expressions through immaterial capacities. NASA's (National Aeronautic Space Administration) recurrent funding crises resulted in a satellite gap when the space agency could not simultaneously fund technical and software system development. The resultant public–private collaboration resulted in NASA satellites' running software developed in the commercial sector. Data acquisition and remote sensing became part of the 'high frontier' identified as crucial to the United States economic and military security the protection of which was vested in a specially created institution 'Space Command'. Satellite telemetry became central to forms of mineral exploration, environmental monitoring and border security expanding the systems surveillance capacities far beyond those envisaged by Giddens (1987).

In Latin America these systems were used to regulate and police subsistence 'slash and burn' forest clearings as McDonalds clear felled huge areas legally. Thermal sensors detected the fires of slash and burn cultivators relaying co-ordinates to helicopter born interceptors. This asymmetrical deforestation excludes the poor whilst permitting the corporate sector to maximise profit extraction. Such actions underline *The Ecologist's* adoption of the notion of 'enclosure' (*The Ecologist* esp. Vol. 22, 4 & 6) as part of its critique of post-Rio sustainable development practices representing the extension of the historic practice of legally subordinating common law rights (see Notes from Nowhere 2003: 27–28).

As Purdue (2000) argues, other forms of immaterial enclosure were also underway through the establishment of trade related intellectual property rights (TRIPs) via the GATT/WTO. These rules subordinated other regimes of patent protection to those laid down by the WTO and enforced through global trade sanctions. In areas where the majority of people earned their income from the land, the extension of TRIPS to Genetically Modified (GM) seed products saw the introduction of license fees and Monsanto's 'terminator gene', which enforced an annual purchase of seed stock by ensuring that crops did not produce viable seed stock (Bowring 2003).

This massive restructuring of trading relations occurred with little recognition or comment in the European and US media. US broadcast and print treatments of foreign news without a significant 'home' angle are extraordinarily limited and the record of the broadsheet press in Europe whilst better reproduces a limited range of prominent and normative frames. Dwyer and Seddon (2002) document the majority world's dissent in the face of these and other assaults on established patterns of production, exchange and circulation of both materials and meanings. Detailed accounts of such resistance and of the lives underlying this resistance were confined to niche products. Even *The Ecologist*, a radical environmentalist magazine from the 1970s which has maintained credibility and 'market share', became a target of corporate global reach when its special issue on GM was delayed because the printer was threatened by legal action (*The Ecologist* Vol. 28, 5).

Outside political economy treatments primarily aligned with the concerns of union and organised labour organisations, feminist output represented the other most significant source of commentary on the simultaneous 'rape' of planet and people for profit. Cynthia Enloe's (1989) *Bananas, Beaches and Bases* stands out as one of the most lucid and accessible accounts of the interrelationships between sweat shop labour in the clothing industry, the formation of union free export processing zones (EPZs) the gendered hierarchy of the diplomatic core, strategic military bases and prostitution. Western feminists were in effect reflecting upon and through network connections established through the women's movement which produced 'sister' organisations across the planet – a process stimulated by US military theatre modernisation.

Of these Vandana Shiva is one of the key figures best known for her prodigious published output (e.g. Mies and Shiva 1993) but equally important for her sponsorship and work within a feminist women's collective in India. Shiva's 'Ten Commandments of Globalisation and Corporate Rule', are a striking example of her word-smithing qualities:

For citizens

1 Thou shalt have no rights to food, to water, to a safe environment.
2 Thou shalt have no rights to work, to a livelihood, to economic security.
3 Thou shalt have no other identity or morality than that of being consumers in the global marker place.
4 Thou shalt elect governments, but the governments shall not be to protect you. They will protect corporations.

For governments

5 Thou shalt give up all functions of protecting your citizens and all duties and obligations required of you by your national constitution.
6 Thou shalt consider your first duty and obligation to be to promote the freedom of transnational corporations and to take away the freedoms of your people.
7 Thou shalt take the environmental wealth of your country and citizens and hand it over for free to transnational corporations.

For corporations and business

8 If you are small and local, thou shalt disappear and make way for transnational corporations.

9 If you are global, thou shalt demand absolute rights in every country to walk in and out as you find profitable.
10 Thou shalt destroy the environment and jobs everywhere to maximise your profits and returns on investment. This will be the end towards which all governments and citizens must assist you as their highest moral duty.

(Shiva 1999: 22)

Harsh as this formalisation may read to liberal eyes it needs to be re-framed in the context of the thousands of deaths resulting from Union Carbides Bhopal explosion, the ensuing corporate denial of legal responsibility and the delays in compensation. On other continents broad equivalents exist, such as the plight of the Ogoni people confronted by the corporate might of Shell in Nigeria – there are no exceptions just repetitions. Where these repetitions are symbolically condensed through the singularity of a named activist such as Ken Saro Wiwa executed in Nigeria for opposing Shell or Chico Mendes the Latin American rubber tapper, trade unionist and environmentalist murdered by 'beef barons' they gain some discursive presence within sections of the Western public sphere. The global local is however, a 'manufactured consensus' passed through the filters of power and 'human interest' before the presses run and consequently the systemic underlying vectors elude all but the specialist reader with access to niche coverage. The laminar character of these flows of information are seldom unpacked, leaving the critical detail of human framing and agency that *produces* the material precursors immanent.

Rendering these processes tangible through deterritorialising acts remains the preserve of the Non Governmental Organisations (NGO), Social Movement Organisations (SMO), social movement and network actors central to this book. Theoretically the work of minoritarian forces within this milieu is absolutely pivotal in understanding the reconfiguration of the public sphere under (dis)informationalised neo-liberal capitalism. Before we elaborate these theoretical stakes we illustrate our argument by recounting the case of Chico Mendes.

Chico Mendes: a death foretold

Chico Mendes was shot through the head and heart at point blank range in December 1988 by a killer working for Sr. Darly Alves a contractor licensed to clear rubber bearing forest. The clearance was part of an ongoing process of land acquisition amidst spiraling prices which cross cut ancient systems of debt peonage. Land acquired under consolidation programmes had to be actively used to prevent reversion to previous from of tutelage. Clear felling and the grazing of beef stock ensured this could not happen whilst simultaneously destroying the livelihood of peon workers.

Mendes had represented the peons in the Brazilian state of Acre close to the Bolivian border. He became head of the rubber-tappers union, championing rain forest preservation and gaining international recognition including UN awards for his environmental activities. Under Mendes' leadership the indigenous workforce became increasingly orgainsed meeting armed gangs of clearance workers in force and occupying the office of the Brazilian Forest Development Institute. Armed attacks upon workers and occupiers continued with the Brazilian state failing to apprehend Darly Alvel who was wanted for murder in Parana.

In *Chico Mendes in His Own Words* he emphasized the importance of support from 'first world' environmentalists in establishing and maintaining his position within Brazil. His struggle was for social and economic justice for both landless Brazilian rubber tappers and the Brazilian environment, home to an estimated two million species vital to bio-diversity and site of bio-prospecting by big pharmaceutical companies.

(After Hecht 1989, see also Mendes 1989, Revkin 1990)

The national: Brazil

The case of Chico Mendes is theoretically interesting in the way it highlights the simultaneous pursuit of collective labour and environmental rights. This case breaks decisively with linear models of development which effectively project the assumed experience of developed nations on to the developing world. In this model, 'work place' struggle, class formation and union representation precede the development of environmental activism, which in traditional accounts is a reflection of a privileged middle class attempting to enter a greener world whilst pulling up the ladder behind them to conserve it (Tony Crosland 1974). This has been an influential stance in work addressing the relationship between social movements and development (Foweraker 1995). Mendes and the Latin American case more generally does not fit well with such stances, which are also challenged by cases within other continents where work and environment have been linked around water disputes and a range of development projects.

The global network domain

Critically the Mendes case demonstrates how CMC interventions began to be used before the World Wide Web reached its current state of development. Members of Friends of the Earth (FoE) groups were amongst those distributing e-mail, phone and fax numbers of not only Embassies and Departments of State in Brazil but also specific police stations holding activists associated with Mendes and the rubber-tappers movement. The arrival of multiple faxes declaring support for detainees and asserting their legal rights in remote

Proposals for a campaign against neo-liberalism summary:

This is the first discussion document in a process aiming at starting a worldwide campaign against neo-liberalism and globalization, which we propose to focus on the World Trade Organisation. It is addressed to networks and organisations sharing (1) a strong criticism of the globalisation process, and (2) interest in engaging in international campaigning and on trying more and better collaboration between South and North in these issues.

This proposal has been done by people within...but does not represent the opinion of these organisations. These are also involved in this discussion process, which will go on until November, where a large group of activists and representatives of different organisations will meet in Rome, in an activists' gathering parallel to the World Food Summit. For more information about the gathering in Rome, about this proposal or about the organisation involved in the discussion.

Amazonian police stations communicated not only an external social force but the prospect of external accountability. Such interventions did not save Chico Mendes but were part of an accumulating repertoire of CMC interventions. Their use by FoE groups also illustrates the overlap in the affective affiliations of members alerted to such initiatives through their overlapping involvement in other organisations. In the United Kingdom, such crossovers were significantly enhanced as direct action against road and airport developments grew through the activities of Earth First! and London RTS.

These same networks were constitutive of European wide networks (Welsh and McLeish 1996) active in the creation of the AGM. These networks included a range of NGOs, SMOs, Social Movements and Network Actors. The fusion of local, national, geo-regional and global activist communities through CMC was consolidating and subject to rapid expansion as 'word spread'. Proliferating weak ties were particularly important during this phase of network extension with casual word of mouth in face-work contexts being prominent within urban centres in the United Kingdom. Within this mixed resource base, network connectivity was already global. Exchanges within these networks formalised the initial anatomy and objectives of the nascent AGM. By 1996 e-mail lists associated with this network were actively discussing this overall strategy, including the most appropriate venue to launch the movement. Text boxes 'n' contain the substantive content of one ten page e-mail circulated early in this process. Dated June 1996 the e-mail has been anonymised to protect the originating source.

Taken together these extracts reveal something of the intent, analytical range, process orientation, South–North network ambitions, and inclusionary commitment present within the network of networks which we deal with in more detail later in this book (see Chapter 6). In terms of our account of CMC and reflexive framing we would emphasise that e-mails such as this one illustrate the process of information circulation constitutive of plateau activities. This one proved particularly potent in identifying the 1999 Seattle trade round as a potential point of intervention.

The ambition of this proposal in terms of the breadth and depth of envisaged initiative is particularly marked. The text also illustrates how this network actor situated their call within the interstices of established events which, in this case, provided a convenient future meeting point. Given the membership crossovers between NGOs, SMO and network actors, such interstitial points maximise the availability of actors, from within such organisations.

The document declares itself as a consultative discussion piece and formalises both an active agenda and background principles emphasising bottom-up approaches and the importance of not replicating 'post-colonialism' within the movement milieu.

These instances empirically demonstrate the active negotiation of meaning and common goals which takes place in what Melucci (1989, 1996a) terms 'latency periods'. During such periods movement activity is almost indiscernible in the public sphere limiting academic accounts based on scrutiny of mainstream media accounts (Rootes 1992). This underlines the methodological importance of longitudinal, qualitative engagement within the movement milieu, particularly during periods of apparent quietude.

Discussion document

1 Motivation and objectives
2 Lines of action
3 Responsibilities and participation
4 Finances
5 Possibilities for the future
6 Proposal for the discussion process.

1 Motivation and objectives

The campaign we propose, according to its motivation, would try to achieve two kinds of objectives: (a) the denunciation of globalisation and neo-liberalism, and (b) a better knowledge and a change of the perception of each other between people's movements and solidarity/environmental organisations. . . . we believe that if we want to involve organisations of such different character in a joint political work against neo-liberalism, we will also have to create a real basis for their cooperation.

For this reason, we believe it is necessary to invest part of our energies (at least at the beginning of the campaign) to facilitate a more complete and integrative analysis within the Northern solidarity/ environmental organisations, with the purpose of challenging paternalist attitudes (charitative, eco-imperialist, etc.) that are sometimes found within them. These attitudes too often assume that social change must come 'from above' (i.e., from the paternalist action of Northern organisations), undervaluing in this way the capacity of people's movements to produce positive change. This implies a real barrier for the cooperation between people's movements in the South and solidarity/environmental organisations in the North.

2   Lines of Action

To achieve these objectives, we propose a campaign with three lines of action:

A   Denunciation of neo-liberalism and globalisation
B   Mutual support
C   Educative work.

A. Denunciation of neo-liberalism and globalisation

We propose an international campaign based on non-violent direct action for denunciation, and addressed to the media. This modus operandi is based on our belief that 'gentle and diplomatic' lobby and conscientisation work has no chances of success (if done in isolation), in front of the aggresivity and power of those interested in boosting the globalisation process.

We propose to concentrate the denunciation work of the campaign on the WTO because it is the organisation with the most important role within the globalisation process, because it affects almost all countries of the world, and finally because currently there exists no international campaign against it.

In the case of the WTO we propose an 'attack and demolish'-like attitude towards the public opinion, in order to ruin its public image, combined with specific and more specialised demands within it, concerning topics such as food dumping, etc.

We think that until November we will not be able to develop (as a group) very elaborated internal demands, but we should be able to at least agree on (1) the external demands, (2) a minimum of internal demands and (3) a methodology of 'distance discussion' to keep developing demands (external and internal) in a participative and democratic way. Direct action is not a new contribution of the campaign; there are plenty of organisations involved in it. The contribution of the campaign would be: (i) offering a framework and a common platform for decentralised actions addressed to the WTO (or the institution(s) we finally choose), as did the campaign 50 years is Enough! for the actions addressed to the World Bank and the IMF; (ii) facilitate joint actions that one organisation wouldn't be able to do alone. For example, in 1999 a new negotiation round will start within the WTO. For this date we propose preparing decentralised actions and/or a big action to wish bad luck to the round.

B. Mutual support

This action line proposes mechanisms for bilateral and multilateral support among the organisations involved in the campaign.

The bilateral North–South support is no novelty in itself; many Southern organisations have cooperation agreements with NGOs in the North, which are in general structured along development cooperation projects. However, what we propose is another thing: it is about long-term institutional and political support to people's movements, a support to the strengthening of their social and political role.

At the multilateral level the campaign should – in our opinion – offer also support in the sense of securing the basic conditions that make international campaigning work possible. To this aim, we propose that it includes the access to:

1   informatic equipment and access to the internet for the organisations lacking it,
2   training in the use of electronic mail and the internet in the cases it is needed (already included in the programme of Rome).

These two points should to a great extent be covered by the potential already existing in the different networks that participate in the campaign. These networks have already built means of communication and information spreading, and hence their participation could reduce these needs, which would enable us to use more resources to cover other needs.

C. Educative work

We believe that the coming together of several networks and organisations in a common campaign offers very good possibilities to engage in supraregional educational work, which has in our opinion a high potential impact. In this sense, we propose to do:

- Joint publications (magazines, leaflets, posters) with a broad distribution
- Speakers' tours like the one planned for right after the Hunger Gathering
- Introductory seminars on social and environmental issues targeted to interested youths from large regions, with the active participation of representatives of people's movements
- Videos, exhibitions, slide series with explanatory texts.

3   ....

4   ....

5   Possibilities for the future development of the campaign

In order to explain our proposal for the long term, we must shortly analyse the kind of organisations that we would like to invite to take part in the campaign.

You will have observed that in the whole document we've proposed these to be people's movements only from the South, and solidarity/environmental organisations both in the South and in the North. We didn't even mention Northern people's movements due to several facts, mainly due to the fact that neo-liberalism has (up to now) affected the South in a much more destructive way than the North, which has caused the development of what we call here people's movements in the South much more than in the North. In fact, in our opinion these still do not exist in the North, at least in the way they do in the South.

In the North there are, in our opinion, three kinds of groups that could play a role in the campaign:

- The solidarity/environmental organisations mentioned throughout the document.
- Political parties and groups (in the traditional sense) which share the criticism of neo-liberalism, but differentiate themselves from the above mentioned by the fact that they base this criticism on traditional ideologies (exclusivist and confrontative), or by their end-goal of gaining political power. Several of these groups would probably be willing to participate in the campaign, but our position about this is

that the campaign should not be open to this kind of groups, due to previous experiences of instrumentalisation from their side.

- Finally there are groups which, being directly affected by globalisation, have not yet achieved the level of analysis and organisation that similar groups in the South have achieved. We refer to the unemployed and to small producers (both agricultural producers and small firms). These groups have the potential of creating something similar to the Southern people's movements. But we believe that this potential can only be developed by an internal process which will probably last quite a long time.

6 ....

Such engagement is central in discerning both specific repetitions and innovations and the patterning of systemic responses *both* within the movement domain *and* the public domain. The public domain responds most promptly through front line police operations, formal political debate and legislation which tends to structure dominant public discourses (see Chapter 4). At the local level the sites of concrete contestation, particularly those associated with longstanding environmental camps, attracted significant support within local communities divided over the contested development. In the United Kingdom road protests achieved iconic prominence through activists constructing tunnel complexes to avoid eviction akin to those of the Vietcong underground systems.

Carnivalesque street parties and other playful forms of protest featured in a period of prominent innovation in repertoires of action. In Seattle, the dramaturgical presence on the streets played a significant role in terms of public sphere registers with much emphasis being given to the slogan 'Teamsters and Turtles Unite' reflecting the presence of union contingents and activists dressed as turtles. Such carnivalesque performances reflect complex relations of trust and the ontological positioning of actors towards prevailing authority structures. Public performances parodying, caricaturing and lampooning 'the system' have to be understood as historically persistent forms of protest during phase shifts in public quiescence.

Entering such spaces is a step into another world, a world where symbolic coding inverts the meaning and sign value of the familiar (see Chapter 4). The genealogical engagement with this domain requires some sense of these sedimented historical states and the associated street dynamics.

Culture, carnival and critique

> To be loosely caught up in festival is to be ambivalently (dis)positioned at the *borderlines* of a given social order and its ritual (re)construction. It is to be at the crossroads between order and chaos
>
> (Pfohl 1992: 214)

The cultural domain assumes a centrality within post-modernism as a domain of critique and deconstruction, a theme also addressed from theoretical traditions derived from Marxism. Culture is simultaneously a sphere of material products and relations *and* innovative expressions of wider social contradictions and conflicts.

This ontological (re)positioning of individuals enables performative modes of intervention unthinkable in isolation and provides a vehicle for challenging elements of prevailing ideological and discursive structures. In the hands of groups whose singularity challenges normative and majoritarian identities such as white hierarchic heterosexuality, carnival is at its most potent. The continuity between pagan celebration of nature and Christian holidays reflects the religious absorption and containment of competing socialities.

In launching repertoires of action as a 'carnival against capitalism' (18 June 1999) the AGM tapped directly into the Achilles heel, the soft symbolic underbelly, of the contemporary social (dis)order around the world (*Notes from Nowhere* 2003). The historic sanitisation of carnival involved the separation and commodification of the component elements constitutive of commonality. Carnival is typified by the simultaneous public consumption of food, wine, other intoxicants, music and expressive acts of a bawdy, rebellious, celebratory nature. The control of carnival is reflected in apparently mundane cultural codes such as those governing what and how food and drink can be consumed in public places. In cases regarded as particularly threatening, cultural code is replaced by rule of law and becomes an issue of public order (Roberts 2003, Donson *et al.* 2004). This is a process which has been significantly extended since the closing decades of the twentieth century actively linking those pursuing 'green critique' with 'terrorism'. The contrast between these symbolic codings and the associated flows of meanings could not be starker.

One of the features of this book is its ability to address the production of symbolic codes through the use of qualitative data derived from multiple sites using digital recording techniques. This treatment makes explicit examples of innovative agency within movements which generate significant repertoires of action and 'frames'.

Analytically we are suggesting that carnival represents a mode of protest which invokes at a micro-interactive level the kinds of power relations associated with the theatrical by Goffman (see Chapter 1). In Foucauldian terms a 'micro-physics of power' is played out on the street as a strategic encounter between protestors and the 'security state' in ritualised forms where there are no 'untouched' passive observers. By creating a 'time between times' the AGM renders them in a particularly condensed form through the work of highly skilled and committed individuals – whom we term 'free radicals'. This is a critical form of immaterial cultural labour which teaches transferable techniques of self, acting as a conduit transposing workplace bio-politics into and onto the public sphere.

Free radicals[1] are not to be conflated with the movement entrepreneur or intellectual who promotes mobilisation around the objectives of defined social movement organisations or a consolidated political ideology (see Chapter 3). The free radical is committed to the promulgation of inclusionary processes optimising consensus decision making *not* the clearer articulation of an *already* formalised interest. The resultant interest representations are *the product of the process* resulting in a temporary formalisation open to further refinement. This sediments a process of 'becoming' within the AGM which is one reason why the work of Deleuze and Guatarri (2002) is so central here.

There is an explicit foregrounding of 'civilisation' in the work of Deleuze and Guatarri, derived in part from engagement with psychoanalytic theory where the term assumes analytical significance, rather than society. Here, Deleuze and Guattari's prioritisation of difference diverges from the Freudian emphasis on the achievement of a sound gendered identity through the resolution of the underlying tensions of polymorphous sexuality. Desire for Deleuze and Guattari is thus not centred on a pervasive sense of 'lack' as in the work of Lacan but as an active affirmation of life, embracing and producing difference. The celebration of difference and libratory potential of desire were prominent features of the Situationist International (Jappe 1999), and were linked to practices of détournement and the construction of 'situations' intended to destabilise the dominant coding of signs. Such practices raise issues of subjectivity, the conscious and unconscious mind which we acknowledge but have no intention of engaging with here. Notions of the conscious/sub/unconscious mind are of course present in the classical sociological cannon – 'conscience collective', 'false consciousness' and a plethora of other terms evoke this domain resulting in the centrality of contemporary debates about identity (see Chapter 7).

For present purposes, the important point is that the enactment of carnivalesque repertoires as public protest enables acts of re and de territorialisation through symbolically coding wider social stakes. Embodying and performing the death of the planet as a consequence of the prevailing capitalist axiomatic produces laminar flows of meaning. Following Appadurai's notion of 'scapes' (1990) the notion of flows have been central to discussions of globalisation (Lash and Urry 1994, Urry 2000) despite its tendency to subsume agency. Whilst laminar flows appear smooth, they are composed of multiple layers which interact at a molecular level. Changes in these interactions can precipitate significant 'phase shifts' in the anatomy of a flow introducing turbulence, for example. Throughout this work we approach the agency of particular collective and individual actors as analogous to these molecular prompts. This is particularly important in relation to flows of meaning which are collectively constituted and enacted whilst containing the residues of other minoritarian meanings subsumed through the process of consensus formation. When such flows encounter obstacles their laminar nature can lead to the re-emergence of residual meanings which become appropriate in changed circumstances.[2] Paying attention to the resultant discourses and discursive contestation in terms of repetitions and iteration between global, national and local levels is a key genealogical task.

Globalisation and discourse

> Humanity does not gradually progress from combat to combat until it arrives at universal reciprocity, where rule of law finally replaces warfare, humanity installs each of its violences in a system of rules and thus proceeds from domination to domination...The successes of history belong to those who are capable of seizing those rules...so as to pervert them, invert their meaning, and redirect them against those who had initially imposed them; controlling this complex mechanism, they will make it function so as to overcome the rulers through their own rules.
>
> (Foucault 1997b: 151)

For Bouchard, Foucault formalises the means through which 'we' can 'question the "value of our values"' (1977b: 17) via a 'genealogical method' such as that underpinning the work of Deleuze, which makes possible 'the re-evaluation of the past traditions and the real possibility of the present' (23). This theoretical move offers an escape from the wheel of history, which perpetuates inter-state wars, by pitting the war machine against the state. It is our argument that the ascendancy of neo-liberal globalisation renders this possibility more tangible.

Neo-liberalism and complexity

We have already alluded to some of the ways in which the social has become more complex through it's (re)constitution in open systems and hinted that this applies to systems of signification. By reasserting the universal primacy of core elements of classic liberalism, the neo-liberal turn foregrounds some key 'past traditions' in an era when the 'possibilit[ies]y of the present' are more readily present(able) through computer mediated communications than ever before. The genealogical task continues to 'require patience and a knowledge of detail' depending upon 'a vast accumulation of source material' sought 'in the most unpromising places' (1977b: 40–41) but now extends beyond text to include moving images, sounds, rhythms, intonation and body language. In part what we write comes from immersion in these kinds of materials gathered in sites associated with the AGM – which in the eyes of most would appear 'unpromising places' in terms of significant social change.

Contemporary neo-liberalism re-emphasises the individual in the context of a global process of economic deregulation which extends government through governance so that market mechanisms, messages and signals become rhizomatic forms of a control society orchestrating day-to-day life. Further, neo-liberalism promotes these rhizomatic forms through 'democratic' institutions responsible for trade agreements, regimes that codify a system of rules. Citizens have no direct role in electing members of these institutions which are part of 'high politics' – a politics which in the view of AGM actors proceeds from domination to domination. The ascendancy of the religious right within the American political class added 'violence' to the contemporary system of rules by adopting the strategy of pre-emptive use of military force against significant *perceived* threats to democracy. Combined with state building and the assertion of inviolable basic values this represents a claim of primacy as the benchmark for human civilisation.

Global regulatory reach: deterritorialisation

By combining Giddens's (1987) notion of administrative reach and Shiva's (1992) notion of global reach, Welsh (1996, 2000) developed the term global regulatory reach as a generic term for scientific and technical regulatory regimes introduced in the post-war era. The term applies equally well to the extension of economic and financial regulatory regimes of the WB and IMF, some of which are tied to technical aid programmes. Global regulatory reach is characterised by the need to establish global regulatory standards across both space and time in order to achieve the intended benefits of a programme. Whilst such regimes typically leave some leeway in terms of how they are implemented to accommodate cultural differences, they are primarily shaped by Western forms or rationality through expert communities. The proliferation of global regulatory regimes exercising such reach represents key instruments for the creation of what Hardt and Negri (2004) term smooth space.

Global regulatory reach assumes that the substantive rationality under-pinning a particular programme can be realised irrespective of the cultural and social composition and traditions of recipient states. Further, there is an implicit assumption that the citizens of Western 'donor' states will accept both the products of such regimes and the necessary life style adjustments. The increasing attention given to 'governance' issues and 'civil society questions' reflect the increasing resistance of actors in both South and North to such exercises in global regulatory reach.

In this process States become increasingly torn between competing externalities as they attempt to simultaneously align themselves with the smoothing and striating forces of capital, science, technology and citizen demands. The clear-cut notion of states as guarantors of national capital(s) – the executive committee model of the state – becomes decisively fractured. The modern state is increasingly fragmented as different departments of state, align themselves differentially in relation to the range of external and internal pressures. The classic functions of the state interact with the global institutional nexus with the security state, finance state and political state both constituting and becoming subject to top-down regimes. These lines of fracture are reflected within the global institutional nexus as part of the struggle to de- and reterritorialise global agendas. Hardt and Negri approach this nexus as an integrated *Empire*; however we argue that this results in an over-hegemonic depiction of the prevailing power relations. There are in effect competing *Empires* as different *fractions* align in the pursuit of competing agendas. The interpretation of these fault lines and the alignment of 'domestic policy' within particular nation states produces increasing fragmentation of the 'national'.

In the United States the generalisation of the state–corporate enterprise has extended to public institutions such as schools transforming and diminishing the 'public sphere', a process paralleled within the United Kingdom. The spread of shopping malls as private developments restricts rights of assembly within urban centres, persistent protests against controversial corporate activities result in the definition of legitimate 'protest zones' distant from the actual sites and state surveillance agencies increasingly target citizens in a wide range of social movement activities. The enactment of opposition in these concrete sites results in myriad instances where the *symbolic stakes* of state–corporate activity coordinated through a global institutional nexus are contested exposing more and more citizens to the increasing array of carefully targeted laws which seek to discipline and punish.

This is nowhere more pronounced than in sectors perceived as central to future economic prosperity such as genetic research. In the 1970s 'anti-nuclear' movements were denounced as dupes of the Soviet Union, amidst claims that they were recipients of 'Russian gold', aimed at denying the 'West' 'the benefits' (billions of dollars and pounds of public money in nuclear clean up operations) of nuclear energy. From the 1980s onwards anti-roads protestors, anti-vivisectionists and a range of other groups have been targeted as enemies within in an era dominated by the fear of network actors – a fear rendered material by the events of 9/11. There is a certain 'repetition' here worthy of some elaboration.

Margins and meanings

The discursive targeting of margins now occurs in a very different context compared to the 'late corporatism' of the 1970s. The neo-liberal market message 'maximise share holder value' is apparently decoupled from the dual identity of shareholders – whether as direct investors or contributors to pension funds – as citizen/subjects confronted by multiple and frequently contradictory demands. The better value a stock has the more ruthless its corporate culture must be in the entrepreneurial pursuit of innovation. The investor citizen may prosper in terms of dividend rates but must live with the consequences of the increasingly *pathological* divisions of labour required by deregulated, flexible labour markets, something that is reflected by shifts in the structure of language to incorporate these changes – such as when *Karioshi* or death from overwork entered the Japanese language (McCormack 1991).

Adults in an average dual income UK household have two hours of free time together each day, including time spent watching TV. The children they nurture live in a world where the chief government scientist considers global warming a greater threat than terrorism whilst the government relaxes emission criteria so that industry is not penalised under the rules of climate change conventions. Amidst intense academic debate about the effects of media product upon behavioural patterns, the pragmatic fact that Berlusconi's children are not allowed to consume the product of their father's media empire apparently means little.

Corporate executives held responsible for misappropriation of pension funds, fraudulent liquidity statements, misrepresentation of research on product health impacts and so on leave with enhanced severance packages. Corporate employees meanwhile work on insecure short-term contracts in flexible labour markets – an intensely competitive and insecure environment where the right to hire and fire is fore-grounded within a climate of corporate governance encouraging employee cooperation and participation. Within this 'mad house' of 'casino capitalism' (Hutton 2002) talent migrates rapidly to the highest bidder, labour market turn over increases and ever more elaborate job titles and descriptions are conjured up to make people feel valued.

Whilst the British Government emphasise the acts of animal rights protests in terms of undermining the science base, their actions are far less important than labour market conditions. Short-term contracts and comparatively modest salaries promote scientific work nomadism to countries with better remuneration. At the 2004 London Social Forum a female speaker opened a session with the observation that having just completed her PhD in biotechnology she was going to become a school teacher as she knew that having children was not compatible with laboratory work (Welsh *et al.* 2005).

As labour markets become increasingly global, nomadism will grow as individuals with relevant transferable skills seek to maximise their life chances outside the container of the nation(state). The relocation of sectors of the biotechnology industry to developing nations inverts the flows of ethnically constituted labour associated with Fordism and Post-Fordism by taking the techniques to the subjects. Comparatively relaxed ethical standards in Southern Asia are easier and cheaper to comply with in areas like stem cell donation and transplant procedures and these are processes in their infancy.

This is the logic of deregulation – it is something our economic and political leaders negotiated within the G8, IMF, WB etc. These are the same people who now assert that 'globalisation is the only game in town' – they invented it, they are the notional ringmasters, they *would* say that – their political parties increasingly rely on corporate sponsorship, they *have* to say that. It is a message dressed in the benefits of individual choice heralding the introduction of more and more areas of life where citizens have no choice but to make choices as high quality *universal* provision is brought to an end in sector after sector.

The freedom of enforced choice is linked to responsibilities to be effective choosers within the market options on offer. In their two free hours per day the adults of the United Kingdom middle class dual income households *must* exercise informed choices about their children's education, their pension plans, their life style health impacts, etc. whilst being invited to participate in endless consultation exercises on how to implement new techniques and technologies they had no part in originating. The imbalance between the cash rich/time poor and time rich/cash poor in the developed north grows. Such is modern 'democracy'. The unelected nature of the state nexus highlighted since the 1970s (Urry and Wakeford eds 1973, Urry 1981) is extended to the global domain where it assumes *predominantly* economic and technical forms (Stiglitz 2002).

Neo-liberal ascendancy elevates discourses of the economic, the individual, and free choice to positions of renewed prominence in the context of a 'knowledge economy' where information and information workers are elevated to a position of prominence once enjoyed by the 'commanding heights' of the industrial economy – such as miners and car workers. Perfect competition within this model continues to be underpinned by belief in the possibility of perfect knowledge, a possibility increasingly promoted through the elision of knowledge and information. This naive doctrine dismissed all counter factual argument through the There Is No Alternative (TINA) principle which in effect asserts the primacy of market rationality in all spheres of life. The relationships between knowledge, power and information thus assume positions of central analytical importance in terms of public trust in the institutions of 'representative democracy' increasingly subordinated to 'unelected' global decisional fora.

The intended and unintended collective consequences of global neo-liberalism are most evident to those individuals least able to insulate themselves and their dependents against the negative impacts of modernisation. The degrees of separation between the 'developed' and 'developing' world are reduced as the global flows of material and immaterial production go into reverse siphoning jobs to the 'developing' economies. As in all phases of transition between modes of production associated with intense techno-scientific innovation, there is a massive preponderance of 'poor people's movements' (Fox-Piven 1979), marginal social actors, dispossessed and disenfranchised. Amongst such groups withdrawal represents a strategy of resistance. We are suggesting that material acts of withdrawal such as withholding labour have extended to immaterial acts such as withdrawal of trust. The pervasive withdrawal of trust was a major feature in the 'hollowing out' of Soviet communism as active expressions of 'living in truth' developed to include active dissident networks.

Unlike previous instances this 'exodus' (see Chapter 7) exists in a network society which significantly transforms the possible axes of solidarity, the density and dispersal of information, and the density and dispersal of the individuals/actors in novel ways. The discrete, constituent nation states of international relations become inhabited by significant diasporic communities, for example. These communities experience the acts of discrete states towards their homelands both as denizens of the perpetrator state(s) and via CMC as 'distanciated' members of the target states through familial and friendship networks as well as more formal media channels. Korea's expatriate citizens thus marched through the streets of Paris as part of the 2003 European Social Forum.

The outsider/insider/other nexus central to the imagined community and identity of nationhood becomes attenuated and the task of constituting boundary conditions infinitely more complex. Put another way, difference becomes increasingly manifest and omnipresent at precisely the moment in which a return to 'traditional values' is foregrounded as a response to increasing social tensions. Freedom of speech, association and assembly – corner stones of the enlightenment national bourgeois public sphere – and the right to civil disobedience (Habermas 1985) – become increasingly problematic and *multi-vocal* raising issues of inter-subjectivity and identity as central concerns for social theory.

Deleuze asserts the centrality of difference for the social and philosophical understanding of both social relations and social forms as the universalism associated with science increasingly confronts difference. Einstein's universal constant, the speed of light, is now in question given recent evidence suggesting that the speed of light must have changed if current models of the universe are correct. The debate extends into questioning how many parallel universes exist if quantum theory is to hold. Whilst there is disagreement about the number of universes there is a reasonable consensus that the laws of physics operating in each universe are different, and possibly contradictory. The universe continues to exist while science enters a renewed phase of becoming as sense making is renewed. Metaphorically, we would liken the AGM to a universe within which different and sometimes contradictory rule bound social universes coexist.

Deleuze as 'difference engineer' (Pearson 1997) formalises issues of difference in terms of the ontological primacy in knowledge formation and the significance of minute biological variances which make every organism unique. This is timely in a century where universal truths, universal values and universal economics are increasingly recognised as contested and problematic. As Thomas Khun (1996) and before him Susan Stebbing (1937) argued paradigms shift when the accumulated exceptions to prevailing theories/laws can no longer be ignored. In Deleuze's words: 'No theory can develop without eventually encountering a wall, and practice is necessary for piercing this wall' (Foucault 1977b: 206).

The practices of science will advance scientific agendas in the face of difference just as social practices will advance social agendas in the face of difference. In Deleuzian terms these result in 'machinic' and 'social' assemblages – movements are playing their historic role as 'agents of innovation' once more and complexity theory is one way of theorising the global movement milieu independent of the teleogical assumptions of modernist approaches. For this reason Deleuze emphasises the potentiality of 'teleologies' (1977b: 206) as entirely consistent with an emphasis on 'becoming' rather than 'being'. This emphasis is implicit in the AGM slogan 'One no. Many Yeses'.

Conclusions

These examples of prefigurative emergence are included here for several reasons. Methodologically we would emphasise the importance of 'latency periods' in reconfiguring movement dynamics and declaratory objectives. For social movement studies and social theory more generally, currents of critical public engagement typically 'disappear' with the resolution of a dominant focus. Such disappearance has been incorporated in terms of 'mobilisation cycles', here we are arguing that this diverts attention away from the invisible work of continually constituted movement networks. Urban centres in the United Kingdom and elsewhere represent the densest configuration of durable movement engagement (Doherty 2002).

In terms of the argument we develop, these network hubs are important precisely because they reveal the multi-layered engagement of the network of networks constituting the AGM. As we go on to argue network actors engage via multiple 'lines of flight' through this permanent presence. Put simply there are global, national and local sites of contestation and co-operation with transformative potential at each of these levels. The AGM thus operates as a strange attractor across the entire spatial spectrum. The balance of effort expended at each of these levels is dependent upon a wide range of factors ranging from individuals' 'biographical availability' to a strategic evaluation of the significance of different points of purchase offered by a prevailing parallelogram of forces (see Chapter 7). A primary focus upon movement actions as they engage within national political opportunity structures diverts attention away from the over-lapping nature of contemporary movement activities.

Another striking feature of the e-mail detailed in this chapter is the explicit embrace of direct action as a preferred means of intervention. Traditionally this has been regarded as a 'tactic of last resort' (Welsh 2000) after all other avenues of engagement have been exhausted. The contemporary movement milieu's prioritisation of direct action as a primary means of engagement reflects the presence of long-term actors and their collective ability to learn from previous engagements.

Direct action has been recognised as a necessary means of engagement in an age where media exposure provides a major source of public sphere presence. It is however, important to recognise that orientation towards mainstream media exposure does not express the totality of movements media impacts. As we have indicated, movements are media, in and for themselves acting in ways, which do not leave any unaffected bystanders. The development of autonomous movement media capacity has had some impact on mainstream media reportage categories and has also been actively targeted by state actors (see Chapter 4).

Our representation of the state as a fractured nexus differentially networked to the global nexus of neo-liberalism and national civil society and its actors is theoretically important. This importance stems from the manner in which key elements of states constitute the global institutional domain. The Finance state is central here in terms of multiple memberships of circles within which market forces are socially constructed through decisions about loan conditions, return rates and so on. As we go on to argue, the finance state demonstrates a more flexible and dialogical relationship with the AGM than other fragments of contemporary states. The response of the Political state is far less sophisticated representing reflexivity in Beck's true sense – the application of more of the same – namely the policing of crisis as a primary response. This is a reflection of the contradictory location of the Political state in simultaneously constituting a global power nexus whilst striving to represent the interests of a national civil society.

3 Reflexive framing
Identities, protest dynamics and technology

Introduction

This chapter gives *an* account of the Prague plateau, a carnivalesque contestation of the IMF WB meeting held in September 2000. Our account draws on a range of sources including direct observation and video capture, interviews with activists from the Czech Republic, United Kingdom and United States, Czech, print media coverage, samizdat materials, activist video accounts and Indymedia sites. Through these diverse sources, we are able to capture something of the multi-layered nature of the meanings and processes structuring this plateau, rendering the underlying complexity visible. Analytically we focus upon the relationship between various forms of technological mediation widely regarded as central to global protests. CMC technologies are central to theoretical accounts emphasising the importance of network actors (Castells 1996, Hardt and Negri 2000, 2004) as emergent phenomena. Our account reveals the continuing importance of technologies that are more 'mundane', face-work contacts and mobilities through which a 'virtual network' is transformed into concrete acts of contestation. In this context the representation of acts of contestation within the public sphere assume a position of centrality in a struggle for legitimacy over world (dis)order. Understanding the dynamics of such contestation is dependent upon a degree of immersion within the network of networks operating as a 'shadow realm' (Welsh 2002) constituting subterranean structures which otherwise remain invisible.

'Protests' with a carnivalesque or dramaturgical element are complex social events expressing multi-layered cultural meanings which are symbolically coded and enacted with the potential to resonate or clash with wider social representations and perceptions. The action against the WB/IMF bank meeting in Prague on 26 September 2000 contained all these familiar elements, but brought together 'national' protest repertoires from across Europe and beyond. Such events are typically 'known' and 'framed' through their appearance within the public sphere in print and broadcast media. Media 'snapshots' such as these even form the methodological basis for some comparative social movement studies, despite being based on analysis of one newspaper per country. Such monochrome renditions lose the underlying event richness which arises, in part, from the multiple acts of definition and meaning found within such milieu (McKechnie and Welsh 2002).

The Prague WB/IMF summit was the first major summit to occur outside the United States. The event had been identified as a site for a Czech action long before this but the consolidation of the AGM transformed this 'national local' event creating a 'new' phenomenon on the streets of Prague. Claims of 'newness' are always problematic within the social sciences, but this one is justified. The Czech Republic had just emerged as one of the transition democracies of Eastern Europe, a transition within which many of the high profile figures from the 'dissident' movement formed under Communist domination became figures of state, including the Czech President Vaclav Havel and the late Joseph Vavroušek as federal minister of the environment (Tickle and Welsh 1998). The action on S26 was the first by the AGM in a country where English was not the primary language. Since the 1989 'velvet' revolution, when the streets of the capital city had been occupied by crowds for days on end, S26 was widely predicted to be a significant protest event. For the post-transition Czech Government it was certainly the most significant street event to have taken place since 1989. There are many 'firsts' here and this underlines the symbolic stakes associated with the event for *all* parties.

Initial conditions and the 'new democracies'

In terms of complexity theory, the founding of the transition or new democracies throughout Eastern Europe is a particularly clear example of the importance of initial conditions in understanding subsequent events. Here, two important factors are our understanding of the foregoing state of civil society and the degree of inclusiveness achieved during the transition period. Many accounts of the transitions assumed that under communist domination, the associations of civil society did not exist (Schöpflin 1993). Tickle and Welsh (1998: 164–167) demonstrate the existence of nascent civil societies of differing compositions throughout the period of communist domination. Here, environmentally orientated citizens initiatives formed a kernel around which much broader social and political concerns became articulated. Even in Poland, where Solidarity formed an apparently clear example of a transition dominated by religious and trades union forces, the role of far less formalised network actors using innovative direct action repertoires was central in reinvigorating Solidarity's 'stalled' initiative (Kenney 2002). The existence of civil society actors at the point of transition has to be recognised as part of the initial conditions making the issue of inclusion critical in terms of understanding the contemporary milieu. Here we depart from the influential idea (Elster *et al.* 1998) that the degree of institutional inclusion achieved during the transition period realised the full expression of these nascent civil societies (see Baker and Welsh 2000).

In the Czech case, there was a clear incorporation of prominent dissident and environmental concerns within the formal political arena. The incorporation of significant 'dissident' demands relating to democratic freedoms and environmental issues arguably 'decapitated' or 'incorporated' key radical constituencies (see Andrle 2003, Fagin 1999). In the new democracies, particularly in Poland and the Czech Republic, there is a widespread view that the dynamism of civil society actors that prevailed during the transitions has disappeared. Given the extent and vibrancy of the civil sphere documented by Kenney (2002) such dissolution is highly unlikely.

The insight that civil society engagement with the institutional dynamics of neo-liberal capitalist societies is a process requiring significant time and effort in terms of identifying, formalising and declaring 'the stakes' (Melucci 1989, 1996a) underlines the importance of remaining alert to emergent social forces within the new democracies (Baker and Welsh 2000). Within this complex domain, issues of gender, ethnicity, and environment become articulated within historically new market relations where they unfold in the context of radically changed processes. Significant here are issues of mobility, transformed communication and information exchange (Urry 2000) and the introduction of private property relations.

As Havel noted long before the transition phase commenced 'capitalism... is struggling with the same problems' of alienation resulting in 'depersonalization and the loss of meaning in work' combined with 'the general manipulation of people's lives by the system' (Havel 1990: 14). To Havel, the maintenance of human scale and a positive orientation towards the 'inventiveness of nature' capable of 'inscrutable complexity of [its] interconnections' were vital to avoid people becoming a 'herd' as a consequence of commodification and 'consumer television culture' *regardless* of the underlying 'socialist'or 'capitalist' form of ownership and control (Havel 1990: 15). The arrival of the new democracies marked an entry into a new phase of struggle where 'living in truth' (Havel 1989) assumed new forms representing expressions of in 'plurality of social association from below' considered by Havel to be the truly important features of high profile events such as the Prague spring of 1968 (1989: 21).

The Prague IMF World Bank action

As host to the IMF/WB summit the Czech state was firmly placed in the eye of a hurricane of global protest rendering the state as a node of network convergence from 'above' and 'below'. As we go on to demonstrate, global political, intelligence and policing networks became increasingly focussed upon the Czech Republic just as AGM networks also 'colonised' activist space. Much of the framework involved in defining the stakes enacted on S26 thus precedes the actual event by at least 12 months. The Czech

Republic was determined to portray itself as a mature host to the event whilst maintaining order and freedom of expression associated with a democratic polity. The dissident background of President Václav Havel accentuated a desire implicit in selecting Prague,[1] for the meeting which was preceded by a state-sponsored critical forum on globalisation and a 'solidarity march' on 23 September. The intent was to produce a 'win–win' (Interview Czech Activist [9]) result producing both a successful summit and protest event.

The fledgling democracy's relative lack of experience in policing such protests precipitated politicians and police chiefs into a series of high powered meetings with representatives of intelligence and law enforcement agencies. These included meetings between delegations from the FBI, headed by deputy director Thomas Packard, and members of Washington police (*Pravo* 29.8.00, p. 2). Significant know-how and equipment specifications were imparted in this process to the satisfaction of US agencies (*Lidove noviny* 31.08.00, p. 2). By September 2000 the operations of activist 'radicals from the USA' and 'west European countries' in 'training their Czech colleagues' (31.08.00, p. 2) for the event appeared under the headline 'Police and demonstrators are preparing for a "war"' (*Lidove noviny* 21.09.00, p. 2).

S26 Strategy and the streets

A core concern here lies with network multipliers arising from the S26 action in terms of the quality of interaction between Czech activists and 'internationals', the dissemination of repertoires of action, the seeding of organisational forms either weakly represented or absent within the Czech Republic and the long-term bottom-up implications of these processes for emergent forms of 'living in truth' consistent with a neo-liberal global order. These analytical themes require a brief account of the main co-ordinating hubs and a detailed account of selected events on the streets as they unfolded.

The Prague protests were the first occasion in Europe where anti-globalisation and anti-capitalist groups from diverse social and cultural backgrounds attempted to work together to mobilise against the same target in a particular geographic location. Previously, 'days of action' had consisted of simultaneous, de-centred protests in many different locations, such as those timed to coincide with 18 June 1999, the first day of the G8 meeting in Cologne, and the day when the City of London became host to the first 'Carnival Against Capitalism' (Chesters 1999). The arrival of these loosely organised groups with different protest repertoires and heightened expectations derived from the Seattle protests combined to make assimilation within the process and facilitation of dialogue extremely complex. Somewhat inevitably those with prior organising experience of large-scale protests, connections to more than one group and English as a primary language quickly became prominent in the organisational process.

The presence of activists associated with PGA a network founded in Geneva in February 1998, to act as 'a world-wide co-ordination of resistance against the global market, a new alliance of struggle and mutual support',[2] was also significant (see Chapter 6). Some of these activists had already established a degree of trust from prior personal contact and communicated the significant interest and mobilisation taking place across Europe to local activists. The PGA commitment to values of autonomy, decentralisation, democratic participation and direct action in opposition to neo-liberal capitalism, formalised during the Zapatista uprising in Chiapas Mexico, were manifest concretely in the efforts of 'internationals' to keep the process 'open'. This commitment to 'unity in diversity' through the fusion of different political perspectives and protest repertoires was central.

> Consensus regarding the action to be taken was reached after a complex process of debate in general assembly, small groups, and in INPEG meetings.
>
> (Minutes of the International Organising
> Meeting, 16–18 June 2000)

This consensus was the product of a meeting of over 70 people participating as 'simple individuals' or 'representatives of organisations', collectives and coalitions from the United Kingdom, France, Germany, Netherlands, Spain, Italy, Finland, Norway, Slovakia, United States and Czech Republic. However, subsequent 'international' meetings were complicated further by the participation of international Trotskyist organisations (International Socialists/Socialist Worker's Party) that opposed extensive deliberation and consensus processes prioritising the recognition of difference. These 'bourgeois' traits were regarded as fragmenting the old unity associated with class struggle defined through relations of ownership in classic Marxist terms.

Despite these political and philosophical divisions, there was broad agreement amongst our respondents of an emerging consensus during these discussions which was subsequently assimilated within the action plan. This position was, as might be expected, a negotiated compromise, involving a mass gathering at a central convergence point, followed by 'a unity march' (favoured by the IS/SWP) during which the assembled protesters would be divided into separate marches each of which would be assigned a colour. The 'coloured' marches would be characterised by political affiliation, ideological standpoint or affective links determined by regional identity, language or affinity with particular protest repertoires.

The presence of internationals or 'free radicals' underlines the significance of individual free acts in shaping social form, action and dynamics operating as attractors 'dissolving old dualisms' (Eve *et al.* 1997: xii–xv). The adoption of colours – yellow, blue and pink – drew upon experience within London RTS (Reclaim The Streets) of providing 'condensation symbols' to which individual allegiance could be temporarily aligned producing a temporary collective. In Prague the process originated in the selection of 'empty signifiers' by using colours 'that didn't have a [local] political resonance' though one interviewee 'liked the idea of Commies having to say they were Pink' (Interview UK activist 2). Despite this, the Pink march produced a lasting allegiance initiating a contemporary reformulation of playful confrontation, previously used by peace and anti-nuclear movements (Welsh 2000), and at subsequent summit sieges (Chesters and Welsh 2004).

On 26 September, the intricacies of this plan proved unworkable and the marches diverged immediately taking different exit routes from the initial meeting place in Namesti Miru (Peace Square). This outcome resulted from a combination of factors including the obvious affinity between certain groups, confusion amongst those attending 'on the day' and the attraction of being party to, or observing some of the more puzzling or obviously confrontational protest repertoires about to be deployed. Thus, the visibly padded, white suited, and multi-coloured helmeted ranks of Ya Basta!/Tute Bianche! set out with an unexpectedly large contingent of followers/ onlookers including the majority of the IS/SWP grouping on the 'yellow' route. Two other groups – blue and pink set off almost simultaneously.

The Blue march was distinctively international in character and included the Infernal Noise Brigade, a uniformed anarchist marching band from Seattle complete with baton twirlers and flags. This march was largely comprised of the widespread anarchist/autonomist movement who have used a 'black bloc' tactic (wearing balaclavas, black clothing and being prepared to defend themselves and confront the police) throughout northern Europe over the last 20–30 years (see Katsiaficas 1997).

The Pink or Pink and Silver march as it had now been labelled left almost simultaneously, variously described as 'pink fairies', 'carnivalistas'[3] or 'samba',[4] in actuality a combination of various Earth First! and Reclaim The Streets activists from the United Kingdom as well as a recently assembled Samba band and the self-declared 'Tactical Frivolity' group, a combination of women activists from Lancashire, Yorkshire and the South West of the United Kingdom, part of whose journey was documented for *The Guardian* newspaper.[5]

As the day progressed the clear demarcation between the colour coded marches began to break down as groups from each manoeuvred to provide support and seek tactical advantage. Towards the late afternoon the majority of people still on the streets marched to the Opera House where IMF/WB delegates were due to meet arriving just as the performance was cancelled. During late evening the first damage to 'global brand' outlets and banks[6] began to occur in Wenceslas Square and riot police clashed repeatedly with groups of protesters that were now becoming dispersed around the city centre. At this point the first mass arrests began to take place, people, including locals, were trapped in various side streets where they had taken refuge from police percussion grenades, they were then made to enact subservience and subordination by kneeling or lying down, before being handcuffed and arrested. Having contextualised events we can now consider the analytical themes focussing on primary data gathered prior to, during and after S26.[7]

The locals: INPEG

On the ground co-ordination fell to the Czech group INPEG – an acronym derived from the Czech for Initiative Against Economic Globalisation. The group originated in Prague in September 1999 being derived from pre-existing environmentalist, feminist, anarchist and socialist groups. Pre-dating Seattle, the groups' agenda envisaged a domestic event but this expectation was overturned following the 'successes of Seattle'. Active contacts with groups in England and throughout Europe had been in train since spring 2000 with key 'internationals' taking up residence in Prague several months prior to the event.

Our respondent within INPEG had been involved from the start of the coordination process in late 1999 witnessing the increasing involvement of 'internationals'. The initial stages, involving Czech participants, had consolidated their networks as 'Czech activists know each other much more than before' (Interview Czech activist [4]). Like Kenney (2002) we found that this process extended across national borders with network linkages to Slovakia, Germany, the United Kingdom, as well as hubs within the global networks mentioned earlier.

The small number of INPEG activists, their youthfulness and limited experience combined to limit the effectiveness of the group confronted by a very steep learning curve. Experienced activists arriving in Prague found it difficult to see what had been achieved in three months of preparatory work, with one respondent recalling

> What I really noticed was the cynicism and the hopelessness of a lot of the local activists.... The real sense of you know, we are not going to get many people the police are gonna kill us. Nothing is possible.
>
> (Interview British Activist [2])

An atmosphere of pending violence permeated the city and quickly diffused through the movement networks fuelled by Government calls for residents to leave the city and the closure of all schools (Welsh 2004). Conformity to official warnings was a norm even amongst the friendship networks of active participants 'people obeyed police and newspapers and media, they really left, lots of my friends left, took holiday, left Prague (Interview Czech activist [6]). Combined with speculation about policing practices in this ex-communist dominated police state there was a widespread fear of repressive 'state' violence.

These fears are reflected in the sophistication of the legal briefings provided by the organization OPH which provided details of participants' rights. Another important 'local' actor, the 'third element', with an ambiguous relationship to the Czech state proved to be a critical channel of communication between protestors and authorities and was prominent within respondents accounts.

The third element

The 'third element' arose through the concerns of ex-dissident, turned journalist Jan Urban over the Czech state's lack of knowledge of contemporary protest repertoires and policing techniques. Through foregoing dissident associations a meeting with members of Vaclav Havel's friendship networks and key Ministers took place in March 2000. At this meeting Jan Urban emphasised the importance of dialogue, conflict mediation and conflict resolution, themes which finance Minister Pavel Mertlik was particularly supportive of. The 'third element' was thus conceived as a 'communication channel' as 'even in war time, warring parties communicate' (Interview Czech Activist [9]) and gained financial support from Comercni Bank, one of the largest Czech clearing banks.

The third element scrutinised video footage of events on the streets of Seattle and Washington and actively sought to mediate between the police and INPEG, eventually focussing their efforts through a key British 'International' having failed to gain the trust of Czech activists. The presence of 'free radicals' thus played a central role in structuring communications throughout this particular plateau. The third elements' extensive video capture during S26 contributed significantly to their interpretation of events and subsequent views on the actions of both protestors and police authorities, themes addressed below. Most importantly, the third element effectively communicated their 'win–win' strategy across the AGM/Police boundary. This was based on the protestors blockading the IMF/WB delegates inside the meeting whilst demanding the self-dissolution of their organisations. The protest would thus appear successful whilst the meeting could be concluded with delegates leaving via the public transport links beneath the conference centre. Accounts of the event suggesting that the aim was to 'storm' the conference centre are profoundly misleading.

Internationals or 'free radicals'

Computer mediated communications are central to network analyses through the constitution of virtual activist communities across geo-political borders. S26 illustrates some of the key strengths and weaknesses associated with communicating within 'cyber-space'. These are addressed here in terms of their impacts upon the event and subsequent networking.

Prominent internationals learned of the Prague event through either personal communications or internet postings with five such individuals familiar with PGA arriving in the Czech Republic in the months preceding the event (Interview British Activist [3]). A male UK activist with significantly more experience than anyone else within this network node assumed the role of 'prime mover' despite arriving with other intentions and agenda. This is a common feature of such events frequently raised in terms of accountability and the exercise of power compared to formally convened and minuted bureaucratic organisations. Such criticisms fail to grasp the impossibility of following such formal models faced by the conjuncture of multiple movement actors. The field of relations and demands constituted by a diverse constituency with varying degrees of familiarity and fluency within such milieus are too fluid and complex to be bureaucratically contained.

In such circumstances pre-existing network trust relations, personal cultural capital, activist skills and demeanour combine in ways which 'precipitate' particular people into the 'thankless' places from whence movement leadership is exercised. Movement dynamics ensure other forms of accountability through the evaluation of leaders' roles in relation to abstract movement values and principles (see Barker *et al.* eds 2001).

All the internationals initial communications with Czech activists utilised CMC. Interviews reveal how embedded assumptions mediate such interactions in the absence of face-work exchanges. The history of Czech resistance to Soviet Communism raised internationals expectations that they would be entering a sophisticated activist community. In the words of a highly experienced activist respondent

> I think I expected it was going to be massive. I expected that the organising would be really good, that the local organising would be really sorted. I suppose I had a romantic notion that they had seen the success of the Velvet Revolution.... and Oh this must be a hot bed – what all these people who were in their late teens and now must be well my age really (i.e. 30s).
>
> (British Activist [2])

This was not an isolated view

> You know, there was a revolution basically ten years before and yet we seem to be in a complete vacuum and having to relearn and invent everything. Where are those people now and what are they doing? All those things were crucial to us.
>
> (British Activist [6])

The disparity between this expectation and the material reality was marked. Despite extensive e-mail contact one experienced international wandered Prague for more than a day failing to make physical contact with anyone. When contact was established locals pre-occupation with the potential for failure and police brutality produced very different pre-event 'frames' and the rapid reconfiguration of internationals CMC perceptions

> I immediately felt like this colonial activist arriving in this in an alien culture so it was difficult to be optimistic or try and push optimism that one felt, not knowing the situation.
>
> (Interview with British Activist [2])

Others considered that 'it was quite racist actually that they were coming in and imposing their own agenda on this thing' (Interview British Activist [4]). The 'internationals' commitment to non-violence intensified these differences as training sessions began

> the person who was asked to do the training was this woman called Starhawk...She had been brought over and she is a great trainer but coming from such a different cultural background there was already a real difficulty there between this total commitment to non-violence, totally committed to process, all the stuff that was really alien to the Czech activists, really really alien.
>
> (Interview British Activist [2])

The establishment of the S26 convergence centre[8] provided a physical space within which street techniques deploying elements of carnivalesque confrontation were discussed, negotiated and rehearsed. Negotiation and communication required translation into a variety of languages and over time the primary language used switched from Czech to English – a significant transition in terms of local co-ordination of the event.

The 'micro-physics' of power in convergence spaces are critical to the negotiation of collective identities within plateaux melding social, physical and affective factors. In Prague the convergence centre was a large disused factory/warehouse space where the acoustics limited effective communications in large groups. Language barriers and acoustics combined to produce a frustrating environment within which to work. The importance attached to non-verbal communication by Bateson become tangible in such contexts. Several respondents emphasised the importance of music, dance, and shared activity in establishing trust relations. The rehearsal of a Samba band contributed significantly to the consolidation of a group ethos and the creation of a positive energy – processes with military parallels in terms of morale and motivation. This gamut of exchanges introduced repertoires of action and their philosophical underpinnings from London, Washington, Seattle and elsewhere to Czech activist circles through the cultural capital of key movement figures acting as 'free radicals'.

The street tactics on S26 found guarded support from within the Communist Party of Bohemia and Moravia (KSČM) a significant political party holding 41 parliamentary seats in 2000. Their formal participation was limited to the unified march on 23 September in an attempt to avoid further depictions of the party as a return to communism, re-nationalisation and a centralist state (Interview with Czech Activist [3]). Our respondent, with 40 years of experience within the organisation viewed the media campaign preceding S26 as 'psychological war against our people, against this demonstration and this protest'. The official recognised the need 'to learn more in the new condition, in the class condition'. In particular, it was clear that any attempt to mount other significant mass protests over neo-liberalism in the face of the new policing tactics required ways of protecting protestors, an area where the activities of the Italian tuti bianche, or white overall movement, were held in a favourable light and jokingly referred to a model for a 'new vanguard' (Interview with Czech Activist [3]). The repertoires of S26 thus exerted influence within established communist organisations.

Tactical Frivolity and hybrid communication techniques

The trajectory of Tactical Frivolity's (TF) from the United Kingdom's Northern Green Gathering to Prague involved the nucleus of the group driving across Europe in an old van. Their departure was delayed by the adoption of direct action techniques by those protesting at the price of fuel in the United Kingdom. Their progress across national borders had been facilitated by the press credentials of the Guardian reporter who also paid for the diesel. Unlike the internationals, TF were newcomers to AGM events, marginal actors with little standing outside the United Kingdom. Despite remaining marginal to convergence centre exchanges their stance embodied the commitment to non-violence and carnival which became a prominent feature of the Prague plateau. Their use of pink and silver carnival dress codes, rehearsed at various stopovers during their journey time, was combined with a determination to tactically utilise frivolity as a means of engaging directly with Kevlar clad riot police. Their en-route discussions prioritised the importance of manoeuvrability and communications to maximise their impact and resulted in one of their number gaining access to the fortified IMF/WB conference complex. To observers associated with the third element, their resultant progress across Prague appeared chaotic and uncoordinated as they lacked local guides. This perception belies a lack of understanding of the sophisticated hybrid communication strategies in use during S26.

INPEG and convergence centre discussions had initially focussed on acquiring sophisticated radio communications system to facilitate events on the street. This reflects the wider tendency to prioritise 'modern' technologies including CMC in accounts of AGM activities. TF's progress towards the

IMF/WB conference centre was guided by a hybrid combination of ancient and modern communiation techniques. On the ground, runners and bicycle scouts sought out weak spots in the police cordons reporting back directly to the Pink and Silver march. These ancient time-honoured techniques were supplemented from 'Centrum' – a group of activists located in a hotel with a number of mobile phones operating on local sim cards. Centrum was established as a secure communication node at the insistence of internationals not prepared to undertake this work from an INPEG office subject to surveillance. Centrum mapped the location of the main marches and police concentrations and co-ordinated movements between the various marches in a number of languages. Guidance was relayed to the street marches using grid co-ordinates for ease of communication given the limited command of the Czech language. The anonymity of the hotel room meant that communications could only be interrupted by tracing call locations or disabling mobile phone networks.

These ancient and modern communication techniques were 'fused' on the streets through the use of flags or standards which would be raised signifying various needs. As one activist put it

> So suddenly this flag with a fish on it would go up and ok so you knew it was time to huddle and come to some agreement about which way to go.
>
> (Interview British Activist [3])

As TF came under increasing police pressure 'Centrum' was able to inform other marches and seek to reinforce their numbers. Underlying the apparent chaos of Pink and Silver lay a parallel form of what is known in military terms as command, control and communication Intelligence (C3i). In contrast to this multi-layered communication process the mainstream Czech print media carried articles speculating that the demonstrators' success could be attributed to highly sophisticated jamming of electronic communications (e.g. *Lidove noviny* 30.09.00, p. 2). Accounts of the multi-layered communications strategy were initially confined to activist circles as the ensuing mainstream coverage of the event focussed upon the violent clashes which occurred towards the end of the day. The multiplier effects of these innovative street tactics were thus initially confined within the network of networks finding expression in a variety of movement media (e.g. *Do or Die*, 9 and Prague Indymedia).

Tactical Frivolity: carnival in Yer face

TF is an area where we are data rich and can add significant depth in terms of the ontological positioning of key members, group motivations, aims, objectives and social support networks. Like Greenham Women (Roseneil 1995) TF were enabled by men willing to take on familial duties and act as 'honorary women' during the action and were motivated by deeply held, biographically sedimented concerns, quite distinct from the declared objectives of the Prague action.

Whilst a primary respondent within the group is used to represent these themes, here we would emphasise that these are consistent with a group view contained in the video *Tactical Frivolity: protesting against the IMF and World Bank in Prague* (Mirrabelle Productions 2000).

The complexity of the Pink Frame arose from a combination of deeply considered personal reflections on the nature of conflict within contemporary society with a significant gender dimension. One respondent related her sense of frustration at what can be characterised as the historical wheel of violence dominated, though not confined to, exchanges between groups of males.

> Throughout history we have like a whole human history of like people fighting each other and righteously fighting each other and going well, I'm fighting you because you're evil and you're wrong and so that means that I have to fight you, you know, and it's like somehow trying to get away from that and kind of play it differently so that we're saying well we don't like what you're doing, we don't agree with what you're doing and we're here to voice our concerns about what you're doing. But that doesn't mean that I'm going to get out a bigger stick than you've got and beat you dead with it. It's just like, symbolically like to have two groups of people dressed in black, fronting each other off, to me it's just like a continuation of history, a continuation of people fighting against people and saying we're right and you're wrong and yes it is a fight and it is a struggle and it is a battle and I think that we're all warriors as well in a sense. But just by dressing up and making ourselves vulnerable, to me it was sort of symbolic moving us out of that war like space in a way, you know, trying to get away from the total black and white, them and us, you know, we're gonna win or you're gonna win or, you know, and it's just trying to move the whole thing from there a bit. And I think just dressing up makes it a bit more, we're not faceless, you know, it forces it to become a little bit more human.
>
> That is what I'm ultimately frightened of. I'm not frightened of being on my own or of nature, you know, I'm frightened that some man is going to hurt me and I was aware of the fact before I went to Prague that I was actually in some way going there to like face this fear because I was going there and I was going to end up facing a man in black who had an intention to hurt me at the end of the day. And so it's quite a sort of like I was up for taking this challenge on board, I was up for like confronting my fear and so these riot police protecting the World Bank and the IMF had sort of become symbolic for all my fears, all the men out there that might hurt me, you know, and I was actually quite up for,

to face that, I want to see what happens, I want to go there. Do you know what I mean? I want to go and stand up against the faceless man and just see what happens, you know. But we all got dressed up in our pink and silver and we went on the subway and we were all dressed up and whooping and excited. We get to the park and there's just pink and silver everywhere at the park and that's all really exciting. And yeah, I mean, the whole day, I did enter a space where there wasn't time to be fearful, there wasn't time to think, it was just a time when you were getting on with it and you're reacting and you're doing and I very much wanted to be there at the front. I had a few like close shaves where I should have got whacked and I didn't and I did feel blessed on the day and there's footage on the video where this coppers throwing bits of wood at me and I'm just like dancing away like this and they just sort of like bounce in front of me and go over my head. We're looking at it afterwards and going that's amazing.

(Interview with British Activist [3])

TF's frustration applied symmetrically to *both* police and security personnel and protestors, particularly those engaged in 'black bloc' tactics that include the use of violence. Such set piece encounters oppose groups of young men dressed in black, their bodies representing the 'front line' of a conflict situation stimulating the release of fight and flight hormones. There is thus an active rejection of violence in the Pink approach which regards this as a problem for both 'sides' engaged in conflict. Visually this symmetry was best captured in images early in the Prague action where police clad in black confronted demonstrators holding placards declaring the assembly illegal whilst the black clad demonstrators lofted their own placards bearing a range of slogans (see Figure 3.1).

To TF this contact zone was precisely the field of action where their selected repertoires of intervention *had* to be targeted as it was here that the contravention of the prevailing norms of interaction carried most meaning. By inserting playfulness into the front line TF achieved both personal and collective aims by simultaneously perturbating the dominant media discourses associated with anti-globalisation actions by using means that embodied the desired, non-violent, ends. A group of women dressed as 'pink fairies' (see Figure 3.2) thus sought to insert themselves into the contact zone between the opposing black clad men in the midst of an event that local and international press coverage predicted would be typified by extreme violence and destruction of property – 'war'.

The apparent vulnerability of TF evoked a 'masculine' impulse to protect the group which was related by their spokesperson detailing the efforts being taken to shield them from police lines eliciting the response 'we don't want to be protected. We're not princesses in distress, we really don't want protecting, we don't need people protecting us, in fact we want to be at the front...we're here to be front line' (Interview British Activist 3: 185–189). Emerging from behind a huge pink banner, bearing the slogan 'SAMBA!',

Figure 3.1 Police and protestors parade their posters, Prague 2000.

Figure 3.2 Tactical Frivolity launch Pink and Silver in Prague 2000.

TF danced their 'way down to the police' emphasising that their dress code combined with rhythmic drumming 'takes you into a different space' enabling them to take 'a different energy to the front line.' Armed with nothing more than a 'presentation of self' expressed through costume, song, dance and pink feather dusters they 'spring cleaned' police armoured personnel carriers oblivious to the rain of projectiles directed towards them.

The desire to be at the front left TF occupying the 'in-between' spaces twixt police and protestors lines 'And this sort of like stage space appears, like a performance space seemed to appear between the rows of policemen and the rows of people like blockading...we found ourselves like going into this gap and tickling policemen's' toes [using] your feather duster on the side of their face and just like performing' (Interview British Activist [3]).

In this account the theatrical dynamic was tipped into another modality when from behind the SAMBA! banner male protestors produced pieces of timber and started beating the police. 'I was disgusted that they'd got those sticks out because they set the whole agenda.... I was really angry because they didn't even use the violence productively (i.e. to break through to the conference centre)...as soon as they started getting a beating they were off...and we were left like dancing in our pink and silver and the water canon comes out' (Interview British Activist [3]).

The onset of violent confrontation quickly eroded the cohesion of the Pink march as communication became difficult to sustain and the limits of pre-event strategising were reached. Transcripts describe the rapid transition in police personnel from 'ordinary', through 'normal riot police' to 'these other police who looked like storm troopers...like something out of Star Wars'. One officer raised 'a thing like a sword in the air...and they all start charging down the hill'. The absence of a collectively agreed set of strategies to respond to a police charge and the fragmentation of a march of 'hundreds' in the face of a charge by 20–30 Darth Vaders' left no option (see Figure 3.3). 'I was expecting to go there and get hurt, you know, and I just did not want to run away from them but standing on my own was pretty pointless anyway...But in the end I had to [run] and then there's this bit on the video where this storm trooper is like wrestling me for like possession of my pink feather duster and like whacking me across the arse' (Interview British Activist [3]). The interviewee's reflection upon this was 'Well, its like that's my stick isn't it...so he's got to take my stick (laughter) in case I hit him with it...It's like sticks and stones...it's just like that's the thing that I've got that is like a gun or a truncheon, it's my feather duster so he's got to have it' (Interview British Activist [3]).

In terms of complexity theory this account renders visible the potency of free acts in terms of emergence and the heterogenesis of a strange attractor with the potential to strip legitimacy from the institutions of law and order. Personal understanding of and engagement with the fear associated with

Figure 3.3 Pink and Silver in retreat, Prague 2000.

'Empire' resulted in a group of thirteen women marginal to established actors within the network of networks becoming the nucleus of a street 'swarm' (Chesters 2003) several hundred strong. Having performed their particular version of TF the wider trope of pink and silver was donated to the movement of movements. Following its debut on the international stage in Prague, Pink and Silver and carnivalesque performativity became recurrent features of subsequent summit sieges in a process of continuing hybridisation extending to the London European Social Forum meeting in October 2004 (see Figure 3.3). CMC played a central role in the creation of the Pink and Silver diaspora as part of the process of reflexive framing, themes we return to in concluding this chapter. Before this can be done it is important to offer an account of the Italian group Ya Basta, a clear example of a well-established actor within the network of networks.

Yellow – Ya Basta

'*Ya Basta!*' led the 'Yellow March' towards Nusle Bridge, the main traffic artery to the Congress Centre, that was heavily fortified by the Czech Police and Military using security barriers, officers in riot clothing and gas masks, armoured personnel carriers, water cannons and buses (see Figure 3.4). Ya Basta! were by their own admission coming to Prague to 'Liquidate the

Figure 3.4 Ya Basta! Head for Nuselsky Bridge, Prague 2000.

International Monetary Fund', presenting a formidable spectacle dressed in heavily padded white overalls. However, the playful and reflexive capacity of this social movement network was soon manifest. This 'liquidation' was to take place via water pistol and water bomb and was coupled with the release of hundreds of balloons bearing the slogan 'liquidate IMF'.[9]

> We are criminals, delinquents, outlaws: using our weapons we shall take what is ours. And if the booty we are after is a universal citizens' income, where should we strike, if not at a meeting of the World Bank and the International Monetary Fund? And if we want to liquidate them, what better weapons than water filled weapons?
>
> Ya Basta! Agit-prop

This performance of protest as play combined dramaturgical presence, courage and a clear declaratory posture linked to a confrontational stance leading to their portrayal in media reports as 'the most disciplined, stylish and effective of all Europe's direct action groups'[10] (Vanderford 2003). Ya Bastas! stance was adopted by some activist groups[11] but was also subject to some critical movement commentary (e.g. *Do or Die*, 9: 11).

Ya Basta! became locked in a confrontation which conformed to a predetermined plan involving the playful use of bodies to symbolically challenge the global economic institutions protected by police lines. Third element video capture also revealed members of the group throwing less playful projectiles at police lines.[12] The emphasis on bodily engagement is part of a strategy to parallel the relations of capital under neo-liberalism. Members of Ya Basta! also travelled without passports as part of their insistence on a symmetrical freedom of movement for people as well as capital. Their media strategy included carefully prepared explanatory statements which were rehearsed and delivered straight to camera before the enactment of a interventions such as the destruction of a McDonalds' outlet. There was thus a conscious identification, declaration and engagement with a range of stakes including symbolic registers, making accusations of mindless violence problematic. Continuity of engagement and a base within established social centres in Italy enhanced solidaristic cohesion contributing to Ya Basta!'s high profile within the Prague plateau.

The denouement of S26

S26 was widely perceived as a 'success' within the movement milieu and an important formalisation of issues revolving around both the definition and use of violence within plateau mobilisations. Our interview data and research process revealed to some key participants the extent to which the inevitability of *some* violence had been 'bracketed out' within the (dis)organisational processes constituting this plateau initiating further critical reflection.

Public sphere accounts were however, dominated by the primacy of violence frames inside and outside the Czech Republic (Welsh 2004) repeating patterns evident in London (Donson *et al.* 2004). Attempts to secure media coverage for the underlying concerns and aims of the movement were not considered 'newsworthy' (Interview Czech Activist [2]). Complexity was subordinated to unambiguous reporting of violence consistent with pre-event story lines about 'war' fuelled by official press releases. In the United Kingdom *The Guardian* was an exception carrying extensive coverage based on John Vidal's experience of accompanying Tactical Frivolity to Prague. The adage 'If it bores it floors, if it bleeds it leads' remained applicable to the majority of coverage.

On this the third element were definitive.

> at the end I think it was 26 shop windows broken. The next morning all major dailies used the word 'war' in uh.. the headlines on the front pages so hell for Czech's 26 shop windows equals war. Um.. this was revolting.
> (Interview Czech Activist [9])

Through their communication work with the security services the third element were engaged with a policing operation constituted by different forces and operational emphases. Their work had been based 'on personal, individual contacts and trust um...with police on one side, we would have our phone tapped, we would be followed by some elements, the other policemen would tell us about it' (Interview Czech Activist [9]) they concluded that:

> part of the police command even welcomed the violence because it proved they were right and uh...later on we have studied more, or near to seventy hours of videos, we have a written analysis of it and it proves very clearly that Czech police, excuse the expression, fucked up completely.
>
> (Czech Activist [9])

Reflexive framing and the S26 Diaspora

Melucci's insight that movement are media (Melucci 1996a, Atton 2002, Chesters and Welsh 2004) is rendered tangible by the dissemination of events in Prague through personal and collective CMC networks such as Indymedia, these immediate representations being followed by print (e.g. *Do or Die*) and video products (Praha 2000: Rebel Colours, Tactical Frivolity, Crowd Bites Wolf) within the national movement milieus of participating network actors. Public viewings, discussions and debate of video accounts become central to post-event interpretations, refinement and finessing central to the process of reflexive framing (Chesters and Welsh 2001). Within the shadow realm such autonomous media product blurs the producer/consumer dichotomy dominating media studies accounts of media production and consumption power relations.

These subterranean networks are part of the process of encoding/decoding (Hall 1980) which formalise *oppositional codes* and frequently coincide with moments of crisis within mainstream broadcast organizations.[13] As Hall concludes, 'Here the "politics of signification" – the struggle in discourse – is joined' (1980: 138). These processes have intensified as withdrawal of public trust, weakening political media management capacities, and fragmented audiences reading niche products combine with increasingly diverse global media.

The ensuing siege of the signs is conducted through the definition and contestation of symbolic stakes which simultaneously 'hollow out' the state (Held 2000) and erode the 'imagined communities' (Anderson 1989) created by national media. The increasing reliance of reporters upon indymedia, with key centres receiving more 'hits' than CNN websites during significant events reflects this struggle as mainstream media begin to recognise the need to incorporate voices from the street (Cottle 1999).

Plateau effects

In terms of the themes addressed in this chapter it is important to sketch some of the network consequences arising from reflexive framing of the Prague plateau paying attention to both 'national local' and 'global' domains.

The Prague plateau increased the network cohesion of activist groups within the Czech Republic and actively tied them into European and Global networks multiplying the potential for 'weak ties' (Welsh 2004). The presence of Czech, and other Eastern European groups, within the European Social Forum testifies to this aspect of capacity building. Protest repertoires from S26 were integrated within subsequent protest events in Prague as the government of the Czech Republic increasingly aligned itself with the 'new Europe' identified by American interests.

Perhaps more fundamentally S26 consolidated and spread the questioning of the 'freedoms' associated with the transition to market economies. In this sense the social associations from below, prioritised by Havel, began rendering the working of business political under the 'new conditions'. The Czech political executive's increasing alignment with American initiatives began to be viewed as rendering Czech citizens 'passive victims of international capital' (www.ce-review.org/00/32/culik32.html).

Discovery of information about the WTO, WB and IMF represented a prominent theme in interviews which emphasised apparently trivial personal exchanges: the loan of a book; attendance at a talk or meeting via a friendship network; involvement with elements of the global networks such as Vandana Shiva's community (Interview Czech Activist [6]); personal contact with people present in Washington, Seattle or London. In this manner the complex process of defining stakes, identifying key institutional pressure points and viable means of political engagement relevant to the prevailing cultures *begins* constituting a 'cultural politics' distinct from political culture (Lash and Urry 1994).

Within Prague the activists involved in S26 established the Infocafe Anarres (www.ainfos.ca/) to provide, an educational and cultural resource for the local community; a space for the Czech movement to use for its political and cultural needs; and as a space for social and political projects. The associated website carries information on libertarian and self-help events translated into 12 languages illustrating a significant transformation of local activist capacities when compared to the run up to S26.[14] These developments more than outweigh the initial deficits arising from S26 which included the closure of the La Dronka squat. Prague Indymedia ceased operating in July 2004 leaving Infocafe Anarres substantially replicating the groups, functions. The global movements' articulation of environmental damage and capitalist economics introduced Czech 'greens' to a set of concerns which had not been linked prior to S26.

> After ten years of a civil drowse the public somewhat clumsily learnt that criticism and a public display of dissent, as long as it does not break a letter of law, is a legitimate instrument of democracy.
>
> (Interview Czech Activist [6])

By November 2000, a group of MEPs wrote formally to Vaclav Havel protesting against the actions of the Ministry of Interior urging him to personally secure the release of the remaining prisoners.

Subsequent actions in Prague, such as those associated with the 2002 Nato summit illustrate the transfer of repertoires of action seeded through S26, including the presence of a carnivalesque samba band and the use of an 'Argentinean style noise protest' (www.indymedia.org.uk/en/2003/09/278096.html). Press accounts of the Nato summit replicated frames prominent in reportage on S26 emphasising property damage, violence and disruption (e.g. *The Prague Post*, 27.11.02). The Czech government reportedly spent \$20.6 million on security for the Nato summit (*The Prague Post*, 20.11.02) and ultimately ceded control of national security to America for the duration of the event.

In terms of the wider AGM, 'Pink & Silver' became a prominent feature of subsequent summit sieges and social forum events throughout Europe resonating with other network actors committed to playful or dramaturgical protest. Given available performance space such repertoires of action are symbolically potent and difficult to police as the energies released in such exercises resonate with wider public sentiments which historically explains the century's long effort of state agencies to fragment, oppress and contain such forms of protest (see Chapters 1 and 4). In this sense 'fear' and the playful engagement with the 'agents of fear' performed in Prague reformulated an historically sedimented, potent form of public protest reconfiguring it in the context of the AGM. This positive multiplier effect added to the potency of the AGM as a strange attractor around which increasingly diverse constituencies condensed within networks influenced by the over-arching values of the PGA.

Conclusions

The global milieu has significantly transformed the potential of minoritarian voices through enhanced mobility and communications which amplify and accelerate the processes by which 'social force' (Welsh 2000) becomes mobilised around these emergent agendas. Multiple network actors will continue to amplify these issues, not through a unified collective identity (Stallings 1973, McDonald 2002), but via the melding of multiple identities: national; regional; local; gendered; disabled; parental and so on within fora such as the PGA and ESF, conceived from the outset as expressions of global civil society (see Chapter 5). In terms of our theoretical arguments this chapter empirically demonstrates significant claims relating to communication, energy, mobility and weak ties as processes constitutive of socially organised expressions of complexity indicative of emergence.

Communication utilising weak ties structured the event enabling mobility on the street. An extremely experienced activist commented that it 'was a miracle we were not just corralled in Namesti Miru Square as the entire march had been declared illegal'. There is strong inferential evidence in our interview material that no such action was taken because of the third elements success in communicating the blockade as a win–win strategy. This was a process which the Czech legal support organisation OPH also participated in (Interview British Activists [4 and 5]). Police forces appear to have been concentrated upon the Blue and Yellow marches associated with the highest probability of violent confrontation. This combined with the view that the Pink March lacked cohesion and direction created a significant freedom of manoeuvre which was accentuated by the hybrid communication strategy developed in the immediate pre-event phase. The apparent 'chaos' or 'flow' of Pink was in fact a form of deliberative and dialogical action based on observation, communication and reflection upon events in more or less real time within which individual free acts played crucial roles. In Kenney's words: 'The actors are not the famous dissident intellectuals [and the ruthless communists], but hundreds of lesser-known individuals' (Kenney 2002: 16). We have been able to relate this account through the use of multiple qualitative and textual techniques predicated upon presence on the ground during the event, reinforcing the importance of Touraine's commitment to direct engagement with and within movements. The themes and analytical concerns presented here are simply not available to accounts derived from mainstream media coverage of the event and are only present in a fragmentary form in movement media. The fusion of sources and interpretation is *ours* and we acknowledge that this is an inescapable part of the process of sense making involved in the interpretation of qualitative data. This process requires time, immersion and interaction.[15] In particular, we take responsibility for locating the data within the theoretical debates addressed throughout this book.

Theory and praxis

Theoretical accounts of the global movement contestation (Hardt and Negri 2000, 2004) emphasising the ascendancy and autonomy of capital over state forms stress the importance of 'smooth space', with deregulated global neo-liberalism representing this over-arching axiomatic. Smooth space enables network actors to sort circuit forms of interest representation associated with state forms delivering direct challenges to Empire. In this process technological mediation plays a central role in both the exercise of disciplinary effects within divisions of labour through the associated techniques and practices. These same techniques and practices are central to the radical uses of bio-power by the multitude operating as a network actor constitutive of unity in diversity. In this constitutive process multiple small world networks coalesce.

Our account of the Prague plateau has emphasised the importance of both cutting edge and mundane technologies within this process. As Urry (2004) argues face-to face interactions remain central in maintaining and renewing network connections necessitating travel and a range of techniques of self. Urry differentiates between 'aristocratic' and 'egalitarian' network forms contrasting the World Wide Web with social networks to argue that approaches to small world phenomena need to be more sociological and more complex. As this account demonstrates plateaux are constituted around multiple axes including biographical availability; physical mobility; communicative competence; ontological security; spatial competence and the courage to engage in free acts.

In this process the theoretical postulate smooth space is revealed to be more complex than the term implies. This is particularly evident in terms of physical movement where national borders represent potential choke points. The mode of physical movement across space is also significant in qualitative terms. Tactical Frivolity's extended journey enabled a process of negotiated meaning and bonding which underpinned their performative integrity on the street, unlike taking a flight to Prague. Another significant feature of the interactions dealt with in this chapter is the dissonance between internationals' expectations formed within the smooth space of CMC and their experience of prevailing conditions upon arrival in Prague. The outcomes of Prague were also clearly dependent upon pre-existing social networks constitutive of the third element, reinforcing the importance of the local in configuring AGM plateaux.

Such 'irregularities' in smooth space arise through active struggles over meaning associated with 'event density' (McKechnie and Welsh 2002) and can be thought of in terms of degrees of abstraction, resolution or pixellation. National borders, offering barriers to physical mobility in this context, define the containers of nations, a role which includes the opportunity to apply trade tariffs and extract excise duty crucial to state finances. Autonomous capital seeks to avoid such fiscal choke points whilst states continue to limit the mobility of labour amidst the free flow of tourist nomads. Smooth space is in effect criss-crossed by multiple and shifting striations etched through the activities of multiple actors with implications for both 'local' and 'global' domains. Plateaux as sites of concrete contestation formalise both issues and the iterative evolution of process through reflexive framing. Irrespective of mainstream media's pre-occupation with violence (see Chapter 4) the implications of smooth space a la Empire become embodied in acts which are broadcast, debated and reflected upon over extended periods of time through the use of recording and communication techniques which reconfigure the framing process constituting an ecology of action (Chapter 5).

4 From carnival against capitalism to death at high noon
States fight back

Introduction

The AGM has been dealt with as a network of networks engaged in conflictual and co-operative movement capacity building at a global level acting as a strange attractor in the process of emergence associated with global civil society actors. Within this process we have argued that the strength of weak ties and significance of small world networks are critical factors in the ability of the AGM to perturbate normative repertoires organising political discourse. These processes are technologically enabled and mediated through CMC and physical mobility. As we explored in Chapter 3 technological and face-work networking at a global level also typify the activities of state and supra-national actors responding to AGM activities, particularly those associated with 'summit sieges'. Whilst the technical mediations are common in kind if not scale, this chapter argues that their use by 'security state', 'political state' and 'financial state' reproduces established and dominant discourses through 'strong ties' consolidating established 'habits of mind' associated with Western nation state actors on the global stage understood as an arena of international relations.

In particular, this chapter considers the replication of political discourses utilising fear, terror and the identification of outsiders as dangerous 'others' in attempts to discredit and marginalise the AGM. These 'moves' were in train long before events of 11 September 2001, which merely added impetus to an established trend rather than precipitating a new era in which 'nothing would be the same again'. This is a point of fundamental importance as the 'war on terror' cannot be adequately theorised or engaged with if it is approached as a 'new phenomenon'. Here we argue that the application of terror tropes to AGM actors is an extension of deviance tropes (Martin 2002) in the attempt to create a new 'folk devil' aligning AGM actors with 'evil' and creating an 'enemy within'. Such moves legitimate harsher policing regimes, erosion of civil rights, the need for 'strong security states' and organs of global surveillance.

As we show, the portrayal of apparently fixed activist identities as an 'evil enemy' within the public sphere are problematic in terms of public resonance, when trust in political, economic and scientific institutions is withdrawn or severely attenuated through the day-to-day experience of neo-liberal 'progress'. The extension of terrorist tropes to AGM actors creates 'enemies within' implicitly linked to generic network evils associated with stateless terrorist actors, both of which are constructed as enemies of progress as conceived within Western 'advanced barbarism'.[1] In the United Kingdom these themes are particularly prominent in relation to animal rights campaigns against the rearing and use of animals for laboratory experiments. The attribution of 'anti-science' stances threatening future economic prosperity arising from sunrise genetic industries emphasises issues relating to substantive rationalities associated with modernity.[2] This highlights the disparity between these and activist attempts to extend 'rights' based arguments to animals, reflecting ethical arguments formalised by Singer (1979) and developed from a range of philosophical stances (O'Neill 2002).

O'Neill's (2002) recognition that the human animal is the only one able to formalise the interests of other species and exercise choice over quality of life issues and species existence adds a critical dimension to human choice in the constitution of sustainable futures. Societal choices in such areas are reflections of the moral and ethical worth attributed to the organic realm with implications for intergenerational equity associated with sustainable development and bio-diversity. These debates are currently in a state of further extension as the mapping of the human genome raises issues of human diversity when confronted by the prospect of 'neo-liberal eugenics' (Habermas 2003).

Other forms of extension accompany the security states' attempts to police the 'siege of the signs'. Policing and surveillance operations increasingly ensnare 'ordinary citizens' as measures conceived in relation to an imagined enemy reveal the heavy hand of the security state in more and more sites. The actions of the security state are complemented by the asymmetrical use of the legal system by corporate actors attempting to silence concerns expressed by movement actors and 'ordinary' citizens. The prosecution of two London Greenpeace activists by McDonalds, the McLibel case, is a particularly prominent example of this wider process of 'legal intimidation' (Donson 2000).[3] The United States' unilateral disregard for human rights in the context of stateless terrorist networks adds a further dimension to these concerns, threatening to contaminate and erode progressive rights based discourses within the international community.

In the context of *Empire* these developments represent the enactment of a US orchestrated imperium modelled upon Rome intersecting with and eliding a number of key discourses through terror tropes. Once constituted, such discursive forms result in multiple readings constituting *both* discursive and material contestation that *is outside* the security state's control. The attempt to create an hegemony of terror tropes encounters numerous obstacles including the historically sedimented memories of previous security state attempts to suppress the exercise of popular democratic will.

The global ambitions of the current imperium rekindle memories of *both* nationalist liberation and domestic class struggles both of which were cast as law and order problems. The re-emergence and re-formulation of these discourses within right wing think tanks towards the end of the twentieth century called for a league of forceful civilised nations to police Third World movements described as 'extremist', 'terrorist', and 'criminal' (Fukuyama 1992).[4]

This so-called 'Clash of Civilisations' requiring 'Western military vigilance to defend itself against Eastern civilisations' (1992) consolidated rapidly in the following decade. Under the leadership of a tightly networked neo-liberal intelligentsia,[5] the global institutional nexus continues to advance an agenda underpinned by a notion of freedom to profit and prosper sedimented within American culture since the seventeenth century (Welsh 2005). In the twenty-first century, this process of 'terrorist' extension now includes civil society actors inside the 'advanced' economies but simultaneously networked as global civil society actors advancing global interests transcending national systems of interest representation. State responses to delegitimise the messengers as a contemporary 'folk devil' (Donson *et al.* 2004) and subject them to extreme sanctions have broad similarities but are enacted in a variety of ways reflecting both national and regional custom and tradition.

These extensions are important and on-going and this chapter concentrates upon the period between 1999 and 2002 where we are able to remain true to the Deleuzian genealogical detail underpinning this work. We thus draw heavily upon material relating to events in Seattle 1999, London 2000, and Genoa 2001 in support of our argument that there has been a conscious attempt to construct a new 'folk devil' despite the absence of the 'moral panic' traditionally associated with the term (Donson *et al.* 2004). In this process, prominent politicians and senior police officers identify activists as 'violent', 'mindless thugs',[6] views widely reproduced in print and broadcast media (Wahl-Jorgensen 2003).

Seattle connections

As we noted in Chapter 1, Seattle was identified as a potential site of emergence within movement networks from at least 1996. The modus operandi advanced at this time was substantially realised through nomadic exchanges central to the diasporic spread of repertoires of action through enhanced mobility. Far from being an unexpected event, the Seattle plateau condensed a diverse range of practices, albeit leading to unpredicted and unpredictable emergent outcomes. It is important to offer an account of these precursors to give the reader some sense of the agency lying behind the 'flows' of meaning that coalesced to structure this action. The role of European and UK movements is foregrounded here as an exemplar of a process paralleled in multiple global sites and enacted via local customs. However, we would emphasise the situated partiality of our account, as academically, we are adhering to our sense of Deleuzian detail in working from examples where we have empirical depth. This enables us to illustrate the importance of network immersion in order to access events otherwise invisible within the public sphere.

The realignment of politics beyond left right binary divides following the collapse of communism was preceded in the United Kingdom by an apparently hegemonic neo-liberal Thatcherite politics from 1979 onwards. The hot cold war became a major focus for social movement actors within the context of defensive unionism. With the collapse of the Soviet Union, the UK movement milieu entered a period of apparent quietude leading to claims about 'UK exceptionalism' in the context of widespread mobilisations on mainland Europe (Rootes 1992). This view had barely surfaced when vibrant actions became visible within the public sphere (Welsh and McLeish 1996). Activists targeted road programmes, airport construction, animal rights, and supermarket locations, marking a significant transition to movement engagement with mundane developments associated with modernity. These defensive movement actions were paralleled by vibrant expressions of cultural innovation associated with musical genres articulating more proactive versions of life style politics (McKay 1996, 1998).

The establishment of Earth First! UK (Wall 1999) as a distinctive variant of its US progenitor introduced an over-arching theme that resonated positively with the dispersed emphasis on direct action across the United Kingdom. Earth First! and derivatives, particularly London RTS, became central network actors orchestrating some particularly high profile events. Of these J18 – the day in June when trading was brought to a standstill in the City of London – assumed international prominence. In the run up to Seattle key individuals associated with this and other UK events were invited to the United States to act as trainers and resource persons. The Seattle event thus drew upon a wide range of experience but was enacted in a US context within a particular urban environment and an established law and order regime and culture.

Seattle

The Seattle WTO meeting was scheduled to produce a new trade round including the inclusion of China, a move with significant backing from President Bill Clinton but opposed by international labour organisations on human and union rights grounds. American Labour and Union concerns over the impact of global free market initiatives had been shaped through experience of the North America Free Trade Agreement (NAFTA), which had also contributed to the Zapatista mobilisation. In Seattle American leadership within the WTO's 'QUAD', an agenda setting core including the EU, Japan and Canada, failed to secure the passage of a new round, meeting significant opposition in open meetings from Latin American and African countries. Inclusion of China in the WTO offered to integrate a dynamic, expansionist economy within global markets stimulating demand, reducing production costs and intensifying the creation of global labour markets (Obando-Rojas *et al.* 2004). Capital restructuring, union and labour rights issues were combined with prominent environmental concerns including the threatened extinction of sea turtles and Monarch butterflies. The resultant slogan 'Teamsters and Turtles Unite and Fight' rapidly established itself as the leit-motif of the event acquiring far more meaning outside the AGM than within (Tabb 2000).

The long traditions of the American movement milieus associated with labour, anti-war, peace and environmental activism interacted with European direct action repertoires communicated by 'free radicals' and disseminated through workshops in co-operation with US trainers. The RTS experience of carnival resonated positively with elements of the 'domestic mix' and the convergence of global networks in Seattle. Other actors, particularly those associated with organised labour movements were less comfortable with these new repertoires. Accommodating the 'new movements' within an action structured and funded by organisations with a 'traditional' American 'new left' orientation resulted in significant tensions and widely competing interpretations of the event (Hardt-Landsberg 2000, Yuen *et al.* 2001).

Irrespective of this 'diversity', a number of common themes consistent with recognition of accumulating 'social force' are evident within these accounts. These include:

- The diverse range of people on the street.
- The significance of street presence in bolstering the resolve of delegates from 'the South'.
- The growing recognition of common experience and common cause between workers and citizens in North and South.
- The simultaneous expression of economic and environmental concerns.
- The relationship between formal labour organisations and vibrant social movements as mutually dependent conflictual actors.

The result was a 'global social force' deploying a range of repertoires to declare the stakes through occupying 'the street' in a manor analogous to events in East and Central Europe during the transitions. The valency of these concerns resulted in encounters that exceeded the experience of both local organisers and police authorities (St. Clair 1999, Tabb 2000, Yuen *et al.*, 2001).

Event novelty confounds established habits of mind leaving engaged actors confronted by the 'unknown' associated with heightened complexity within the point of emergence. Some sense of this in terms of operational policing can be gleaned from a police radio transmission in Toronto during the first 'Global Street Party' on 16 May 1998. 'This is not a protest. Repeat. This is not a protest. This is some kind of artistic expression. Over' (Klein 2000: 311). In Seattle, a carnivalesque event that virtually controlled the streets from dawn disoriented familiar forms of police engagement, which was now confronted by multiple repertoires of action. This 'unknown' was significantly structured by tensions between Federal and local security services. The FBI attached primary importance to President Clinton addressing the meeting resulting in the operational imperative that 'the President must get through'. Accounts of the event reveal how policing strategy became increasingly aggressive as the time of the Presidential arrival approached with the use of tear-gas, pepper sprays and riot batons increasing throughout the day.

The post-event dénouement is more important to present purposes as events on the day are the subject of extensive treatment elsewhere (Cockburn *et al.* 2000, Yuen *et al.* 2001, *Notes from Nowhere* 2003). In post-war United States, the relatively unrestrained use of riot police and state troopers is historically associated with labour disputes, 'race riots', student revolts and anti-war protests. US 'freedoms' of assembly and speech have always been open to the ultimate use of force, something sedimented within popular culture and collective activist memory through events such as the shooting of students on University Campuses during the late 1960s and early 1970s. In Seattle, force was used against a coalition of predominantly white[7] union and environmental activists in a sufficiently unfocussed manner to impact directly on citizens about their daily business. The 'local' outcome of this Federal Imperative included the end of the career of Seattle's police chief and initiated a steep learning curve for police and security agencies in coming to terms with an emergent 'protest' phenomenon (Canadian Security Intelligence Service 2000).

Media coverage of Seattle

Solomon's (Solomon 2000) study of 22 articles and editorials in the *Los Angeles Times (LAT)* and 35 from the *New York Times* between 21 November and 21 December 1999 reveals some marked similarities with media coverage of subsequent events in other countries. Both papers emphasised the marginality of protestors with the *LAT* asking 'Who on earth were they' (3.12.99, p. A1) and the *NYT* drawing 'Dark Parallels with Anarchist Outbreaks in Oregon'[8] (3.12.99, p. A12) describing them as 'a Noah's ark of flat-earth advocates' (1.12.99, p. A23). To protestors the WTO appeared as 'a handmaiden of corporate interests' representing 'the tyrannical symbol of a global economy that has shoved social priorities aside in a relentless quest for profits' (Solomon 2000: 14–15). Public support for protestors by Seattle residents was expressed through chants of 'Let them go!' as police pursued activists.

Media reports did however, follow Bill Clinton's public statements supporting the cause of many of the peaceful protestors and the need for dialogue, identifying a 'small knot' of 'more militant elements' who had used police behaviour as 'a cue to go on a rampage' (Solomon 2000: 15).

Seattle police were criticised for failing to discern the true intent of protestors and were urged to follow the example set in Washington DC where police had made use of 'informants and undercover officers' (Solomon 2000: 17). Solomon emphasises the way in which key market precepts like 'free trade' and 'liberalization' were not elaborated or questioned within media commentary being accepted as facts of life 'like gravity' and certainly 'not a continuation of colonialism and imperialism', with the *LAT* declaring that 'Economists regard free trade as just about as controversial as motherhood' (Solomon 2000: 17).

Solomon argues that the US press depicted the failure of the Seattle trade round as the consequence of internal dissent with Clinton's proposals having 'collapsed...after a rebellion by developing countries and deadlock among America's biggest trading partners' (*NYT* 5.12.99, p. A1). This is consistent with US foreign policy stances which typically integrate national economic policy and specific economic sectors within their declaratory posture, making opposition to US economic and business freedom an act of opposition to the United States (Welsh 2005).

Seattle was a rude awakening for both political and police leaders as the influential but misguided 1990s slogan 'Think Global Act Local' was decisively abandoned in favour of global contestation drawing on multiple locales. Seattle was a point of emergence for the AGM and operated as a strange attractor/symbolic multiplier drawing together a range of actors within a complex collaborative venture (see Gillham and Marx 2003). Whilst comparisons were drawn with the radicalism of the 1960s and 1970s the 'global reach' of this action, particularly the conscious alignment with issues of 'the South' far exceeded the limited critical mass achieved in Paris in 1968 (Singer 2000, Purkiss and Bowen eds 2004). Significantly, Solomon (2000) notes that the global nature of Seattle went uncommented in US newspapers whilst receiving coverage in *The Guardian* and *Observer*. This is attributed to the independence of these UK papers by virtue of their ownership. As we detail later these titles are far from representative of the remainder of the UK press in terms of the treatment of AGM actions. However, representations of such actions are widely reported as part of global protests suggesting that corporate ownership is not a sufficient explanation of US myopia. Tendencies amongst the US media toward insularity and weak coverage of world events with no direct US angle suggest themselves as relevant cultural and political factors.

May Day 2000 Guerrilla gardening

The euphoria following Seattle suffused activist networks bolstering confidence and ambitions. In the United Kingdom, where like most industrial economies, May Day holds particular significance in terms of popular struggles dating back centuries; network actors went 'guerrilla gardening' in Parliament Square. The event, conceived as a celebration, set out to 'green Parliament Square' by planting verges and ornamental areas with vegetables, a horticultural use of public space not seen since the rationing associated with the Second World War. We have examined the portrayal of this event by police and politicians as the creation of a 'new folk devil' elsewhere (Wahl-Jorgensen 2003, Donson *et al.* 2004). For present purposes the important features of this work are, a media portrayal of AGM activists consistent with Cohen's original (1972) folk devil thesis; their depiction as the 'the personification of evil' (Goode and Ben-Yehuda 1994); and the use of such images to enable 'ideological exploitation' by a range of commentators (Thompson 1995: 39). Significantly, we found an absence of the usual 'moral panic' associated with a new 'folk devil', which is often central to the mobilisation of public fear and acquiescence in the face of new policing methods and public acceptance of stereotypic representations (McRobbie 1994: 199). Despite this, prominent politicians and police commentators acted *as if* such a panic was underway in terms of public order issues *without* explicating the anatomy of the underlying crisis, largely *because* this would involve them in accepting central tenets of the activists' arguments as legitimate concerns.[9] Here, we suggest that subsequent revisions to legislation on the detention of terrorist suspects has *begun* to make the normative symmetry between democracy and freedom problematic.

The 'Devil' is in the detail

Cohen emphasised three key stages in the media portrayal of a social actor as demonic. A particular word or phrase – anti-capitalist protestor – becomes associated with a delinquent or deviant status; key objects – hairstyle, clothing – come to symbolise the word/phrase – resulting in these objects becoming symbols of the attached status and the associated emotions (Cohen 1972: 134). The life style attributes of targeted social actors in the UK have been subject to a process of legal incorporation since direct action made the legal definition of 'breach of the peace' problematic in the 1980s (Welsh 2000). The 1994 Criminal Justice and Public Order Act (CJA) represented an initial consolidation of this judicial drift re-defining trespassory assembly and naming specific life style attributes as public order issues. 'Rave' culture and other urban musical innovations were also incorporated within the CJA by reference to music characterised by a 'repetitive beat'. Within movement circles, this was inverted to include the repetitive beating of police batons' on riot shields, a rhythmic repetitive sound frequently preceding raids and evictions. The adoption of such tactics varied across police authorities reflecting chief constables prioritisation and interpretation of national legislation.[10]

As direct action sites spread across the United Kingdom, the number of police authorities confronting movement activists multiplied with the use of 'civil contractors' and feudal legal institutions such as County Sheriffs increasing.[11] The Prevention of Terrorism Act 2000 represented a further consolidation of state powers but remained inadequate in the eyes of senior police officers. Sir Charles Pollard, Thames Valley Chief Constable from 1997–2002 considered that 'If anything we have not been bold enough in seeing where the line is and going right up to the line to stop people who are basically criminal people doing serious things – and it is that robustness we have still not quite got' (BBC 2 *True Spies*).

Chief constables continued lobbying for more powers, something confirmed by Amanda Webster, Deputy Sheriff of Lancashire, commenting on her experience of running training sessions at the Metropolitan Police Academy at Hendon, London. In her view amongst the police the 'the will to stamp out extreme protest has intensified', producing an 'effective lobby...to curb the Movement'. The inclusion of animal rights and similar protests within the Terrorism Act 2000 was part of a 'backlash against extreme protest', to which she adds 'similar draconian legislation will not be far behind' (Webster 2002).

Underlying the fractured and episodic media representation of public order issues within the public sphere lay police and movement cultures interacting on a day-to-day basis. Asymmetrical access and media credibility structures the images of these interactions, which become dominated by 'newsworthy' events (Wahl-Jorgensen 2003). A repetitive cycle of representation has been established revolving around Cohen's tripartite schema.

In the run up to a protest event, police and senior politicians issue public announcements emphasising the violent intent of protestors and the likelihood of damage to property which are implicitly and or explicitly linked to a more abstract threat to democracy and or civilisation. Such statements are justified retrospectively through past examples of riotous assembly and warn of future repetitions. Whilst political figures typically defend the right of citizens to legitimate protest, there are also appeals for ordinary citizens not to participate in 'extreme' AGM actions.

As we showed earlier (Chapter 3) this cycle of representation owes much to global networking within and between police, intelligence and political offices of state, foregrounding 'fear', 'terror' and 'anarchy'. Once established as dominant discourses within the public sphere, these tropes *tend* to silence participants' substantive grievances and motivations, collapsing complex multiple identities to a 'mob'. This discursively constructed 'mob' then becomes the 'object' of policing strategies and operational practices. The application of this label conceals the presence of numerous 'respectable' and thoughtful citizens committed to positive change within society. Attempts by activists to gain mainstream media coverage for systematic debate on contested issues such as social justice, rights of assembly and freedom of speech is effectively foreclosed by their 'deviant' construction.

Traditionally this silencing process has been part of the establishments' capacity to manage and control political debate and shape public expectations (Middlemass 1979), something made increasingly difficult by modern media technologies (Thompson 1995). Generally, politicians also attempt to trivialise activists' substantive claims as naïve, irrational, dangerous, un-democratic, self-interested etc. The subordination of AGM activists through dominant discourses within the bourgeois public sphere effectively blocks public engagement with the contemporary equivalent of the 'crisis' identified by Cohen (1972). To engage with the substantive issues raised by the AGM would mean implicitly accepting the existence of a crisis in institutional trust amongst the general public and the need to radically alter mechanisms of interest representation.

Creating 'new' folk devils – May Day 2000 and 2001

The largely peaceful demonstration in Parliament Square on May Day 2000 tipped into limited violence and property damage after police allowed protestors to leave Parliament Square and enter Whitehall. Some shops, including a McDonalds, were damaged and, more controversially the Cenotaph and a memorial statute to Winston Churchill were defaced. There were 30 arrests and 5 reported injuries on the day. Despite these low figures the dominant representation of the event on the following day's front pages was that of a 'riot'.

Headlines included 'Anarchy thugs riot in central London' (*The Times* 02.05.00), 'Rioters dishonour war heroes' (*The Daily Telegraph* 02.05.00), 'Protests erupt in violence', (*The Guardian*), 'May Day Mayhem' (*Daily Express*), 'Riot Yobs desecrate Churchill Monument' (*The Sun*). Prime Minister Tony Blair reportedly described the protesters as being 'beneath contempt', portraying 'The people responsible for the damage caused in London today' as 'an absolute disgrace' and their actions as having 'nothing to do with convictions or beliefs and everything to do with mindless thuggery.' (*The Guardian* 2.05.00).

The Home Secretary, Jack Straw, whilst recognising the distinction between 'legitimate' protest and criminal action, portrayed the demonstration as 'criminality and thuggery masquerading as political protest' (*The Guardian* 2.05.00). The subordination of protestors' motives to mindless violence proved difficult to maintain even in apparently 'strong' cases which were pursued via the public sphere regardless of the consequences for individuals' targeted in this manner[12]. Three instances of criminal damage became the condensation symbols around which appeals for public denunciation were orchestrated. Two of these, damage to the Cenotaph and the decoration of Winston Churchill's statute with a grass Mohican, transgressed 'war heroes' whilst the ransacking of a small McDonalds outlet reaffirmed the targeting of global corporate brands.

The protestor photographed spray painting Churchill's statue gave himself up amidst a nationwide police hunt for more than 200 people. However, far from being a 'mindless thug' the protestor was a 25-year-old former soldier with an active service record in Bosnia. As *The Guardian* pointed out he did not fit the stereotype of a protester or eco-warrior, views strengthened when he appeared in court, justifying his actions as follows:

> The May Day celebrations were in the spirit of free expression against capitalism. Churchill was an exponent of capitalism and of imperialism and anti-Semitism. A Tory reactionary vehemently opposed to the emancipation of women and to independence in India. The media machine made this paunchy little man much larger than life – a colossal, towering figure of great stature and bearing with trademark cigar, bowler hat and V-sign. The reality was an often irrational, sometimes vainglorious leader whose impetuosity, egotism and bigotry on occasion cost many lives unnecessarily and caused much suffering that was needless and unjustified.
>
> (*The Guardian* 8.05.00)

When asked by the stipendiary magistrate what he had wanted to achieve by his actions he replied, 'I thought that on a day when people all over the world are gathering to express basic human rights and freedom of expression it was acceptable to challenge an icon of the British establishment.' (*The Guardian* 10.05.00). An ex-soldier with a sophisticated understanding of the role of political leaders in fostering inequalities in the world cannot be easily dismissed as the stereotypic thug of media portrayals.

Other individuals prominent in the protests also confounded simplifying folk devil epithets as *The Sun* headline of 4 May declared 'Eton Boy is Riot Thug' describing the University Professor's son as a 'Self styled Anarchist' who had apparently thrown a plastic bottle at the police (*The Sun* 04.05.00, pp. 1 and 5). *The Daily Telegraph* preferred to focus on those they could easily classify as 'outsiders' reporting 8 of the initial 13 individuals appearing in court 'were born overseas, others were unemployed and one was a Kurdish refugee' (4.05.00).

The McDonaldisation of protest?

The only property damage of any significance occurred in Whitehall when an unguarded McDonalds outlet was 'trashed'. The destruction of this retail outlet featured prominently in establishing dominant discourses within the public sphere. Given that the ambitions of the Guerrilla Gardening event were largely confined to Parliament Square, this event raised significant speculation and debate about the underlying reasons for this action. Parliament Square is one of the unique spaces[13] in terms of public order and freedom of speech within the United Kingdom. A Sessional Order of Parliament instructs the Commissioner of the Metropolitan Police to maintain unimpeded access to the Palace of Westminster. Guerrilla Gardening raised the prospect of riot suited police fighting with 'gardeners' beneath Big Ben, an eponymous symbol of democracy recognised around the world. The police operation on May Day was as much about managing the political theatre of people staking their claim to this piece of land, as it was about any objective sense of threat posed by 'guerrilla gardening'. The police found themselves in a double bind, compelled by political imperative to defend a particular space, described in police parlance as a 'ditch' in which they feel compelled to 'die' (Waddington 1994: 66). As an alternative allowing the crowd into Whitehall created the opportunity for those who wished to vent their frustrations on a McDonalds – this was an operational police decision that reinforced a public order strategy. As an eye-witness subsequently recounted:

> The inevitable happened and for a full quarter of an hour those who wished to, had a free hand to smash up the restaurant. It was only when surrounding shops were started on that the police miraculously reappeared and swiftly and easily corralled everyone in that section of Whitehall into the secured pen of Trafalgar Square[14]
> (http://www.urban75.org/mayday/015.html accessed 01.03.05)

This was not an isolated view. Although *The Evening Standard* tabloid newspaper incorrectly reported that the McDonalds restaurant had been guarded by '12 police officers' (http://www.indymedia.org.uk/newsite/text=softly_policing.txt accessed 18.10.01) John Vidal reporting in *The Guardian* noted, 'The confrontation had to happen. The first 400 people went past McDonalds barely believing it was there, unboarded and unguarded. The second 300 gathered round it' (1994: 66).

The eyewitness, quoted, posed the question 'Who stood to benefit from the day ending with a small, totally contained and 99.9% ineffectual disturbance?'. The eyewitness's conclusion was that a kind of 'give them enough rope and they will hang themselves' conspiracy had taken place, because the police, the politicians and McDonalds would all benefit from images of the destruction of yet another McDonalds restaurant. Such a conspiracy, if real, would justify the police tactics, allow politicians to 'rail against those advocating direct action' and give the burger company free publicity.[15] In effect, the Mayday 2000 carnival against capitalism became transformed from a 'peaceful celebration of the growing global anti-capitalist movement'[16] into a riot. Francis Wheen, writing in *The Guardian* summed up the incredulity of such a label when he described the events as being a 'Small Riot Near Trafalgar Square: No One Dead' (3.05.00). For present purposes the intent and agency behind the photo-opportunities which became the dominant iconic representations of May Day 2000 are irrelevant. The importance of this iconic praxis lies in the ready availability of symbolic expressions that condense and fuse an event around a deviant social actor. Such condensation symbols are retrospectively retrieved and repeated to predict the behaviour and motives associated with future events reinforcing the need for firm action.

May Day 2001 – the devil incarnate?

As May Day 2001 approached media reports emphasised impending violence with The *Sunday Telegraph* reporting:

> more than 15,000 dedicated, hardened activists from all over Europe [who] will descend on just one target, central London.... Among the anarchists who are likely to attend are those from the Black Flag movement and German terrorists. These are the same people who caused trouble at the meeting of the G8 group of economic powers... at Seattle
> (18.02.01)

Such accounts were reproduced across the spectrum of print media (see *The Observer* 29.04.01). Photographs of suspected ringleaders 'intending' to cause violence were circulated to the press during April 2001 (Vidal and Branigan 2001), despite none having been identified as offenders. Newspaper accounts intoned that anarchists were thousands strong, would carry samurai swords, had links with the Real IRA, had been to training camps in United States, and were 'battle hard'. Political figures including the Mayor of London, Ken Livingston warned protesters to stay at home and backed the police in arresting anyone whose intention was 'to engage in criminal activities' (Vidal and Branigan 2001). Tony Blair considered that:

> The limits are passed when protesters, in the name of some spurious cause, seek to inflict fear, terror, violence and criminal damage on people and property.... There is a right way to protest in a democracy and there is a wrong way. Britain and its people are not just tolerant of peaceful protest but see it, rightly, as part of our democratic process.
> (*The Guardian* 1.05.01)

The Guardian, reported that 'more than 100 often hysterical articles have been printed in the mainstream press hyping the violence, with few suggesting that the protesters have any valid point. The unbalance has been remarkable. No one wants to look at why people are protesting (Vidal and Branigan 2001).

Given the expectation of violence the police adopted a 'zero tolerance' stance, mobilising 6,000 officers with a further 3,000 in reserve (*The Independent* 2.05.01). Predictions of a large protest committed to violence were confounded when only 3,000 to 5,000 turned out to participate in a fluid action that envisaged carnivalesque events in areas of London associated with the board game Monopoly. The policing operation was clearly intended to maintain control of the streets and limit mobility and resulted in protestors being 'kettled' in Oxford Circus. The police cordon was strictly maintained for over six hours during which no one was permitted to leave without being photographed and giving their personal details. Some small skirmishes broke out as water, food and personal comfort all ran out. The predicted demonic assembly did not materialise leaving senior Metropolitan Police Officers in evening TV news studios justifying their operations in terms of 'plastic bottles' having being thrown at officers.

The tabloid media emphasised the success of the police action. The *Daily Mail* ran under a headline reading 'Day the Law fought back' (2.05.01) with *The Mirror* announcing the result as if reporting on a football match 'One Nil To The Bill' (2.05.01). Both front pages carried the same photograph depicting a protester being beaten over the head by a police baton. *The Sun's* coverage announced 'Mayhem Across The World – Going Nuts in May' depicting the 'Face of hate' as protestors clashed with police in London, Australia, France, Korea, Germany, Pakistan and Russia (2.05.01, pp. 12–13). Participants were variously described as being a 'mob', 'anarchists' and 'thugs'. The broadsheets carried images of police surrounding protestors in Oxford Circus, with *The Daily Telegraph* headline declaring 'Police quell May Day threat' (2.05.01) whilst *The Times* considered 'Rain rescues capitalism from spike-haired hoard' (2.05.01). *The Independent* and *The Guardian* headlines declared 'Scuffles mar May Day protest' and 'Police set trap for protests' (2.05.01 respectively).

Despite attempts by Liberty to pursue the police for 'unlawfully detaining' activists (*The Guardian* 12.06.01) the Metropolitan Police's position remained virtually unchanged in 2002, with assistant commissioner Mike Todd reportedly instructing officers to use 'in your face' tactics with protestors regarded as potential rioters (Hopkins *et al.* 2002). Such views resonate with US government thinking which has seen the introduction of 'free speech zones',[17] specially designated areas within which dissent can be voiced, that are frequently far-removed from the source of protestors' concerns. Similar restrictions have been applied in the United Kingdom.[18]

The dominance of images depicting damage to war memorials in 2000 contributed to a widely held view that London RTS had been significantly damaged and their credibility undermined. But pessimism within activist circles overlooked polling data suggesting a far more complex public stance. A Democratic Audit survey (http://www.fhit.org.democratic_audit) sought responses to the statement 'If governments don't listen, peaceful protests, blockades and demonstrations are legitimate ways of expressing people's concerns'. Amongst respondents 49% agreed strongly whilst a further 32% tended to agree, a combined total of 81%. Such polling evidence leaves interpretation of 'peaceful' open but taken with other indicators, such as not guilty jury verdicts in trials involving activists from Trident Ploughshares charged with criminal damage on military bases, point to a public sphere which resonates with aspects of the anti-capitalist movements' case and moral principles.

> If you have got something to say, say it democratically. Come out and vote, but don't end up trying to beat the place up because your politics aren't shared by the vast majority of people.
>
> (Hopkins *et al.* 2002)

Such public ambivalence is key in understanding the importance of the 'incitement to silence' typifying media non-coverage of topics 'uncomfortable to dominant forces in society' (Wahl-Jorgensen 2003: 133). In order to maintain the silencing process there needs to be no accompanying debate about the activists beyond their deviancy and naïveté. Unlike the traditional folk devil the AGM has a voice within civil society, albeit a liminal one, but this is denied in the mainstream press by their portrayal as folk devils.

This is important because it re-affirms Melucci's (1996a) argument that most political discourse seeks to deny the existence of fundamental conflicts about the production and appropriation of social resources by reducing everything to a question of grievances or political claims. Finally, the demonisation of activists militates against large sections of society identifying with their actions. By removing the identity of the individuals and focussing on the group as 'anarchists' and 'thugs' they become associated with the violence that the media chooses to focus upon, not the message their activism seeks to advance.

One possible outcome is that politicians seek the social–democratic assimilation of these movements through some new political settlement. However, it seems more likely that the criminal justice systems will be left to 'police the new crisis of interest representation' in democracies confronted by the pressures of neo-liberal globalisation. In the United Kingdom, New Labour is reported to have created more than 600 new criminal offences since 1997 (Kettle 2004) whilst media reportage on terrorism since 9/11 has proliferated despite there being fewer actual terrorist events per year since 2001 (Lewis 2004). It would appear that the extension of terrorist tropes to less marginal social locations is set to construct more rebels with a cause who will appear within the criminal justice system leaving judges and juries confronted with the task of reconciling underlying motivations, 'deviant' behaviour and what constitutes legitimate forms of protest. Precedents from relevant jury trials in cases brought against Trident Ploughshares activists in the United Kingdom suggest that citizens are more than able to balance international and national legal concerns to arrive at verdicts embodying the 'lesser evil'. All such cases have been dismissed to date intensifying Home Office attempts to limit trial by jury.

The incremental extension of legitimate offences under public order legislation and the creation of arrestable offences requiring the exercise of judgement by police personnel appears set to multiply cases in which citizens experience an intensity of feeling opening out onto a need to exercise judgement and conduct 'free acts'. The tension between state legislature and the judgement of citizens reflecting upon the actions of apparently marginal actors will increasingly perturbate the distribution of institutional trust within the United Kingdom. One of the fundamental and inescapable consequences of the AGM and associated movement networks particularly those opposed to the illegal military assault upon Iraq has been increased public and institutional questioning of seats of legitimate decisional authority. The scale of the social force attached to issues is critical here.

The attempt to dismiss protest as deviance in effect sows the seeds of upstream consequence that arise in part from government statements and press releases which are then fed back to Whitehall via focus groups resulting in legislative responses. In the jury room, citizens appear to make finely balanced discriminating judgements in cases that will become more frequent given legislative programmes. The Serious Organised Crime and Police Act, 2005 contains provisions to prevent protests within one kilometre of the House of Commons and to secure the visual enjoyment of Parliament Square. News coverage of the Act set it in the context of the vandalisation of Churchill's statute on May Day 2000 with Nicholas Soames MP describing a four year peace vigil opposite the House of Commons as an 'offensive encampment…defacing a principal focal area of tourism' (Today, BBC Radio 4, 28.01.05).

This is tantamount to making aesthetic preference a basis for legal sanction and extends the power of judges to prescribe appropriate dress codes in the courtroom to the public sphere. More importantly, moves to harmonise UK terrorist law in terms of its treatment of foreign and native suspects clarifies the stakes of pushing the legal defence of democracy to the limits. At the time of writing the British security and political states continue to refine strategies of confinement for protest events, the spatial separation of protestors from sites of contention and a proliferation of criminal offences. The British tradition of tolerance towards 'eccentric radicals' appears to be at an end.

Genoa – death at high noon

This final account is the most tragic and charged of the chapter, following the shooting and subsequent death of one young Italian activist, Carlo Giuliani, and the systemic beating of activists in Genoa. Activist accounts of these events make harrowing reading (On Fire 2001, Neale 2002, *Notes from Nowhere* 2003). The sense of shock, fear, bewilderment and disbelief arising from the intensity of assaults incurred in a Western Democracy is tangible. We present this material as dispassionately as we can having absorbed a significant amount of video capture, written, verbal and media accounts all of which have been triangulated and filtered, a process assisted through the presence one of the authors on the streets during the event.

The divided nature of Italian civil society, characterised by 'the Southern problem' has been a significant issue since its formalisation by Antonio Gramsci. Events in Genoa in 2001 were suffused with the long shadows cast by the history of tensions between the formal associations and organisations of the Fascist right and Marxist left in a particularly volatile European democracy. Some sense of this history is necessary to make sense of the particular shadows cast in Genoa.

Despite the ascendant neo-liberal paradigm, a vibrant left remains a feature of Italian political life. The Worker's Power (Potere Operaio) movement established the idea of a plural left through 'autonomy at the base' during the 1960s and early 1970s. This central principle was enshrined within the Autonomia movement in 1973 as the basis for both work place and social, notably housing, issues. In 1979, the Italian state crushed Autonomia arresting and imprisoning 1,500 intellectuals and militants in a single year. The establishment of social centres throughout Italy and the reinvention of autonomist repertoires through movements such as the *Tute Bianche* coincide with robust union organisations and the Communist party. The Italian left is characterised by a significant diaspora of 'civil society' associations, more formalised social movement organisations, unions, and political party representation. This network continues the centuries old struggle for ascendancy within Italian civil society underlining the importance attached to hegemony by Gramsci and approaches emphasising the centrality of culture to political life (Hall 1980).

Fascism, formally defeated in Italy following the fall of Mussolini after Second Word War, remains a barely submerged sub-text in terms of formal politics, key state security services, and 'Southern' civil society associations. Within contemporary debates the alignment between Prime Minister Berlusconi's political and business interests, the role of Berlusconi owned media in the portrayal of both the global and Italian 'good life' and the relationship between the political and security state are all prominent issues.

These left/right traditions are differentially sedimented across state institutions and urban administrations resulting in a variable geometry of political alignments. The meeting in Genoa represented a return from the isolated citadels for world summitry with the Berlusconi government keen to maximise material and symbolic gains. There was a particular emphasis on achieving a secure summit where world leaders would be safe from acts of terror. Airport security was particularly intense and the reported arrival of body bags in the run-up to the event underlined the potential for violent confrontation. The Genoa Social Forum had been central in organising the event negotiating key resources including dedicated convergence space, information and media centres in municipal buildings. Despite this, the sheer scale of the event represented a significant challenge given the diversity of participating groups.

Italian security services in collaboration with US and European security and intelligence networks created a secure 'Red Zone' as a no-go area within which the summit would convene. Area denial was achieved through the construction of a double wire perimeter fence and the use of shipping containers to limit access to the labyrinthine side streets. This ring of steel was defended by around 18,000 armed personnel drawn from a range of police and military units. The mobility and manoeuvre used to advantage by 'Pink and Silver' on the streets of Prague was extremely limited with only main thoroughfares remaining as obvious conduits.

Irrespective of the underlying issues about chains of command, it is the policing of the Genoa plateau that is of central importance to this chapter.

Accounts of the event from a remarkable range of commentators reveal some consensual points that can be summarised as follows:

- The established coloured zones depicting 'types' of engagement were not adhered to by police and security forces.
- The defence of the red meeting zone was accompanied by wide-ranging police actions across Genoa.
- Systemic and brutal beatings were inflicted upon any and all categories of protestors.
- The police raid on the Diaz school was an attempt to seize images of the foregoing police violence and demonstrate that officially sanctioned spaces were not beyond the reach of force of 'law and order'.

To these it is worth adding that the actions of the Italian state were seriously in conflict with the legal definition of human rights enshrined within the European Union. The exercise of such brutality by a nation claiming to be part of a superior civilisation reminds us of Habermas's descriptor 'advanced barbarism'. We make no attempt to conceal our point of reflexive departure here – the tacit standards and established best practice for the policing of public order situations were breached in Genoa. A member of the BBC World Service Spanish Division is reported to have said 'I know this well, it was like this before, in Chile under Pinochet' (Porter 2001: 79).

The policing of Genoa differed from previous plateaux where resources had been targeted at containing 'black bloc' elements. In Genoa, the 'black bloc' remained relatively free and unrestrained by police intervention. Numerous accounts suggest the presence of agent provocateurs within the ranks of the black bloc pointing to the relative ease with which commercial properties were attacked and destroyed. Video footage of police and security personnel dressed in plain clothes and a mixture of uniform and plain clothes testifies to the use of both clandestine and explicit presence on the streets. Debates on the political accountability of the police operation revolve around the presence of Italy's Deputy Prime Minister in police headquarters during two days of escalating police violence. Claims of personal affiliation with Fascist organisations and the presence of pictures of Mussolini in police stations are central to such accounts.

Police units operated throughout Genoa repeatedly driving vehicles into crowds at speeds estimated to be in excess of forty miles an hour. One such event resulted in two police vehicles losing manoeuvrability in Piazza Alimondo, which contained a significant number of protestors. Eye-witness accounts describe a fire extinguisher being dumped from one of these vehicles. This was picked up by Carlo Giuliani, a 23-year-old protester who brandished it in the proximity of the rear of the stalled vehicle. Here, mainstream media images reveal a young officer pointing a semi-automatic pistol directly at Carlo. This image dominated print and broadcast media being followed immediately by images of his dead body lying in the Piazza. Broadcast media coverage omitted, however, images of the vehicle reversing and then driving forwards over the prone body. Activist footage and at least one agency source captured such images. Following these events there was an immediate attempt to confiscate cameras in the Piazza by police. After this tragic death, chants of 'Assassini' dominated the day and the word was painted or hung as a banner on police stations.

Non-violence, like military operations, involves the careful weighing of options and the removal or containment of factors likely to harm humans – unlike military operations. Given the summary execution of Carlo and the authorities' demonstrable will to use armed force and terror tactics, the ensuing absence of mass crowd violence and comparatively limited property damage testifies to the commitment to non-violence within this movement. Three hundred thousand people subsequently demonstrated in Genoa as Italian Embassies, Consulates, Multi-national offices and the docking of Italian flagged shipping became subject to citizen sanctions around the world. No political leader condemned the police action though the death was regretted, with violence being attributed to an anarchist bloc. Speaking through the mainstream media the public were invited to choose between a global public sphere run by legitimate elected representatives or permitting an anarchist mob to disrupt 'progress'. The tacit implication being that, whilst deaths were regrettable, this was a small price to pay for the greater good.

Speculation about the alignments between political authority and police actions assume a greater degree of significance in relation to events in the immediate aftermath of the main protests. Following the mass march on Saturday activist accounts (e.g. Neale 2002) reveal experienced individuals debating where it would be safest to spend the night. Such speculation was based on the experience of increased levels of aggressive police activity in the immediate aftermath of previous AGM sieges such as Prague (Chesters and Welsh 2004, Welsh 2004). In light of this, a number of individuals eschewed the Convergence Centre as a safe haven opting for the school established as an official information and Indymedia space for the event. This calculative decision proved ill-founded as the Diaz school was raided by a mixed force of around 150 police.

At the time of the raid, the majority of people in the building were asleep or settling into their sleeping bags. Accounts detail brutal and repeated beatings, resulting in multiple fractures, extensive bleeding and concussion (*Notes from Nowhere* 2003: 361–367). One UK activist centrally involved in Indymedia work sustained eight broken teeth and several broken ribs. Initial assaults were followed by cursory paramedic triage and treatment with the more seriously injured being moved to a variety of medical facilities. Here, Carabinieri and prison guards continued to intimidate protestors who remained unclear about their custodial status. Accounts include interactions in which officers praised Mussolini and Pinochet, the cropping of hair, infringement of legal rights, loss of personal property, inadequate medical attention and misapplied deportation orders (*Notes From Nowhere* 2003). Five days after the raid on 25 July 2001, 90 of the 93 people initially reported as detained were released on grounds of wrongful arrest.

At the time of writing these events remain the subject of an on-going trial of 28 police, Carabinieri and revenue guards alleged to have been involved in the raid. Those charged include Fransesco Gratteri who was subsequently promoted to become head of the police 'anti-terrorist unit'. Italian interior Minister Giuseppe Pisnau welcomed the trial as in everyone's interests 'above all the police' who he was confident would 'be able to confront and overcome even this test' (*The Guardian* 13.12.04, p. 13). Further legal action over alleged police brutality at a detention camp at Bolzanetto, used after the main protest, reached a preliminary hearing in January 2005. The 47 named defendants included senior police, doctors, nurses and prison guards including General Oronzo Doria. General Doria was promoted to head Italy's penitentiary guards, a force involved in the raid on the Diaz school, after events in Genoa. Prosecution charges include the enforced chanting of songs praising Mussolini and Pinochet, although torture charges cannot be brought as Italian law lacks any relevant provisions. The protracted nature of Italian legal proceedings makes it unclear whether the cases will ever come to trial as the Italian parliament considers legislation which would reduce the time available for legal action following an alleged offence. Such legislation would exempt President Burlusconi from outstanding charges relating to corruption (*The Guardian* 27.1.05, p. 17).

In the public sphere the complexity underlying the Genoa protests was apparently reduced to law and order issues but this appearance conceals the wider social responses sedimented at day-to-day levels. In line with precedents established in 'the south'[19] marginal social groups in Genoa were 'cleansed' before the summit to present a positive urban image. As part of this drive to conceal unsightly aspects of daily life (street prostitution) citizens were also instructed not to hang laundry on the lines criss-crossing the narrow streets. As the clashes in Genoa intensified, more and more washing lines were bedecked with 'pants'. In Havellian terms, these citizens of Genoa were 'living in truth', symbolically declaring that the official edict to cleanse the public sphere in the name of capitalism was 'pants'.

The 'siege of the signs' identified as a major strategy of engagement in 1996 was responded to by the use of 'decisive force' in Genoa. Subsequent summit sieges continued to be frustrated by the selection of remote heavily defended locations. Police actions continued to jeopardise the lives of activists[20] increasing the sense of being at risk through participation. The decline in summit actions can be explained in part through the adoption of more extreme forms of policing but even in Italy the use of force has not blunted the process of movement capacity building. Summit sieges were only part of the network of networks activities and the founding of geo-regional social forums has provided a focus for proactive nomadic mobility. Florence hosted the first European Social Forum (ESF) in 2002 amidst fears of a repeat of events in Genoa. An estimated one million people attended the closing march at the end of a meeting containing sessions on every 'issue' conceivably relevant to a modern society. During this plateau, the idea of a global day of action against the looming 'war' on Iraq was proposed seeding a process that has proved particularly problematic in terms of political legitimacy and trust in the United Kingdom and United States. Subsequent ESF meetings in Paris 2003 and London 2004 (Welsh *et al.* 2005) continued the process of network extension and consolidation through proliferating weak ties.

Conclusions

In terms of the theoretical stakes central to this volume, this chapter has addressed the way in which establishment networks responded to the appearance of the AGM within the public sphere. This engagement has been structured around the networking of established 'strong ties' between national and international political and security organisations. This network has applied a range of historically sedimented frames to the movement of movements emphasising established deviance categories associated with 'the mob' in the context of a global 'war on terrorism'. Whilst state-centric actors declaratory postures typically refuse to negotiate with organs of terror, unofficially lines of communication are frequently opened either directly or via intermediaries. In the United Kingdom, senior media reporters have acted as intermediaries between top tier political offices in an attempt to open such 'dialogue'. It is however, clear that the public sphere remains dominated by the application of negative, deviance-based attributions. These responses are consistent with forms of interaction extending back several centuries and are part of a process of selective incorporation of emergent political actors within national political opportunity structures. This chapter has detailed how the security and political elites within the fragmented states that typify the global era responded to the legitimation stripping activities of the AGM. Whilst we have emphasised the roles of the security and political state in constituting dominant discourse structured around terrorism, the more ambivalent response of the financial state is significant (Chapter 2).

Throughout this book, we argue that the AGM represents a process of global emergence expressing early formalisations of stakes associated with global civil society and combining social and environmental justice approaches within an overarching recognition of difference melded by the commitment to 'unity in diversity'. The fusion of these concerns within the AGM is significant because together they constitute a global network actor which simultaneously bridges and establishes common ground between civil society actors in the 'developed' and 'developing' world which foregrounds Bateson's insight that an organism plus environment paradigm is crucial to human survival and progress. In this sense, the environmental crisis is in effect a crisis of Western civilisation not the organic realm – which will continue irrespective of the fate of consumer society.

The primary collective frames of nationhood and liberal possessive individualism emphasising our/my economy/wealth/prosperity/progress which 'organised' the conflictual and cooperative military, economic, political and development agendas of the twentieth century are extraordinarily limited in terms of their capacity to give expression to collective global stakes. The move from 'disorganised capitalism' (Lash and Urry 1987) to free market complexity and chaos are theoretical expressions of this transition which is structured by human/environment interaction as 'man' (*sic*) becomes a force of nature. Emergence and the complexity sciences assume a position of contested centrality in this transition in terms of both the 'natural' and social sciences. The controversial areas central to our argument relate to the temporal horizons of phase shifts and debates over whether these are bi-polar or multi-polar phenomena. There is no prospect of closure on these debates but we would argue that there are some retrodictable acts of sense making offering durable pointers suggesting 'we' have entered an era typified by order on the edge of chaos.

This is profoundly challenging to linear models of progress and civilisation based on the incremental extension of established scientific, technical, social, economic and political practices conducted under conditions of Darwinian competitiveness and survival of the fittest. The incremental refinement and extension of established techniques underpinning this process has *assumed* a viable organic realm as an environment, something made particularly clear by post Second World War economic science approaching 'the environment' as an external free good.[21] With natural science disciplines increasingly recognising that significant phase shifts in planetary ecosystems can occur within rather short time periods once certain threshold or initial conditions are met, incrementalism based on strong ties is a limited strategy of engagement.

What we have argued in this chapter is that the AGM represents the initial expression – the emergence of the first planetary action system from the bottom-up. Attempting to reduce this multi-faceted social actor to 'mob' represents the failure to recognise emergence by interpreting it through 'habits of mind' derived from the passing era of international relations. As we have demonstrated here national governments in the United States, United Kingdom and Italy have prioritised international summit esteem over citizens' rights, including rights of assembly. Habermas regards respect for such rights as the 'litmus test' of legitimacy for representative democracy, their breach in practice and further erosion through terrorist legislation merely adds to the increasingly pervasive sense of growing democratic deficits in the lands of 'the (un)free'. More problematic for contemporary 'power holders and brokers' is the fact that significant sections of the AGM have no desire to engage with those who are creating the problem and indeed positively eschew such interaction. This is important in terms of the conscious creation of an 'outside' – imperfect as this may be – to the 'the system' – alterity becomes established within the network of networks lying in the interstices of Empire(s).

Whilst the anarchist contribution to the conflictual activities of the AGM has been widely commented upon (Graeber 2002) little attention has been paid to the proactive 'other order' present within and pursued through the AGM (Bowden and Purkis 2004). Anarchism in this sense is a particular habit of mind capable of multiple and infinite expressive forms but premised upon factors immanent within the principles of PGA. The embodiment of these principles in the day-to-day lives of activists ranging from internationals to activists to citizen support groups to casual sympathisers sediment them within countless global locals. Such attempts to 'live in truth' are easily ridiculed and criticised for inconsistency but as puissance (Maffesoli 1996) is withdrawn from formal politics, such lives assume increasing significance and potential.

Under such conditions citizens typically turn to individuals who have 'lived in truth' and 'declared the stakes' despite the 'fear' exercised by the system. This was a process clearly evident in the 'revolutions' in East and Central Europe (ECE see Chapter 3). Free acts by free actors assume positions of increasing significance but rather than replacing one system with another, as was the case in ECE, the demands are for the reconfiguration of the entire system through the application of organising themes compatible with planetary survival and co-operation. The representation of the AGM as anarchic disorder in effect conceals the extent to which the AGM embodies organisational forms and aims that *are* the future. The political stakes are immense as adoption of the organisational form alone and its application through established habits of mind will merely accelerate the descent into reinforcing cycles of chaos. If there is to be order on the edge of chaos then the social and environmental agenda of the AGM is a *necessary initial condition*. These are themes we address in Chapter 5.

5 Ecologies of action within global civil society

Introduction

So far, this work has addressed the changing context of movement mobilisation in a post-cold war neo-liberal climate, the impact of movements on key institutional fora such as the WTO, IMF and WB, the responses of national states and the globalisation of policing actions. In this chapter, we elaborate the *ecology of action* that arises from the system of relations between the various actors – NGOs, social movements and other civil society actors, and the militant re-framing of the concept of global civil society (GCS). Here the changed and accumulated capacities of the AGM initiate a transition to a 'new' mode of networked engagement in *plateaux* – the topographical term utilised by both Bateson (1973) and then Deleuze and Guattari (2002: 22) to describe the temporary stabilisation and heightening of collective intensities. These plateaux: protests, gatherings and social fora lead to the intensification of conflict around the key targeted signs elaborated in Chapter 2.

They also provide opportunity for the multiplication of dynamic movement trajectories and processes, 'lines of flight', 'vectors', 'destratifications' and 'deterritorializations' that in turn constitute a virtual 'plane of consistency' such as that elaborated by Deleuze and Guattari (2002: 266), an immanent field of relations constituted through the overcoming of habitual patterns or hierarchising processes. Theoretically this marks the translation of Bateson's postulated Ecology of Mind into an Ecology of Action capable of adapting to and colonising key niches within complex systems and networks resulting in systemic challenges and changes which are inevitably both intended and unintended. Plateaux also enable certain actors and actions to become symbolic multipliers – strange attractors – that indicate processes of movement capacity building that have been underway in the West since the 1970s (Welsh 2000, 2001). This emphasis signals our departure from approaches which concentrate on specific protest events and their impacts on formalised national power structures.

The chapter proceeds by outlining the renewed importance of civil society within political discourse and examines how this concept has been applied to the global level. It continues through analysis of how actors within the

AGM have sought to frame GCS as a space of contestation and resistance, thereby maintaining links to structures of political representation and mediation whilst opening and maintaining space for antagonistic action by multiple constituencies across diverse milieu. In this sense GCS is an empty signifier which is invested with meaning by those utilising it, a discursive construct that seeks to articulate the 'n' dimensional state space of a global system constituted by a variety of associational relationships conducted by extra-familial and non-state actors. Our argument suggests that within this state space the AGM acts as a strange attractor that perturbates the trajectory of GCS whilst recursively structurating and defining the system of relations described by GCS.

Reframing global civil society

> Its intricate social linkages stretched across vast distances are puzzling, indeed so difficult to grasp that new metaphors are urgently needed to help us to picture and understand them. Perhaps (to take an example) it is better to liken this society to the tens and hundreds of thousands of 'nested systems within nested systems' described in certain versions of complexity theory.
>
> (Keane 2003: 19)

The concept of GCS is deployed as a normative-ideal by a range of political actors because of its considerable rhetorical and strategic utility. In each instance it is presented as a version of the good society stretched to the ends of the earth. Almost uniformly perceived as progressive and democratising, its composition varies according to one's ideological position. Kaldor's (2003) framework provides a useful orientation here. In what she terms the 'activist' definition of GCS, it takes on a utopian quality and is manifest in the interstices between markets and states. In the 'neo-liberal' version it is an essential adjunct to the globalising forces of free trade and privatisation, and in the normative 'ideal-type' she and Keane favour, it is a 'dynamic non-governmental system of interconnected socio-economic institutions' that is capable of pluralising power and problematising violence (Keane 2003: 8).

We would add a further definition: global civil society through the lens of global complexity – where GCS is perceived as a domain contested and variegated by multiple axes of cause and effect, reciprocity and ambivalence, an outcome and effect of 'global complexity', the interaction between 'networks' and 'fluids' that characterise planetary systems of production, mobility, and exchange (Urry 2003). From this perspective, GCS constitutes a 'state space', a field of relations between variables of a self-organising system, including the combination of ideological, organisational, and material investments that are represented in the definitions above. These denote attractors within the system that compete to consolidate their interpretation of GCS, dominate resources, and attribute meanings. We are suggesting that the rise to prominence of the AGM signifies the emergence of a strange attractor within GCS, an 'antagonist' attractor that perturbates relations between GCS actors and opens new directions for action, reflection, and critique.

In doing so we are responding to Taylor's call for a 'theoretical re-articulation' of GCS (Taylor 2004a: 8, 2004b) and to Keane's challenge 'to develop theoretical imagery for better imagining global civil society' (Keane 2003: 24), so we might get 'beyond theories of GCS based on simple unilinear projections' (Munck 2004: 21). We advance these aims by suggesting the AGM can be considered as a heuristic device to accompany that of GCS. This is what Keane considers to be a 'nested system within a nested system' and it involves a typological distinction between the 'antagonistic' (Melucci 1996a) orientation of the AGM and the ideal type of GCS utilised by Keane (2003) and Kaldor (2003). It therefore marks an engagement with a movement that is actively involved in reframing the concept of GCS in order to support conflictual collective action, and goes some way to assessing the impacts and potential of the AGM as an antagonist attractor.

When global civil society actors are differentiated according to their modes of organisation, and their position *vis-à-vis* international systems of production, distribution, and exchange, it is possible to discern an antagonistic kernel within GCS that promotes a fundamental and systemic critique. This is important, as Melucci (1996a) has pointed out, because most political discourse seeks to deny the existence of fundamental conflicts about the production and appropriation of social resources by reducing everything to a question of grievances or political claims. We argue that this antagonism is primarily, but not exclusively visible in the AGM. As demonstrated in Chapters 2 and 3, the AGM has been influential in perturbating existing discourses around trade, the environment, and social justice and through its capacity to re-orient the field of relations between GCS and global governance structures. When we move beyond complexity metaphors to the application of its conceptual framework of 'emergence', 'small world networks', and 'strange attractors' we can begin to discern the reasons for these seemingly disproportionate 'system effects' (Jervis 1997), reasons which suggest new possibilities for our understanding of social change.

Civil society and democracy

Many commentators have remarked upon the reflexive, dialogical and deliberative character of civil society and its potential to invigorate democratic processes (Beck *et al.* 1994, Lash and Urry 1994, Inoguchi *et al.* 1998). This interest has been given impetus by the much-heralded decline of participation in formal electoral processes, indicated by the low electoral turnouts amongst social democratic states and the increasing dissatisfaction with elected representatives indicated by survey data. Research produced by the Democratic Audit of the United Kingdom (UK) funded by the Rowntree

Reform Trust indicates that participation levels in the 2001 general election were the lowest ever. The qualitative data from this study also indicates that the public 'do not believe they possess the power they want through conventional politics' and are therefore becoming 'increasingly sympathetic to direct action' (Dunleavy *et al.* 2001). Such observations add weight to proposals emphasising the need to reassess fundamental questions about the nature of the state and governance in a globalising world and to those calling for a rethinking of democratic structures and processes (Stiglitz 2002, Wainwright 2003, Monbiot 2004).

These developments have combined to provoke a certain anxiety amongst political elites about the degree of legitimacy conferred by electoral processes and have led to a number of initiatives to increase political participation in local and national government, as well as attempts to seek out alternative means of engaging with and addressing the 'democratic deficit'. In the UK these include mandatory classes in citizenship for younger people, experiments with information technology to provide ease of access to polling and a proliferation of inclusionary fora based around deliberative processes. In policy practice, this attempt to revive participation has been expressed through 'new' deliberative processes, which are introduced alongside 'older' democratic institutions. These experiments in deliberative democracy (Dryzek 1990, Benhabib 1996, Elster 1998) include citizens juries, citizens' panels, in-depth discussion and focus groups, consensus conferences, and round tables. Unfortunately, these proposals are subject to, and often frustrated by, the constraints of the framework within which they take place and the lack of institutional means for carrying them forward (O'Neill 2001, 2002).

Disaffection with the political class and non-participation in the political process are compounded by changes to the composition and form of civil society, which have been well documented (Shaw 1996, 1999, Scholte 1999, 2000, Foster 2001). In the UK nationally based civic associations representing particular class affinities have declined with the fragmentation of their bases of support and the advent of post-Fordist restructuring, whilst organised religion in all but its more fundamental guises has declined as an effect of its marginality to consumer capitalism. Two outcomes flow directly from this. First, the capacity of civil society organisations to assimilate conflictual currents within pseudo-state forms is diminished, giving rise to a decline in the legitimation of social norms by civil society (Wolfe 1989, Etzioni 1993, Putnam 1995). Second, there is a rise in new opportunities for disaggregated forms of political expression that challenge the state as a locus of power and which seek other means and opportunities of redress. This includes direct action, self-organised alternatives, and campaigning and networking at an extra-national level.

This has contributed to institutions such as the WB, IMF, and WTO becoming the target of protest. These institutions have been used for critical engagement with civil society institutions closely linked to nation states and embedded in national political cultures, but they are now increasingly besieged by organisations and networks apparently seeking to construct and deepen a counter-hegemonic account of globalisation to which they respond in confused and often contradictory ways. This is primarily because of the multivariate and conflicting demands articulated by this emergent global civil society and serves to demonstrate one of the dilemmas at the core of theorising GCS as a normative-ideal. That is, to describe and account for the potentially transformative and counter-hegemonic challenges posed by GCS whilst considering the underlying question of whether a domain committed to radical pluralism can ever attempt to be hegemonic.

However, the confused response of international organisations such as the WTO, IMF, and WB, which as we have seen in Chapters 2 and 4, frequently results in a default mode of non-engagement and repression is in part due to their previously effective model of instrumentalising civil society participation to legitimise neo-liberal reform and restructuring. This has been combined with ambivalence to the destabilising effects those reforms might subsequently have for nationally based civil society organisations. Thus, the growth of civil society networks that extend beyond the regulation of individual states and that engage in conflictual action (re)presents a new set of problems that were previously mediated at the national level. This is one of many unexpected outcomes of globalisation, which include changes to the role of the state in international relations and the rise of GCS (Eschle and Stammers 2004).

Globalization, civil society and the state

> Anti-globalization activists understand that sympathetic and mutually beneficial global ties are good. But we want social and global ties to advance universal equity, solidarity, diversity, and self-management, not to subjugate ever-wider populations to an elite minority. We want to globalize equity not poverty, solidarity not anti-sociality, diversity not conformity, democracy not subordination, and ecological balance not suicidal rapaciousness.
>
> (Albert 2001, www.globalpolicy.org)

The idea of the nation state as the principal organising unit of political and economic life is called into question by the growth of extra-national administrative bodies, transnational corporations, and the liberalisation of capital and investment flows (Strange 1996, Hardt and Negri 2000, Held 2000). This has led some commentators to the conclusion that 'global networks' (Castells 1996), 'scapes' (Appadurai 1990), and 'flows' (Urry 2000) should be the primary focus of investigation in the social sciences. These are the 'true architectures of the new global economy' (Castells 2000: 61), an economy that has catalysed a marked acceleration in the disparity between rich and poor along a number of axes: hemispherically from south to north, regionally between 'peripheral' and 'core' countries, and nationally across class and ethnic boundaries (Castells 1996: 66–150).

This marks a break with the conception of civil society as channelling conflictual impulses towards resolution within state structures and the beginning of the opening out of multiple avenues, audiences, and opportunities through which to exercise conflictual relations, including the targeting of corporations and international systems of governance, and the possibility of self-organised alternatives. Add to this the enlargement of international communities of interest and affinity facilitated by computer mediated communications and the rise of issue-based networks that integrate virtual and real campaigning and we can begin to get a sense of what this emergent global civil society might look like.

The implications of these perspectives are that one must look outside the state at networked processes of interaction between state and non-state actors. This does not mean that the state is no longer important, but rather that we must consider the meshwork of national and extra-national political institutions, corporate, and civil society actors that co-produce the effects of the 'global'. As Burawoy argues:

> The dense ties that once connected civil society to the state are being detached and redirected across national boundaries to form a thickening global public sphere. Yet these connections and flows are not autonomous, are not arbitrary patterns crossing in the sky, but are shaped by the strong magnetic field of nation states.
>
> (2000: 34)

This 'magnetic field' and its complex effects are observable in the challenges posed to NGOs and other civil society actors trying to develop campaigns and mobilise around a range of issues including trade, agriculture, and health. Invariably these organisations need to apply pressure through the state as well as to attempt to gain leverage within global governance structures. The proximity of NGOs to these processes and their capacity to deliver a wide-range of social goods often ends with their participation in restructuring programmes, where the state rescinds its duty to provide essential services leaving NGOs to pick up the responsibility of care, often in the face of rapid and aggressive marketisation. The apparent ambivalence of some NGOs to their assimilation within this neo-liberal framework of 'development' and their professionalised concern with the 'realpolitik' of aid delivery has led to accusations that they are in danger of becoming 'the shock troops of the empire' (Clark 2003: 78). This accusation has been directed particularly at those NGOs who have been instrumental in the management and delivery of economic and social 'development' programmes such as those initiated by the WB.

The assimilation of NGOs by the neo-liberal axiom of free trade raises a number of questions about the potential for social change contained within GCS. The political possibilities of civil society are often inferred from a Gramscian theoretical framework that originally privileged civil society because of a presumed continuity and overlap between the institutions of civil society and the apparatus used for reproducing the state through the transmission of normative values and disciplinary mechanisms. Civil society according to Gramsci (1976) was composed of organisations rooted in both state and people, thereby making it a privileged domain for political contestation. However, as observed earlier, these traditional forms of civil society organisation are declining and are being replaced by newer organisations many of whom are less embedded in everyday social and cultural activity. As such, their transformative potential is limited to the symbolic contestation of dominant social codes often expressed at an extra-national level, rather than with the revolutionary transformation or seizure of the state. Add to this the interpolation of the private into the state and public spheres, and deciphering whether GCS is potentially a transformative domain becomes increasingly problematic.

Consequently, our attention is drawn again to the precise characteristics of what is being referred to within the discourse of GCS. A number of questions are pertinent here. Is it possible or desirable to envisage a domain that operates as a counter-power to the forces of neo-liberal globalisation, a domain that is conscious of itself and that seeks to deepen connections across movements, organisations, and networks? How might it be organised, what forms could it take and where would we look for it? Furthermore, do the established NGOs, trade unions, and newer social actors such as ATTAC, best represent this GCS, those whose challenges are potentially reconcilable within capitalism's systemic capacity for assimilation and mutability? Or, are those who adopt more openly confrontational repertoires equally, or more acutely 'representative' of GCS, presuming therefore that they express some deeper antagonistic conflict? The more interesting question is whether we can perceive this hybrid combination of individuals, movements, and organisations, this networked domain of social solidarities as a unified or unifiable opposition, or whether indeed, we would want to?

Global networks and antagonistic movements

Castells has demonstrated how the rise of 'network society' means that societies are increasingly structured through 'a bipolar opposition between the Net and the Self' (Castells 1996: 3) meaning that 'global networks of instrumental exchanges', international financial organisations, transnational corporations and the like, have the capacity to selectively 'switch-off' groups, organisations, and even countries and regions from global networks.[1] The prevailing logic of economic networks in an era of neo-liberal ascendancy has been to demonstrate this capacity to excess. However, at the same time the impacts upon communities of having been 'switched off' and abandoned to the fate of marginality, have also facilitated a return to the self, in the form of self-reliance and the valorisation of particularistic or 'local' identities, hence the polarisation between 'Net' and 'Self' in Castells' account. The network form is not unique to corporations however, and the evolution of networked relationships between diverse social groups has been an increasing feature of protest and social activism. Increasingly the threat from 'fluid' capital in an era of 'liquid modernity' (Bauman 2000) and its capacity to organise the means of production in dispersed locales without external controls or regulatory frameworks has led to the expansion of oppositional networks which are necessarily international and increasingly global in character (Edelman 2001). These networks are sometimes facilitated through direct contact, but are increasingly maintained through CMC, and such networks have been successful on a range of issues including the 'electronic fabric of struggle' (Cleaver 1998) woven during the Zapatista insurrection and the successful opposition to the proposed Multilateral Agreement on Investment.

As these networks have employed confrontational, imaginative, and highly symbolic repertoires of collective action based upon the ethos of 'direct action for direct democracy', they have generated ripples beyond their obvious impacts upon international trade summits and related policy fora. The militant and participative character of these movements has been significant in catalysing reflection amongst civil society actors, including some prominent NGOs. Greenpeace International, for example, professed to feeling 'outflanked' by the effectiveness of these movements (Greenpeace 2001) and promptly embarked upon a five year rolling programme of internal debate – *Breaking Down the Walls* – with proposals for action and deliberation aimed at addressing both its own democratic deficit and broadening its focus of opposition.

What is being described here is the emergence of an antagonistic current to GCS that is composed of networked actors often in dense national or regional clusters, connected into global affinity structures maintained by CMC and reconfigured during intense periods of social interaction around specific protest events or reflexive gatherings. However, as we have already demonstrated attempts to understand this were hampered by the over-concentration on the 'novelty' of the WTO protests in Seattle in November–December 1999, which belied the prior existence of these international networking processes, without which the 'success' of Seattle makes very little sense (*Notes from Nowhere* 2003, Chesters and Welsh 2004).

Analysis of this antagonistic current can be facilitated through reference to the typological distinction Melucci (1996a) makes between forms of collective action and social movements. This allows us to differentiate between the majoritarian representation of social movements within GCS and the antagonist movement instantiated in the AGM. Melucci (1996a: 28) defines a social movement as a collective action which: (i) *invokes solidarity*, (ii) *makes manifest a conflict* and (iii) *entails a breach of the limits of compatibility of the system within which the action takes place.* This last point appears somewhat ambiguous, until we examine Melucci's definition of the 'systems' within which action might take place. He identifies four differing types of social movement, which are defined symbiotically in relation to the system invested by these forms of collective action; consequently, in elucidating the differing types of social movement he is also describing the four different systems. These systems are unable, by definition, to absorb the challenge of the collective action without substantive change to their internal logic or organisational form. This typology is analytically useful as a means of differentiating between the varied instrumental, purposive, and expressive orientations of the social movements that help constitute GCS.

The first type of social movement Melucci identifies is described as 'conflictual networking' and takes place within the lifeworld. Primarily, he argues that 'forms of popular resistance are always present in society, creating a free space that precedes visible action' (Melucci 1996a: 34). These forms of popular resistance do not necessarily involve challenging the production and appropriation of society's resources. They are, instead, the series of conflictual social relations that are characterised by challenges to normative values and behaviour within everyday life. Beyond this field of action, Melucci recognises three further movements which he terms claimant movements, political movements, and ultimately, and most abstractly, antagonistic movements.

A *claimant movement* is normally situated within an organisational system and seeks a different distribution of resources, roles, and rewards. It might be mobilised to seek or defend a set of conditions and rewards which it has, itself, internally defined as appropriate, thereby pushing the conflict beyond the operative level to the level at which norms are produced. Examples of such movements might include campaigns for disabled access to public buildings and transport, or the campaign for same-sex marriages.

A *political movement* breaches the limits of compatibility within the formal political system, by challenging forms of representation, influence, and decision-making, thereby endeavouring to create new avenues for participation and expression and drawing attention to previously excluded interests. Historically examples of such movements in the United Kingdom would include suffrage campaigns such as those conducted by the Chartists and the Suffragettes, whilst a contemporary example would be the campaign for parliamentary proportional representation.

An *antagonistic movement* is more theoretically abstract in that it challenges the production of society's resources in the most fundamental way, not only in terms of the allocation of resources, but in the very nature of their production, distribution and exchange. Whilst no movement can ever be completely antagonistic, that is, without recourse or relationship to existing formal systems of social and political representation and decision-making, an antagonistic orientation may be empirically observable within certain movements, and might become increasingly manifest in circumstances where organisational or political systems attempt their repression through a process of criminalisation.

The rise of the AGM is indicative of this last category, an expression of a fundamental conflict over the form of production and distribution of crucial social, economic, and ecological goods, a movement(s) that has acquired momentum due to the assimilation and decline of traditional state-centric channels for civil society expression. Thus, the AGM represents a 'new' and distinctive voice, which has attempted to militantly redefine GCS as a constituent space of counter-power, critique, and contestation, giving succour to those seeking a new agent of social transformation. A position most apparent in Hardt (1995) and Hardt and Negri's work (2000):

> Civil society is absorbed in the state, but the consequence of this is an explosion of the elements that were previously coordinated and mediated in civil society. Resistances are no longer marginal but active in the centre of society that opens up in networks; the individual points are singularized in a thousand plateaus.
>
> (Hardt and Negri 2000: 25)

Some of the most strident attempts to re-frame global civil society as a key interlocutor between people(s) and capital are to be found in the communiqués of the Mexican Zapatistas, and particularly those authored by Subcommandante Marcos (2001). His repeated calls upon 'international civil society' to intervene in their conflict with the Mexican state and his characteristically poetic valorisation of the 'disarming facelessness of civil society' (Marcos 2001: 54) led to the first *Encuentro* (encounter) in 1996, held in the Rainforest of Chiapas and styled as an 'intergalactic' meeting for humanity and against neo-liberalism. This was an invitation to their global network of civil society supporters – activists, artists, academics, and others to consolidate their relationship with the Zapatistas and each other and to begin to theorise and implement a global strategy of networked resistance. The *Encuentro* process catalysed by the Zapatistas also led directly to the founding of PGA, an international network of resistance movements, including landless peoples, indigenous rights organisations, small farmers, independent media collectives, squatters, environmentalists, and community organizations. PGA is discussed in depth in Chapter 6.

This Zapatista model of GCS as global public sphere, a space of encounter, deliberation, and exchange also helped to inspire the World Social Forum process (Houtart and Polet 2001) which was eventually manifest in 2001 in Porto Alegre, Brazil (Fisher and Ponniah 2003, Sen *et al.* 2004) as:

> an open meeting place for reflective thinking, democratic debate of ideas, formulation of proposals, free exchange of experiences and

linking up for effective action, by groups and movements of civil society that are opposed to neoliberalism and to the domination of the world by capital.

(World Social Forum International Council, Charter of Principles, Section 1)

The social forum process has since expanded to include regional social fora in the Mediterranean, Asia, Europe, and the Americas. The first ESF meeting in Florence during October 2002 attracted around 50,000 participants and led to a proposal for the 15 February 2003 anti-Iraq war protests. This globally co-ordinated collective action was the singular largest manifestation of GCS and the biggest protest ever to have occurred. The second ESF in Paris during November 2003 attracted similar numbers and scheduled over 1,000 seminars and plenary sessions engaging with major political, policy, and civil society concerns. These actions and events demonstrate the ecology of action within GCS that enables the transformation of deliberative encounter in to a social force constitutive of what *The New York Times* called 'the second superpower'.[2] A 'new power in the streets' that is challenging both the economic orthodoxies of neoliberalism and the 'inverted' totalitarianism underpinned by permanent war (Wolin 2003).[3]

These events and the subsequent commentary on them begin to shed light on the questions raised above about the possibility of GCS constituting a counter-hegemonic domain. They also move us beyond traditional political concerns with the seizure of state power. Instead, in the social forum model we are presented with an alternative vision of freely cooperating autonomous actors engaged in the day-to-day management of their own lives through a vital, open and uncoercive public sphere. At its core, this project desires to dissolve 'political society' into 'civil society' and with it to reformulate a truly democratic and participatory public sphere.

Complexity and global civil society

What has been outlined earlier is the discursive construction of a global field of struggle, constituted by the forging of connections between social movements operating in a context defined by the hegemony of neo-liberalism and the arrival of the information age. GCS and in particular the AGM have proliferated by using inclusive methods of organising, pluralistic patterns of intervention and the targeting of organisations, events, and situations that have a global impact – and as such have resonance for social movements and other sympathetic constituencies globally. An additional success of these targeted actions against the G8, WTO, WB, or IMF has been the enormous cross-fertilisation of ideas, concepts, and collective action repertoires resulting from the express desire of organisers to see politically contiguous actions proliferate in the same spatial and temporal context. The AGM has therefore provided the means through which politically engaged people can conduct the necessarily collective work of deciphering their individual experiences of globalisation and forging from them shared understandings that can become the basis of recognisable needs and therefore political demands.

However, as we demonstrated in Chapter 3 there is a number of methodological and theoretical difficulties associated with analysing subterranean networks comprised of non-linear flows of people, resources, and ideas. Recent ethnographic and anthropological work has taken these problems seriously (Mueller 2003, Chesters and Welsh 2004, Osterweil 2004a, Sullivan 2004) and what this work repeatedly demonstrates is that proximity to specific groups or organisations alone is analytically insufficient. To capture the dynamics of this movement(s), one must literally be adrift within the network, engaging with movement actors in material and immaterial spaces and sensitised to the emergence of qualities that are irreducible to the sum of the parts of that network.

Equally the key to understanding the AGM is not to be found amongst individual actors be they groups or organisations. Instead, we must focus our attention upon the processes of interaction *between* actors, to the iterative outcomes of reflexive framing and to the emergence of an ecology of action within GCS that is actualised through the AGM. If we are to reveal anything about how the AGM works, we must look to processes and to form, for it is within this hidden architecture that something of the dynamic strength of the AGM can be grasped. The AGM displays 'small-world' characteristics (Watts and Strogatz 1998); it consists of hubs and nodes that are typified by a penumbra of 'weak links'. In network analysis, this structure demonstrably allows for rapid communication and is resilient to all but the most focussed of attacks. It is also associated with generative processes that lead to macro-level outcomes which are not always apparent to their participants. These emergent properties are the outcome of complex adaptive behaviour occurring through participative self-organisation from the bottom-up. This organisational form and the behaviour that structures it leads to the emergence of a collective intelligence that in turn drives forward the same processes in feedback loops, leading not to entropy as one might expect in a system of this type, but rather to substantial increases in agency and potential.

The concept of emergence describes the unexpected macro outcomes produced by reflexive actors engaged in complex patterns of interaction and exchange, outcomes that are historically determinate and unknowable in advance. Of interest is the apparent operation of these feedback loops within the AGM. Here the emergent properties of acting in a decentralised, participatory, and highly democratic manner are recognised at a collective level as affording a strength, durability, and interconnectivity that would otherwise be absent and this feedback reaffirms the praxis that gives rise to the emergent properties. Recent work in this field has demonstrated (Barabasi and Albert 1999) that emergent properties are ubiquitous in complex systems, albeit they often go unrecognised. What appears to have occurred within the AGM is that its affinity with participatory and democratic means and its adoption of a decentralised praxis have encouraged organisational forms with emergent properties that are politically and culturally efficacious within a network society. Thus, we have seen the emergence of durable networks that are highly effective at information management, communications, material and symbolic contestation and mobilisation at the local and global levels. This has been coupled with a recognition amongst certain actors of the primacy of process in catalysing these effects and a prioritisation of process as a means to maximise these emergent outcomes.

Emergence in plateaux

In order to analyse these processes of network interaction and emergent outcomes we are suggesting a conceptual framework that allows descriptive and analytical purchase over two key processes in the emergence of global social movements. The process of encounter and interaction and the process of constructing shared understandings within and between movements. So far, we have described the construction and iteration of sense-making processes (*reflexive framing*) and we now move to consider the spaces of intensive networking (*plateaux*), both rooted in a 'minor literature' that begins with Gregory Bateson (1973).

One of the most interesting yet under-theorised concepts to arise from within this minor literature is the concept of plateau(x), originated by Bateson (1973) and subsequently developed by Deleuze and Guattari in their second volume on *Capitalism and Schizophrenia* (2002). Plateau has geological, mathematical and figurative meanings but was used by Bateson to differentiate a preference within Balinese culture for the continuation of intensity over the transcendence of culmination or climax, an orientation that he noted as extending from sexuality to aggression. Deleuze and Guattari (2002) developed this concept as an extension of their distinction between arborescent culture (linear, binary, hierarchized) and rhizomatic culture (multiplicitous, heterogeneous, non-linear): 'We call a "plateau" any multiplicity connected to other multiplicities by superficial underground stems in such a way as to form or extend a rhizome' (Deleuze and Guattari 2002: 22).

In our formulation we use plateau(x) as a descriptor for the process of intensive networking in material and immaterial spaces that occurs around nodal points of contestation or deliberation, such as protest events or social fora. This allows us to focus upon processes of territorialisation – the manifestation of networks within physically and temporally bounded spaces and lines of flight between territories – the reconfiguration of networks through processes of encounter, the proliferation of weak links, the exchange of knowledge and the construction of affective relationships through face-work and co-presence. These processes of physical interaction that characterise global social movements – the protest actions, *encuentros* and social fora are further understood to be dynamically interconnected and co-extensive with a *digital commons*[4] that underpins computer mediated interaction and communications and which co-constructs the rhizome of the AGM. This rhizomatic 'network of networks' (Melucci 1996a) constructs 'new' democratic spaces for deliberation on complex global problems and frames these problems within the discourse of 'anti-capitalism' and 'alter-globalisation'. These participatory fora, including the conferences and gatherings of PGA, the WSF (Fisher and Ponniah 2003) and its regional sub-conferences, are central to the emergence of global social movement networks as antagonistic actors within GCS.

These encounters facilitate the elaboration and exchange of diverse perspectives emerging from specific histories and cultures of struggle which fuse with desires to explore the potential of synergistic forms of collective action that can retain diversity whilst exerting social and political force. Unpacking the dynamics of these interactions requires an analytic descriptive vocabulary able to address how individual and group interpretive schemas are constructed, represented and changed within plateaux. Social movement theory has traditionally used 'frame analysis' as a means of engaging with such processes. Whilst we continue to utilise a frame analytical approach, the concept of plateaux and the centrality of network actors reorients the object of frame analysis underpinning Goffman's (1974) formulation. For Goffman the object of 'frame analysis' is a 'strip of activity' arbitrarily selected by an individual and subject to sense-making activity. This results in a discussion of individual reflexivity 'too removed from fieldwork' (Goffman 1974: 10).

Our use of plateaux departs from Goffman's notion of a strip of activity in two important ways. Through fine-grained fieldwork, using multiple recording techniques that were unavailable to Goffman, we have analysed how individual frames can become group frames within particular movement events (Chesters and Welsh 2004, Chapter 3) and this work suggests that plateaux are typically longer than the notion of a strip suggests, creating multiple event horizons that persist long after the particular event is 'over' (Welsh 2001, 2004). We use the concept of reflexive framing (Chapter 3) to address the iterative process of renegotiating meanings through retrodictive sense making utilising feedback mechanisms including CMC; list-serves, web logs and post-event video screenings. This allows us to advance a conceptual framework for interrogating processes of iteration at different scales (macro to micro, synchronic to diachronic) across the ebb and flows of movement activity permitting further insights into processes of capacity building accentuated by relations of affect and intensity inculcated within plateaux:

> a plateau is reached when circumstances combine to bring an activity
> to a pitch of intensity that is not automatically dissipated in a climax

leading to a state of rest. The heightening of energies is sustained long enough to leave a kind of afterimage of its dynamism that can be reactivated or injected into other activities, creating a fabric of intensive states between which any number of connecting routes could exist.

(Massumi 1992: 7)

Thus we conceptualise plateaux as events of temporary but intensive network stabilisation where the rhizomatic substance of the movement(s); groups, organisations, individuals, ideologies, cognitive frames etc. are simultaneously manifest and re-configured. The study of movement plateaux thus requires a focus upon process, interaction and intensity. The 'object' of analysis becomes the iterative character and fractal patterning of over-lapping networks and the processes of interaction and exchange between global locales, the relationship between the virtual and the real, and the interaction between new social actors and familiar forces of antagonism.

Understood this way plateaux provide a reflexive impetus for movements, an opportunity to recognise 'oneself' and the points of connection between one's identity and actions and those of other participants engaged in similar struggles. They also allow for the expression and exploration of difference (identity, politics, strategy, goals) through theoretical and practical innovation. This includes cognitive and symbolic re-framing (Chesters and Welsh 2004) and the construction of distinct spatialities within the one temporality (e.g. dedicated action zones for different protest repertoires, or autonomous spaces within a social forum).

Interaction of this sort encourages the formulation and shaping of political projects at local and global levels and enables strategic and tactical reflection. Other outcomes include the transmission of 'techniques of self' conducive to collective expressions of solidarity and mutual aid. Plateaux are therefore increasingly the means through which phase transitions occur in movement forms; they precipitate increases in flows of energy, which produce non-linear changes in the system (of relations) conducting that energy. These can include anything from a mundane re-orientation of campaign focus, to changes in the internal dynamics of decision-making within a social movement organisation, or the wilful 'contamination' of leftist parties seeking greater purchase amongst social movement actors.

The WSF and its regional offshoots are one of the most tangible expressions of movement plateaux, eulogised by Hardt and Negri as '*the* representation of a new democratic cosmopolitanism, a new anticapitalist transnationalism, a new intellectual nomadism, a great movement of the multitude' (2003: xvi). This space of encounter was strongly influenced by ideas expressed during the Zapatista *Encuentros* (encounters) of the mid-1990s, where the concept of creating a global 'mirror and lens' (collective recognition and focus) for antagonistic movements was first elaborated (see Marcos 2001). This process enabled activists to 'bridge worlds' through the deliberate construction of spaces wherein links between diverse movements could be made.

The importance of 'weak ties' and 'social bridges' for the elaboration of communication and access to resources is familiar from Granovetter's (1973) work on the 'strength of weak ties' and latterly from those elaborating theories of small world networks (Barabasi 2002, Buchanan 2002). This counter-intuitive argument suggests that it is the weak ties between people, not strong friendships that are most important when it comes to such things as launching a new project, finding a job, and accessing news. This is because weak ties are crucial for being able to communicate beyond one's immediate social (or activist) worlds. Close friends and fellow activists almost inevitably move in the same circles and as such are most likely to be exposed to the same information. Weak ties have to be activated to open new channels of information and maximize potential for agency – ties which might include e-mail contacts, people met during meetings, at protests, and during gatherings. There is also a need to be able to connect with those activist hubs – individuals active within many networks ('spiders at the centre of many webs')[5] networking spaces (such as fora and information exchanges), and social centres – without undue interference from structures and hierarchies or barriers to participation such as class, culture, age, gender, and race that would inhibit such connections.

It is this combination of elements – large numbers of interacting individuals, groups, and movements constituting an open system that adapts to its environment leading to increased reflexivity facilitated by feedback loops and non-linear processes of interaction and iteration that leads to even greater complexity. Plateaux are combinatory expressions of complexity effects realised through assemblages of material and immaterial elements. They are shaped by the material infrastructure of mobility and communication systems that are a pre-requisite of a 'network sociality' (Wittel 2001) and through their emphasis upon co-presence, face-work, meetings, and encounters, they point to how these material assemblages realise the potential of small world networks. What emerges is a network of networks, increasingly shaped by an eclectic mix of minoritarian subjectivities, of *virtuosi*, including net-workers of various kinds – artivists, hackers, mediatistas, and academivists (*Notes From Nowhere* 2003) – whose capacity to resist co-option by party discipline and ideological strictures is growing as a direct result of increasing complexity.

Conclusion: the antagonist attractor within global civil society

The emergence of global social movements characterised by an antagonistic orientation and their organisation through horizontally structured networks of real and virtual relations has profoundly influenced the trajectory of GCS. This is discernable in the effect of movement plateaux, such as the siege of international trade summits or the growth of the social forum process, where the AGM has produced a surfeit of material and symbolic resources that enable the expression and linking of conflictual currents – movements, organisations, groups, and individuals. These plateaux are shaped by a number of ideological inputs, including, liberal constitutionalism (human rights, anti-corporatism, fair trade, democratic representation); socialism (trade unions, welfarism, internationalism); anarchism (participation, direct democracy, direct action); and, ecologism (environment, sustainability, nature) – each of which interacts with the others exchanging, assimilating, and adapting concepts, slogans, symbols and other cognitive, emotive, and affective resources.

From these ideological motifs emerges a hybrid anti-capitalism such as that articulated by the AGM, albeit a minority of their exponents would perceive themselves to be taking an explicitly anti-capitalist position. During interactions between different groups and individuals within these plateaux 'anti-capitalism' acts as a 'strange attractor', it causes a perturbation in the pattern of behaviour and the mode of being of those bodies encountering it as a discursive practice. The iterative communication of experiences and ideas, and the formulation of proposals 'by movements of civil society … opposed to neo-liberalism and to domination of the world by capital' (WSF Charter of Principles) declares the stakes to be fundamental and therefore to concern the production and exchange of crucial social and economic goods. This opens new directions of movement for civil society bodies such as NGOs, charities, and religious groupings that would otherwise tend towards the equilibrium offered by normative forms of political engagement (e.g. institutional lobbying).

This breach in the system of relations and signification allows for engagement, albeit briefly, in more speculative, dynamic, and hybrid repertoires of collective action and discursive democracy. Some of these possibilities, immanent in the plateaux of counter-summitry, social fora, and associated protest events, are realised through the passage of formerly regulated social actors into an open system of determinate chaos where outcomes are likely to be unplanned and unpredictable. In this context, the medium becomes the message. The model of social change implied is constituted in a process of encounter and deliberation sedimented in movement plateaux where critical discourses and affective solidarity can reconfigure non-linear networks and multiply weak links to create a plane of consistency between heterogeneous actors. This does not obviate the need for 'politics', nor does it smooth away the familiar dilemmas of any organisational process (resources, leadership, democracy, and so forth) as we demonstrate in the Chapter 6. Instead, alongside the network form in which they are manifest, it privileges these processes as the locus of political action, suggesting a need for new modalities of investigation and a willingness to countenance theoretical excursus appropriate to the complexity of GCS.

6 Shadow realm

Beyond resistance to global nexus

> There is no centre anywhere that could hope to organize and oversee all this mutual thickening of ties. It would be like trying to instruct a forest how to grow.
>
> (PGA Bulletin Five 2000)

> In order to transcend the current paradigm of new social movements the main characteristics of recent collective action must be identified. Even though I am not in search of the central movement of complex society, I maintain that there are forms of antagonistic collective action capable of effecting the logic of complex systems.
>
> (Melucci 1989: 73)

Neither anti nor pro, but *alter* (alternative and other)

Two of the most common accusations against the alternative globalisation movement are that it amounts to an 'anti' movement with little idea of an alternative vision (Freidman 1999), or that it indulges in 'movementism' (Callinicos 2003) serial protesting that actively excludes political parties because of a misplaced opposition to the party form. The presumption underlying both these positions is that the expression of diverse perspectives through a combination of dialogical encounter, protest and cultural experimentation is insufficiently coherent to mount or maintain an ideological challenge to the status quo. Therefore, those that constitute the AGM are dismissed as either 'a Noah's ark of flat-earth advocates, protectionist trade unions and yuppies looking for their 1960's fix' (Freidman 1999) or they are conveniently reframed as nascent parties to avoid the difficulties of theorising afresh:

> These divergent currents operate like parties, organizing on the basis of what amount to distinct political programmes, even if they spurn the name 'party'.
>
> (Callinicos 2003)

The majoritarian logic behind these perspectives is concerned with efficacy, efficiency and utility. In their construction of potential enemies and allies both these positions recognise that the AGM has opened a discursive space in which fundamental issues of environmental and social justice can be raised, a space that should either be closed off through vitriolic dismissal (Freidman) or accommodated within the existing paradigm of Marxist revolution (Callinicos). In both accounts, the AGM is criticised to various extents for its incoherence and/or lack of organisation. A significant flaw in the reasoning of these commentators lies in the disassociation of the impacts of the AGM and its organisational form(s), as if the impacts that make the movement(s) worthy of comment have little to do with the way the movement(s) organise and relate to each other. In both these accounts, ideological expressions of liberalism and Marxism reduce complex social and political phenomena to established paradigms of interest representation through market or party structures.

Neither position, it would appear, has the political will to engage with the means through which antipathy to party structures, diverse repertoires of resistance and the construction of new affectivities have been articulated through a rhizomatic expansion of networks that provide space for a multitude of social and political programmes, without the need for an overarching ideological narrative. These processes of encounter and exchange facilitate the articulation and exploration of common values and emergent interests that are either taken up and multiplied by iteration through facework and CMC or instead fall back to the level of their initial expression. The effect as we demonstrated earlier in our discussion of movement plateaux is that outcomes are often unpredictable, and frequently spectacular outcomes are the result of actions by seemingly peripheral activities conducted by 'minor' actors.

The interesting question therefore, is the one that is not considered by commentators such as Freidman and Callinicos – to what model of social change does the rhizomatic interlinking of movements give rise and to what extent does this model offer the potential of radical social transformation? Similarly, if the concepts of reflexive framing and plateaux provide us with a means of elaborating the sense making and intensive qualities of movement interactions that lead to unexpected and seemingly disproportionate outcomes, such as the perturbation of prominent discourses on development and global trading, how then might that form be elaborated, communicated, co-ordinated and extended? To explore this question we turn to attempts to co-ordinate the AGM and to those who seek to spread the medium as strongly as the message. In particular, we look at two distinctive attempts to co-ordinate resistance and offer alternative visions to the prevailing model of neo-liberal globalisation, People's Global Action (PGA) and the World Social Forum (WSF) Movement. We examine their roots, organising processes and effects and speculate upon their likely trajectories within the current geo-political context.

Catalysts of encounter

Until the rise of the WSF and the explosion of national, regional and local social fora, the prominence of the AGM arose from its capacity to mount large-scale protests and interventions during summits of international government and finance organisations. This capacity was one outcome of networking processes that were underway for a considerable time before the public emergence of the AGM in events such as the June 18th Carnival Against Capitalism in London or the Seattle shutdown of the WTO during 1999. These protests were amongst the first to explicitly articulate a link between northern movements and the backlash against globalised neo-liberalism that had found its most advanced expression in the resistance of the majority world of the global south to structural adjustment policies and free trade agreements during the late 1980s and early 1990s. There were many catalysts for these links, but the most significant for our discussion of movement forms and co-ordinating processes are the actions of the Zapatistas – the EZLN (Ejército Zapatista de Liberación Nacional), an insurgent movement in Mexico whose military intervention was timed to coincide with the introduction of the North American Free Trade Agreement (NAFTA) on the 1 January 1994.

The Zapatistas are a hybrid of initially Maoist cadre, indigenous movements and civil society supporters, who have successfully created an autonomous zone of self-government in the Chiapas region of Southeast Mexico (Holloway and Pelaez 1998). This was achieved through limited military means and multiplied by their capacity to construct an 'electronic fabric of struggle' (Cleaver 1998), utilising a web-based network of observers and solidarity campaigners to insure the Zapatistas against a military onslaught from the Mexican state. The Zapatistas are crucial to any discussion of the emergence of the AGM (Tormey 2004) because they were amongst the first to articulate the potential of a global resistance movement that valorised marginal subjectivities and privileged processes of encountering the other as a means of building peace and sustaining social change. Their conception and hosting of the 'First Intercontinental *Encuentro* for Humanity and Against Neoliberalism' in 1996 gave a form and expression to the anti-capitalist attractor that was to subsequently animate protests globally. This was the first point at which the logic of encounter, the emphasis upon minor subjectivities and the proliferation of weak ties were formalised as explicit movement goals.

Encounter as method: the mirror and the lens

An echo of this rebel voice transforming itself and renewing itself in other voices. An echo that turns itself into many voices, into a network of voices that, before power's deafness, opts to speak to itself, knowing itself to be one and many, acknowledging itself to be equal in its desire to listen and be listened to, recognizing itself as diverse in the tones and levels of voices forming it.

(Closing Remarks to the First Intercontinental
Encuentro for Humanity and against Neoliberalism,
Subcommandante Marcos 2001: 122)

Something in the world forces us to think. This something is an object not of recognition but of a fundamental encounter.

(Deleuze 1994: 139)

The Zapatistas engaged in a double articulation defending a place-based model of the cultural and natural, whilst expressing that defence as a contributory action to a network of global resistance. They sought to catalyse self-recognition amongst movement actors of the field of potential, the immanent global civil society (GCS) that they defined militantly as an antagonistic force for social change. In Latin America, the concept of civil society had come to stand for strategies 'based on the autonomous organization of society and the reconstruction of social ties outside the authoritarian state' (Arato 1995: 19). The Zapatistas' definition and broadening of the concept to the global emerges in this context, and as such describes something different from the dominant concept of civil society as the associational space mediating between family and state. Instead, the immanent GCS that the Zapatistas sought to actualise is conceived as a networked, self-organised and reflexive project of inter-linked experiments in autonomy and co-operation. A project to affirm the possibility of 'dignity' that 'already exists in the form of being denied' (Holloway 2002: 213) where repression is negated by the diffusion of power and movements strive for dissolution rather than capture of state apparatus. The struggle of the Zapatistas therefore counterpoises means against ends, advocating a form of a radically democratic praxis towards the emergence of a public sphere, constituted by and from struggle:

And its result will not be the victory of a party, an organisation, or an alliance of triumphant organisations with their own specific social proposal, but rather a democratic space for resolving the confrontation of various political proposals.

(Zapatista Communiqué, 20 January 1994)

This conceptualisation prefigures the emergence of the Social Forum movement and it suggests a process model of a participatory and deliberative space that the Zapatistas reasoned might act as a break upon neoliberal globalisation. The Zapatistas' successes in utilising the interventions of this ill-defined sector as a defence against military aggression provided a rationale for this strategy. Once defined, this GCS was invited to Chiapas, to the Zapatista 'reality' in a place of that name – *La Realidad*. Here, in the 'First Intercontinental *Encuentro* for Humanity and Against Neo-liberalism' activists from around the world – trade unionists; environmentalists; campaigners from various NGOs; sympathetic writers and intellectuals, gathered to hear of and respond to the particular situation the Zapatistas had helped create. In Marcos' words:

> Some of the best rebels from the five continents arrived in the mountains of the Mexican Southeast. All of them brought their ideas, their hearts, their worlds. They came to La Realidad to find themselves in others' ideas, in others' reasons, in others' worlds.
>
> (Marcos 2001: 121)

This encounter consolidated links that had already begun to emerge through websites, list-servers and other CMC establishing a new set of weak links born from reciprocal affectivities derived from the participatory, pedagogic and risk-taking inclinations of those in attendance. The *Encuentro* thus acted as a 'mirror and a lens' in the idiom of the Zapatistas, it allowed for recognition of common themes and experiences and sought a collective focus upon whom and what could be described as the 'enemy'. The Zapatistas' combination of paradoxical lyricism and participatory structures caught the mood of southern activists engaged in collective struggles against the damaging economic and delocalising effects of neo-liberalism and fired the imaginations of northern activists seeking to rearticulate a political project in the era of TINA (there is no alternative). In this encounter they discovered their targets were essentially the same, the 'hylomorphic' (Deleuze and Guattari 2002: 407–409) architecture of globalised capitalism. The IMF, WB and WTO, as well as the proxy governance through multi-national corporations facilitated by Free Trade Agreements (FTAs), Structural Adjustment Programmes (SAPs) and the rapacious conduct of the corporations themselves, the only difference was in the form and type of resistances. Although resistance was occurring globally, there was little attempt to co-ordinate and communicate between movements in a cohesive or comprehensive way. In the early 1990s, sweatshop workers were rioting in Manila, Indian farmers were dismantling Kentucky Fried Chicken outlets and land was being reclaimed across Brazil by Movimento Sem Terra (*Notes from Nowhere 2003*). The First *Encuentro* was an attempt to name these struggles as one, to offer space for connections to be made, to construct an inclusive framework and to announce a space for thinking alternatives, albeit these alternatives should in the Zapatistas' words seek 'everything for everybody and nothing for ourselves.'

By promoting a process of encounter and mutual recognition of grassroots movements, in their sophisticated crafting and use of symbolic repertoires of struggle and in their articulation of an immanent GCS, the Zapatistas framed resistance as process – 'preguntando caminamos' (Asking we walk). This framing of solidarity within a terrain of uncertainty and possibility

resonated with similar critiques voiced by movements and peoples struggling to construct alternative networks to those they were peripheral to, or
'switched off' from in the 'network society' (Castells 1996). These subaltern
networks, parallel patterns of resistance rooted in specific social and economic conditions occurred in many locations, and in many instances they
derived from similar, and seemingly incongruous interactions between
diverse constituencies (*Notes from Nowhere 2003*). In Mexico, it was
urban Marxists and Maoist cadre in dialogue with the rural indigenous
population which led to a peculiarly hybrid expression of anti-capitalism.
In the United Kingdom, it was a curious mixture of urban sub-culture, environmental sensibility and the criminalisation of dissent that facilitated the
emergence of Reclaim The Streets as another antagonistic expression of this
movement (Chesters 1999). An eclectic fusion of politics, party and protest
based in London and utilising street blockades, direct action and the recla-
mation of urban space for political and pleasurable ends, it too, soon
became a global phenomenon (Jordan 1998).

Linking and co-ordinating such diverse expressions of resistance was the
explicit aim of the process originated by the Zapatista *Encuentro* and in
1997, the Second Intercontinental *Encuentro* for Humanity and Against
Neoliberalism took place in a number of locations in Spain, including
Madrid and Barcelona. A significant outcome of the second encuentro was
the proposal for a further meeting to consolidate the emerging network and
to derive a means of co-ordinating action between its constituent parts, be
they movements, groups or individuals. In February 1998, the founding
conference of PGA took place in Geneva. It was attended by more than 300
delegates from approximately 71 countries, many of whom were attracted
by the 5 PGA hallmarks drafted and circulated by Professor
Nanjundaswamy leader of the Karnataka State Farmers' Association, one
of the largest farmers' movements in India, and a key advocate for PGA.
The hallmarks originally expressed 'a very clear rejection of the WTO and
other trade liberalisation agreements', but this was amended at the Third
International Conference of PGA in Cochabamba, Bolivia to reflect the
broader concerns of the PGA network. They now read as follows:

1   A very clear rejection of capitalism, imperialism and feudalism; all
    trade agreements, institutions and governments that promote destructive
    globalisation.
2   We reject all forms and systems of domination and discrimination
    including, but not limited to, patriarchy, racism and religious funda-
    mentalism of all creeds. We embrace the full dignity of all human beings.
3   A confrontational attitude, since we do not think that lobbying can
    have a major impact in such biased and undemocratic organisations, in
    which transnational capital is the only real policy-maker.
4   A call to direct action and civil disobedience, support for social
    movements' struggles, advocating forms of resistance which maximise

respect for life and oppressed peoples' rights, as well as the construction of local alternatives to global capitalism.

5   An organisational philosophy based on decentralisation and autonomy.

These hallmarks have become the basis for co-operation between a variety of autonomous groups and movements including those mobilising against the G8 in Scotland in 2005 (see www.dissent.org.uk). Those attending the founding conference of PGA in Geneva included striking teachers from Argentina, Canadian postal workers, women organising against the near slave–labour conditions of the Mexican 'Maquillas' factories, farmer's movements from India, Honduras, Nicaragua, Senegal, Togo, Peru, Brazil and many other countries and indigenous peoples including the Ogoni, Maori, Maya, Aymara, U'wa and others struggling for political recognition and personal and cultural survival. Also present were striking workers from the Ukraine, anti-free trade activists from the United States, environmentalists, peace activists, anti-racists, animal rights advocates and others associated with issues of equality, diversity and autonomy. This encounter was to generate an intense affectivity as a letter from the Geneva PGA Welcoming Committee subsequently made clear:

> It is difficult to describe the warmth and the depth of the encounters we had here. The global enemy is relatively well known, but the global resistance that it meets rarely passes through the filter of the media. And here we met the people who had shut down whole cities in Canada with general strikes, risked their lives to seize lands in Latin America, destroyed the seat of Cargill in India or Novartis' transgenic maize in France. The discussions, the concrete planning for action, the stories of struggle, the personalities, the enthusiastic hospitality of the Genevan squatters, the imapssioned accounts of the women and men facing the police outside the WTO building, all sealed an alliance between us. Scattered around the world again, we will not forget. We remain together. This is our common struggle.
>
> (http://www.nadir.org/nadir/initiativ/agp/en/
> pgainfos/bulletin1.html#1, accessed 25 October 2005)

There is little new in the idea that personal proximity, cultural exchange and affectivity are precursors of powerful forms of solidarity. However, as Massumi (2002: 45) argues it is precisely the 'matter-of-factness' of affect that 'needs to be taken into account in cultural and political theory', because as both psychologists and economists have recognized, emotions are key variables within a number of spheres, including markets (Elster 1998, Shiller 2000).[1] This leads Massumi to assert that 'affect is a real condition, an intrinsic variable of the late-capitalist system' capable of producing economic effects 'more swiftly and surely than economics itself'. If we prioritise the affective, the 'warmth and depth' of the encounters at the

Geneva PGA conference, what emerges at this global level is a process of movement building that privileges encounter and deliberation as ends in themselves. This runs counter to the standard social movement presumption that movement building primarily involves the 'rational' pursuit of episodic claims-making within the structure of political opportunities that is co-constructed by the state (McAdam *et al.* 2001). It also calls attention to the effects of movement plateaux, where the intersection of identities brings into tension previous particularistic definitions of self whilst avoiding the need to transform those tensions into a collective identity (McDonald 2002).

The familiar mechanisms employed in constructing a collective identity (Melucci 1996a) were present in Geneva, including agreement on the PGA 'hallmarks' and the political work of constructing a manifesto. These documents also recognised the need to retain a dynamic and open system maximising the creative tension generated by bringing very diverse groups and movements together. The importance of the event for those who participated seems to originate from its commitment to what Massumi refers to as 'symbiosis-tending' (2002: 255) the capacity of the encounter to retain the tension between agreements upon a common field of struggle and to simultaneously maintain the space for articulation of singularities within that field in a manner that encouraged processes of emergence. In this way, the absence of pressure to 'conform' in order to constitute a collective identity provided the ground for fluid and affective connections akin to Deleuze and Guattari's 'intensive multiplicity' (Deleuze and Guattari 2002: 33). The founding texts of PGA seek to articulate these processes and to elucidate a field of potential that had yet to be actualised, but which was immanent to this process of encounter and brought closer to its effects by the conference.

Therefore, despite the 'traditional' model of a manifesto and 'mission statement', there is little attempt at defining an organisational identity for PGA, instead the organisational principles seem to be paradoxical. For example, the 'PGA is an instrument for co-ordination, not an organisation' the 'PGA has no membership', 'No organisation or person represents the PGA, nor does the PGA represent any organisation or person' and 'the PGA will not have any resources' (PGA website: www.agp.org). These principles are the antithesis of organisation as usually understood and emerge from a desire to valorise encounter around mutually agreed terms – the PGA hallmarks – from which the expectation is that affective bonds established by physical proximity and face-work will enable effective network co-ordination based upon trust, reciprocity and confidence that can be further elaborated through CMC.

The initial outcomes were profound: an email call for action was circulated on 27 February 1998 in which PGA called for 'decentralised and co-ordinated actions 26th April–18th May against undemocratic international economic institutions, corporations and governments promoting economic globalisation.' The G8 were meeting in Birmingham on

16–17 May before moving on to Geneva on 18 May for the Ministerial Conference of the WTO and a celebration of 50 years of the GATT. This was the first time an explict call for the use of civil disobedience against the WTO and G8 had been made and the global response catalysed by the PGA process was dramatic.

On 16 May between 6,000–8,000 people occupied the Bullring area of Birmingham in close proximity to the conference centre where the G8 were meeting. This was a small part of the 'Global Street Party' initiated by London Reclaim The Streets, who were soon to become European convenors of PGA. On the same day in Geneva approximately 10,000 people marched on the WTO building smashing the windows of banks and overturning the Mercedes of the Director General of the WTO. Elsewhere, street blockades and parties involving tens of thousands of people took place in a number of cities worldwide including Athens, Berlin, Berkeley, Bogota, Darwin, Lyon, Melbourne, Prague, Stockholm, Tel Aviv, Toronto and Vancouver. As the protests against the WTO continued in Geneva in the days after the global street party, reports were posted on the internet by PGA including accounts of a mass mobilisation in Hyderabad, India involving nearly 300,000 people marching against the WTO. Whilst in Brazil a 50,000 strong 'star' march converged in Brasilia on the 20th May having set off from the four cardinal points of the country and led by organisations including Movimento Sem Terra (MST) whose representative at the Geneva protests declared 'The mobilizations in Brazil are the logical response of peasants and workers against the policies imposed by the WTO. These policies are being readily implemented by the Brazilian government, and as a result, the social polarization is growing rapidly.' Those marching in Brasilia went on to invade a number of supermarkets and distribute the food to the poor of the capital.

These were the first globally co-ordinated events in the 'field of collective action' (Melucci 1996a, Alvarez 2000) that contextualised the emergent AGM, although the simultaneous and networked nature of these events went largely unobserved by either the media or academic commentators. Amongst those participating however, there was an explicit acknowledgement of the potential evinced by this globally networked and co-ordinated activity. As the PGA's own analysis put it: 'The success in Switzerland has many people asking, "is this the first flutter of a new global social movement?" After so many years of saying "it's no use resisting here, we would have to organize globally", people are thinking "hey, maybe we can!" ' (PGA Bulletin Issue 2).

Co-ordinating encounters: the PGA multiplier effect/affect

> Movements in complex societies are hidden networks of groups, meeting points, and circuits of solidarity which differ profoundly from the image of the politically organized actor.
>
> (Melucci 1996a: 115)

The explosion of internationally co-ordinated protest actions against global governance and finance structures that was initiated by PGA in Geneva grew exponentially through events that have become synonymous with the cities in which they took place. This historiography varies according to the involvement and preferences of those documenting the growth of the AGM, but for most, the key locations include London, Seattle, Washington, Prague, Melbourne, Quebec and Genoa. During these events, the reticular and multi-faceted aspects of this emergent movement became observable and various attempts were made to condense and represent the movements' aims or demands for the purposes of political advantage or assimilation. This included the near universal condemnation of 'violence' within the movement by all parties with an investment in formal political processes, including most NGOs (Benjamin 2000). Despite evidence that violence was overwhelmingly conducted *against* rather than *by* protesters (Donson *et al.* 2004) and the instrumentalisation of that violence by those condemning it, for whom it had opened a space to convey their arguments via the media – the so called 'radical flank' effect (McAdam *et al.* 1996, 2001).

This period of growth and action by the AGM precipitated regional PGA networks as personal enthusiasms, connections and affinities grew; this included the adoption and iteration by numerous groups and movements of the PGA hallmarks as a statement of intent and a condition of participation in protest events or particular repertoires of collective action. During this period, PGA-inspired groups and movements established regional networks in Latin America, Asia, North America and Europe. The idea was that the convenorship for each regional network would rotate between movements and those convenors would form a Convenor's Committee that would organise conferences of the network. This was entirely fitting with the PGA's organisational principles of decentralisation and autonomy and it was also anticipated that the Convenor's Committee would be enabled to manage flows of information and advise on technical issues of resourcing, organisation and communication between regions.

In practice, this proved extremely difficult due to the inability of convenors to fully assume their roles because of existing commitments to local movement activities. This was further complicated by the problems of working at a distance including cultural and language barriers and differentials between northern and southern movements with regard to resources, including Internet access and travel. In place of the Coordinating Committee an informally organised support group, a 'PGA secretariat' (Interview with PGA activist El Viejo, Geneva, 25.03.03) performed the task of co-ordinating flows between and amidst nodes in the network for its first four years. This group was largely composed of those who had catalysed the process, who also had the enthusiasm, time and contacts within the network, and this group tended to be bi-lingual or multi-lingual Europeans with mobility and internet access, with additional support coming from those inspired to promote the network in the other PGA regions. Whilst this group performed an increasingly difficult task out of necessity, feedback through PGA email lists and during conferences focussed on its lack of transparency, accountability and the susceptibility of the network, in security and leadership terms, to the exigencies of an informal and mostly unknown group of individuals, the so-called 'tyranny of structurelessness' familiar to generations of activists (Freeman 1970). This led to the reformulation of the support group after the 2002 European PGA conference in Leiden in an attempt to make participation transparent and to encourage broader involvement by movement actors – groups or individuals who had recently engaged for the first time with the network. This initiative involved additional 'communication tools' including email lists dedicated to 'process', 'strategy', 'resistance' and 'discussion' and the development of local 'info-points' – awareness raising groups who could act to promote the scaling up of PGA-inspired activity.

Although PGA has been cited as an important actor within global civil society (Keane 2003: 61), excepting our own work (Chesters and Welsh 2004, Chesters 2004b, Welsh 2004) and work by Routledge (2004), little attempt has been made to either describe or analyse its form and structure. This is because understanding PGA's role and influence within the AGM is difficult due to the self-organising traits it manifests, including its evolving capacity to adapt its internal structure in order to cope with and manipulate its environment. In this sense PGA is a 'smoothing force' (Deleuze and Guattari 2002: 474–475) a space of intensive processes and assemblages constructed from individual contacts and the flows of information enabled by its 'communication tools'. As a network it puts out 'calls' for action yet is frequently invisible within those actions, its constituent actors forming new links and co-creating temporally or place specific initiatives (DAN in Seattle, INPEG in Prague) before re-emerging after a period of reflexive analysis to undergo a further iteration in the next plateaus. This fluidity is accentuated by its reluctance to be named or represented and its emphasis upon processes of symbiosis through encounter rather than the espousal of a political cause or goal against which its 'successes' could be measured.

Melucci's (1996a) definition of movements in complex societies corresponds closely to the pattern of relationships and activities that typify those movements that constitute and recursively structurate PGA as a mechanism of co-ordination. PGA activity is, in effect, an attempt to grapple with the paradoxical relationship between collective action and the expression of individual demands and needs which exceed the capacity of existing political systems to accommodate systemic change. The PGA is thus a material expression of the social movement form envisaged by Melucci within complex societies. As Lash and Urry argue, Melucci's stance represents the 'birth of political culture' rather than the 'transformation of [existing] political culture' (Lash and Urry 1994: 50). That is to say, social movements in complex societies bring to bear a conflictual pressure upon the symbolic logic of the system of social and economic relations that does not operate through politics alone. Whilst many movement claims are amenable to political articulation and mediation they are not reducible to cycles of grievance – interest representation – or accommodation associated with formal politics (Melucci 1996a: 117), placing considerable weight upon cultural accounts of movements (Alvarez, Dagnimo and Escobar 1998).

These forces help constitute variables in the phase space of GCS wherein attractors form from complex social, cultural and political demands. The formulation of the demand for the Tobin Tax, first articulated within GCS by ATTAC (Waters 2004) or the Jubilee campaign against Third World Debt and the various attempts at political accommodation of these issues by the French and British State, including Gordon Brown's 'Marshall Plan'[2] for the majority world, are key examples. However, by forsaking the organisational accoutrements of membership, representation and resources, and rejecting opportunities for influence through formal political channels PGA has sought to avoid this process of condensing and fixity pertaining to a simple goal, preferring instead to articulate a further set of co-ordinates, to militantly reframe GCS from within. In this sense, PGA is crucial to understanding how the anti-capitalist attractor of the AGM functions within the phase space of GCS, because its emphasis upon sociality, direct action and confrontation has ensured the continuity of an antagonistic orientation within the AGM. However, as Melucci points out (Melucci 1996a: 35–36) if the means of articulating demands within an antagonistic movement are completely divorced from any mechanism of political representation, there exists a tendency to either retreat into expressive escapism or for the conflict to be posed as a zero-sum proposition that elevates violence as a modus operandi.

PGA has instead invoked a shared reference system based upon its hallmarks, which emphasise autonomy, plurality and participation and preclude the contraction of complexity by avoiding the formulation of specific demands or any means of compulsion or forced adherence to a specific 'party line'. By resisting the temptation to consolidate and bureaucratise and deliberately functioning as a distributed network, PGA is still able to mount sustained campaigns, which include focussed activity around militarism, self-determination, privatisation and access to water without PGA being determined or defined by these activities. These campaigns arise from the priority ascribed to them by groups and individuals participating in complex patterns of deliberation in real and virtual spaces. They become network priorities through consensus decision-making processes during PGA conferences where those participating do so freely and according to their 'biographical availability' (Wall 1999) and assessment of the importance or merit of the issue. Inevitably those groups or individuals for whom the specific issue is the main focus of their time and energies are also able to pursue linkages with organisations that would not adhere to the PGA hallmarks including political parties, NGOs etc. In this sense, the globally networked character of PGA allows it to sustain a 'pure' space of antagonism within the AGM, yet precludes the dissolution of such an orientation along the continuum between expressive escapism or violent and obsessive rejection that otherwise tends to characterise antagonistic movements. Movement actors, be they individuals, groups or movement organisations enter into relation with each other in a space defined by the 'pure' antagonism (Melucci 1996a: 36) indicated in the PGA hallmarks and this field of relations constitutes a space of co-ordination for the inter-scalar politics of the AGM, without enforcing or limiting the capacity of movements to act autonomously in pursuit of claims-making in a less antagonistic manner.

The 'co-ordination' of this distributed and inter-scalar politics is an emergent outcome of the voluntary participation in the network and the affinities such participation generates. There are few sanctions within the PGA process for groups or movements participating in more traditional or orthodox political activity. Indeed this is frequently taken for granted, especially where the divergence from the hallmarks is a condition of the individuals' external connection or involvement within social movement organisations that share similar aims but have differing organisational models. This has been particularly true of southern movements where financial means have determined the connection between the movement and the network is conducted through the actions of individuals who are specifically delegated to the PGA and/or leaders of their respective social movement organisations. However, in the context of specific actions the activities of individuals participating within PGA-initiated processes have on occasion been subject to censure. Here the deliberately low-profile PGA presence makes it difficult to determine those spaces/processes, that Routledge (2004) calls 'process geographies' within which deliberate or marked divergence from the hallmarks could prompt censure within the broader PGA network. However, as we have described in Chapter 3 this process of recursive structuration within the PGA network also precipitates individuals engaged in 'free-acts' into unanticipated positions which can lead to frustration where such individuals become accountable to a network which is otherwise opaque.

These considerations resulted in close attention being paid to issues of representation, communication and accountability within PGA at a global level and attempts to formalise self-regulation of Europeans' participation at the global level to avoid 'internationals' mobility and wealth establishing dominance by default. Examples include the criticism and reformulation of the informal support group and the decision taken at the convenors meeting in Prague before the IMF WB protests, where it was agreed that the PGA global conference should have a quota system with a maximum of 30% European participants. However, because of the character of the network and the lack of sanctions available, the application of this quota system comes down to voluntary observance. The combination of 'biographic availability' (Wall 1999) of Western activists with the 'pull' of the symbolic spaces chosen for PGA conferences frequently means greater than 30% participation by Europeans and North Americans. A further factor here relates to the availability of cultural capital central to the performativity of key roles within plateaux.

The Zapatista model of relating the defence of symbolic spaces and localised life-worlds to a project of global resistance has been strongly influential within PGA. PGA has helped multiply the symbolic stakes of action through its use of 'transnational collective rituals' (Routledge 2004) that effectively and affectively link movements through activities where places become symbolic articulations of both militant particularism and global aspirations. These tactics have included speech-making tours and protest caravans that interpolate 'global' actors into 'local spaces', and have included a tour of Europe by five hundred Asian farmers that coincided with the G8 meetings in Cologne during 1999. PGA's International conferences have also been held in symbolically resonant locations including Geneva, Bangalore and Cochabamba, either for their proximity to power (WTO meetings are held in Geneva) or as an expression of antagonist resistance, such as the KRRS (Karnataka State Farmers Association) campaign against genetically modified crops in Bangalore, or the Coordinadora del Agua of Cochabamba's campaign against the World Bank-sponsored privatisation of Bolivia's water. These processes of deterritorialisation and reterritorialisation enable pedagogic opportunities, face-work, trust building and the challenging of sedimented 'habits of mind' whilst facilitating the circulation of people, resources and ideas necessary for iterative refinement of network priorities and systemic feedback.

PGA has thus instituted an autocatalytic process scaling up protests based on the defence of place-based cultural and economic practices to globally co-ordinated activity aimed at transnational actors, from individuals to groups to movements and between virtual and real environments. Whilst we agree with Routledge that PGA is essentially a 'contested coalition of place-specific social movements, which prosecute conflict on a variety of multi-scalar terrains' (2004: 2), we would emphasise the capacity of PGA-catalysed actions or spaces to lead to emergent outcomes at a global level via the AGM. Specifically, the networked form of PGA enables the retention of an antagonistic kernel within the AGM that acts as an attractor within GCS.

The World Social Forum – constructing, maintaining and developing 'open space'

> The World Social Forum is the most recent, vibrant and potentially productive articulation of an emergent global civil society.
>
> (Fisher and Ponniah 2003: 1)

In this section, we argue that as the PGA instantiates the antagonist attractor of the AGM, so also the World Social Forum (WSF) defines a phase space of GCS akin to the militant re-definition of GCS provided by the Zapatistas. The WSF is the largest 'open meeting place' of GCS and provides a discursive arena where movements come to communicate their struggles, to deliberate around possible strategies and alternatives and to network with similarly inclined covalent movements and individuals globally. In this sense, its aspirations for a non-representational domain of encounter are similar to those of PGA; however, there are many differences, including obvious ones such as scale, resources and profile where the WSF has significant advantages. Despite this, both forms of networked organisation underpin the growth in non-representational political theory and politics and both consistently refine and experiment with the theoretical and empirical relationship between the concepts of 'space', 'network' and 'actor'.

The intellectual origins of the WSF are traceable to 1996, at approximately the same time as the first International *Encuentro*, when intellectuals and activists associated with the Tricontinental Centre[3] (Belgium) proposed a counter-summit to the World Economic Forum, the 'informal' gathering of political and business leaders hosted yearly in Davos, Switzerland. Subsequently, participants in this 'other Davos' (Houtart and Polet 2001), buoyed by the success of their meeting, and emphasising the importance of continuity of action, proposed a series of events that would 'feed into the accumulation of knowledge, experience and analysis, becoming part of a long term dynamic' (2001: 115). This proposal was framed by leading activists from France and Brazil as a 'World Social Forum' that would occur in the southern hemisphere, at the same time as the World Economic Forum was being held in the North and this objective was finally realised in Porto Alegre,[4] Brazil, in 2001, where the efforts of a number of organisations came to fruition. These included the Brazilian Justice and Peace Commission (CBJP), the Brazilian Association of Non-Governmental Organisations (ABONG), the Social Network for Justice and Human Rights and ATTAC (France).

The forum was conceived as a participatory, dialogical and pedagogical space that would be non-directed and non-representative and therefore unique as a self-organised space of encounter between civil society actors including social movements, NGOs, trade unions and engaged activists/intellectuals. The conditions of participation and engagement with the WSF process are set out in its Charter of Principles formulated by the Organising Committee (now the International Secretariat) composed largely of the Brazilian organisations that convened the first forum. Politically the Charter represents a clear statement of intent, by identifying and declaring the WSF's opposition to 'neoliberalism and to domination of the world by capital and any form of imperialism' (Fisher and Ponniah 2003: 354). The Charter also emphasises interrelations of knowledge exchange and linking of movements and points towards a 'global agenda' based upon the concept of 'planetary citizenship' (2003: 357).

From the very beginning the WSF has been overwhelmingly successful, according to some of its critics too successful, attracting huge numbers of activists to discuss and debate and to otherwise participate in a vast array of workshops, seminars and plenary events, allowing for a cross-fertilisation of ideas and experiences previously unimagined. The appeal of the 'forum' model has also grown exponentially since the original Porto Alegre meeting leading to the establishment of regional social fora in Europe, the Mediterranean, Asia, Africa and the Americas, as well as the proliferation of autonomously initiated local and city fora. It is by far the fastest growing example of the rhizomatic domain of GCS, which is constituted by and through movement plateaux, and which makes explicit the political importance of spaces of enunciation, interaction and iteration that are co-extensive with the actions of movements, networks and organisations, without trying to represent them, or in turn to be represented by them.

However, this rapid expansion has presented a number of practical difficulties and organisational problems, which have attracted praise and criticism in equal measure. Leading movement intellectuals have suggested that radical activism is in danger of becoming 'a permanent conference' (Grubacic 2003), or being 'hijacked' by the 'big men' of Latin American politics – Hugo Chavez and Lula de Silva (Klein 2003). Others have argued that the WSF has become 'a logo' and 'a religion' that is rapidly alienating its participants through 'giganticism' (Sen 2003). Although a self-declared 'open meeting place', the WSF has retained the capacity to exclude and as commentators from Leftist parties to Indymedia networks have noted, this capacity is most evident in point nine of the Charter, which reads: 'Neither party representations nor military organizations shall participate in the Forum. Government leaders and members of legislatures who accept the commitments of this Charter may be invited to participate in a personal capacity.'

This clause was ironically (given their catalysing role) a reason for the Zapatistas (a military organisation), to stay away from the forum in 2002 and it has been much debated, particularly in India where it became a source of division during the organisation of the 2004 WSF in Mumbai (Sen 2003: 72–75). It was also used, albeit unsuccessfully, by autonomous social movement actors such as Indymedia, Babels (activist translation service) and the London Social Forum to argue against orthodox leftist political parties having organisational influence within the European Social Forum process. The Charter's other ambiguities include its emphasis upon non-violent struggle without specifically defining it or ruling out violence per se. This appears to be a way of avoiding the WSF having to criticise self-defensive actions, or to avoid censure of actions that may lead to property damage or other forms of protest activity that are constructed in dominant and normative discourses as 'violent'.

However, as De Sousa Santos (2003) points out, the minimalist character of the Charter of Principles means that, despite principled opposition to the under-enforced exclusion of political parties or the failure to engage armed groups, in practice, it is difficult for those who would willingly exclude themselves to define what they are excluding themselves from. This applies to both the political parties themselves, who frequently utilise front groups to attend, and those who wish to curtail participation by these parties and front groups. This he suggests is the 'WSF's power of attraction' and is the reason why the WSF has grown so quickly, the minimalist criteria for participation acts as an incentive to participation. The emphasis that the WSF has placed upon process and flexibility and its declared intention to defy temporal or geographical boundaries also strengthens this inclusive trajectory:

> The World Social Forum at Porto Alegre was an event localized in time and place. From now on, in the certainty proclaimed at Porto Alegre that 'another world is possible', it becomes a permanent process of seeking and building alternatives, which cannot be reduced to the events supporting it.
>
> (Point 2 WSF Charter of Principles)

Waterman (2003) describes this as akin to discovering the 'secret of fire', a secret which he describes as the capacity to 'keep moving', to constantly challenge any process of capture or stratification. The construction of the WSF as process rather than event advances these goals of continuous, reflexive critique, which when iterated via CMC result in a situation Waterman describes as 'around the world in 80 seconds'. However, in order to understand the emergent qualities of this system, derived from the 'edge of chaos' or process of self-organised criticality (Bak and Chen 1991, Cilliers 1998) that the WSF exhibits, we must first look to the processes of political competition between attractors within the state space of GCS described by the WSF.

The importance of the 'minor': attractors, margins and peripheries

The rapid growth of the WSF is attributed to a number of factors. These include the cultural politics (Osterweil 2004b) produced through personal and collective outcomes derived from encountering and interacting with an extraordinarily diverse group of people from all over the world. The WSF also provides a partial withdrawal or reprise from the confrontations that feature so prominently in summit siege gatherings where experiences of solidarity, affectivity, mutual learning and cultural exchange are framed by the risk of violence (Donson *et al.* 2004). The massive marches/protests at the end of social forum events have notably attracted little media coverage with police and State agencies adopting low profile approaches. As we detailed in Chapter 5 the period of growth and popularity of the forum concept coincided with escalating State violence against the AGM (Shabi and Hooper 2005). These events, combined with 11 September 2001, raised strategic issues of alignment including how to differentiate 'anti-capitalism' from 'anti-Americanism', mobilising against restrictions on civil liberties and US aggression against Afghanistan and Iraq. In this context, the process initiated by the WSF provides a means to 'catch up', to reflect upon a period of accelerated and sustained mobilisations and to continue to explore the possibilities immanent to the emerging planetary action system.

However, the influence of larger NGOs and the Brazilian Worker's Party – the PT (Partido dos Trabalhadores) who until 2004 controlled the municipality of Porto Alegre led to suspicion within some anti-capitalist networks, including PGA, that the WSF was a comparatively 'top-down' initiative. Whereas PGA was envisaged by its participants as a system of relays to co-ordinate and multiply energies released within protest plateaux at what Deleuze and Guattari (2002: 275) refer to as the 'molecular' level, the WSF process appeared to these same activists as a system of capture, a 'molarising' force that treated groups as aggregates from which norms could be produced and generalised. The subsequent raft of criticisms by those active within PGA and associated networks (Grubacic 2003, Waterman 2003, Farrer 2004) led to a 'one foot in one foot out' approach, leading to a proliferation of events and spaces on the peripheries of the 'main event'.[5] These included autonomous gatherings of various sorts, including peasants' fora,[6] youth camps, social laboratories, cultural events and so on.

Once again, we can observe in this process the importance of the 'periphery',[7] where competing (antagonistic) attractors produce symmetry-breaking behaviour, that in Melucci's terms 'entails a breach of the limits of compatibility of the system within which the action takes place' (1996: 28). In other words, we can see the emergence of movement forms in the phase space of GCS described by the WSF. In complexity terms, the system of relations constituting the WSF has tended towards a point of self-organised criticality, an 'edge of chaos' represented in the balance of attractors constituted by the official forum and the self-organised alternatives. Thus the willingness of antagonistic actors to critically engage and the permeability of the WSF has been its strength, leading to a high degree of sensitivity to external inputs enabling it to assimilate ideas and initiatives whilst internally adapting its structures to move between steady states without violent perturbation. Indeed, we would argue that the constant iteration through reflexive framing that characterises the emergence of feedback loops within the AGM has been particularly apparent within the WSF, where the use of CMC, including wikis and other online publishing by autonomous actors,[8] has crowded out 'official spaces' of articulation in cyberspace. The emphasis placed upon process by both the International Secretariat (IS) and the International Committee (IC) of the WSF also catalyses self-learning and adaptation and there is evidence that the structures of the WSF are flexible enough to enable many of the criticisms originating in the alternative or 'autonomous' spaces to be incorporated into the design of the WSF 'event'. Consequently, the 2005 WSF integrated the 'Youth Camp' within the main body of the forum and dispensed completely with the plenary format to dilute the much-criticised opportunities for grandstanding by political actors seeking a large stage upon which to rehearse familiar arguments.

Thus, the WSF has the capacity to adapt its internal structure as a result of dynamic interactions between its constitutive parts and its external environment leading to emergent outcomes that are unforeseen and unpredictable. This is perceived to be problematic by orthodox political actors who wish to actualise the social and political force immanent to the forum either by means of a manifesto or through aggregation to form a party or campaigning organisation. This has led to attempts to exert control over the direction and outcomes of the WSF by powerful actors, from members of the International Committee[9] to political parties.[10] However, these attempts have been largely unsuccessful because of the competition between attractors and the inability of any actor to hegemonise the process. It would appear that 'control' is no longer an option. This is not to suggest that the WSF process could not be stopped or moved towards a less dynamic state, as either is possible. However, it is to suggest that the cultural–political attraction of the process for its participants is strong enough for it to resist obvious attempts at subversion or control.

These outcomes are the result of the complex and adaptive qualities that the system of relations underpinning the WSF exhibits. When we examine the WSF as a state space we can begin to see how the attractors referred to above are themselves emergent qualities of dynamic interaction between other systems that are nested within the WSF. These are systems of relations that are internal to Social Movement Organisations and Networks (SMOs/SMNs) and systems of relations between those SMOs/SMNs and between those SMOs/SMNs and the structure of the WSF – the IS and the IC. Within these reticular structures diverse motivations, aims and intentions, strategies and expectations circulate. For the most part, they co-exist as aggregations of particular identities, issues or organisational forms retaining their cohesion by organising with those of similar character interactions that represent the familiar, despite the contextual potential for perturbating established modes of action. Thus they often talk *within* and not *between*. However, the discursive 'bleed' that takes place between these aggregations and the growth of affectivity encouraged by proximity and cultural exchange leads to an increased awareness of the immanent qualities of the encounter and its valorisation as a form. In this sense the term 'open space' captures, in a common sense fashion, the complexity of interactions and the diversity of outcomes which do indeed began to feel like the 'secret of fire' and as such prompt strident resistance to attempts to confine or inhibit this process.

Conclusions

> What is new about contemporary movements is first of all that information resources are at the centre of collective conflicts. Conflicts shift to the codes, to the formal frameworks of knowledge, and this shift is made possible by the self-reflexive capacities of complex systems. The self-reflexive form of action is thus another specific characteristic of recent movements. The decline of movements as 'characters' signifies the dissolution of the 'subject', and an increase in the formal capacity for self-reflection. Finally the 'global interdependence' or 'planetarization' of action profoundly alters the environmental conditions in which actors are formed and act; the field of opportunities and constraints of action is redefined within a multipolar and transnational system.
>
> (Melucci 1989: 74)

The emergence of self-organised, participatory spaces of encounter, deliberation and co-ordination amongst social movements at the global level constitutes the shadow realm of Melucci's *planetary action system.* A militantly redefined global civil society that can create spaces that are autonomous from formal and institutionalised processes of global governance, whilst maintaining links to means of political representation and exerting social force through the cultural expression of singularity and difference. This presents unique challenges to social theorists and social movement theory, requiring analysis of material and immaterial flows, including people, mobilities, technologies and knowledge practices as they unfold synchronically in intensive encounters and diachronically through the diffusion of weak links that reconfigure virtual networks.

Using complexity theory as a means of describing nested systems and posing conceptual categories in order to differentiate the field of relations between networks, actors and spaces, we suggest that the WSF is a system that instantiates the phase space of global civil society composed of competing attractors that maintain the system at a point of self-organised criticality, where collective action at the edge of chaos becomes possible. Thus, we are arguing that the 'open space' metaphor that has proven so popular amongst those who seek to defend the forum from processes of political capture and stratification has resonance because of its common sense formulation of an immanent field of potential revealed by processes of self-organisation at the planetary level. In this context PGA instantiates the antagonist attractor of the AGM (Chesters 2004a), a 'pure' space of antagonism that perturbates GCS through its 'co-ordination' of conflictual actors, thereby maintaining the centrality of systemic challenge to neo-liberal axioms, without necessitating those actors lose contact with other means of political or social mediation.

One conclusion we draw from these observations is that the AGM as an antagonistic attractor has played a pivotal role in creating and maintaining an open and adaptive system of relations in GCS through its insistence upon the primacy of process and non-representative practices as a means to resist territorialisation by political capture from above. This prioritisation of process and non-representationality is encapsulated both in the PGA hallmarks and the WSF Charter of Principles and appears to flow from the collective memory (system history) exhibited within GCS that poses the accumulated experience of trading one system of domination (capitalism) for another (authoritarian/ state socialism), against the protestations of orthodox political actors whose linear perspective suggests that representation equals control equals power. In the Chapter 7, we address these issues of power and control through analysis of the complex distribution of forces within the AGM and GCS using a conceptual framework catalysed by the idea of a 'parallelogram of forces'.

7 The death of collective identity?

Global movement as a parallelogram of forces

A force is applied to another force: They form a parallelogram of forces. They do not cancel one another; they are composed, according to a law. The play among forces is reformist: it produces compromises. But the game is never between two forces, it is among countless forces; the parallelogram gives rise to far more complex multidimensional figures.

(Eco 1986)

Introduction

In this chapter we argue that plateaux facilitate the multiplication of forces through artisanal production in subjective, material and symbolic domains with the resultant vectors expressing both *force* and *flight*, thereby exposing the axiomatic of neo-liberalism to challenges that cannot be met by the application of equal and opposite forces within the fashion of a hegemonic struggle. This 'asymmetric' terrain of struggle is frequently addressed by political elites through the application of 'simple' solutions, including violent intervention by the state, such as the pre-emptive attacks against protesters in Genoa (Chapter 4) or populist attempts at assimilation through global governance structures.[1] This chapter explores the force relations within this field of struggle by developing the account of the antagonistic orientation of the AGM (Chapter 5) and further distinguishing the composition of relations and forces constituting the AGM (Chapter 6), by explaining how collective identity approaches to social movements are problematised by the emergence of a global movement milieu animated through plateaux.

We argue that through reflexive framing and plateaux global movements are able to hold in dynamic tension the expressive and transformative potential of a number of ideological and discursive traditions. *Not* as an integrated collective identity but as a *parallelogram of forces* that enables the realisation and multiplication of force relations through the exploration and actualisation by the AGM of the *virtual singularities* (Protevi 2001: 6–10) present within global civil society (GCS). Hybridity, diversity and difference combine here in forms of antagonistic *collective* action rendering *identity and cultural politics* material in a proximate sense and highly visible in terms of the wider siege of the signs that is underway in the public sphere.

Sociology and the social sciences more generally have a remarkably poor record in terms of understanding the dynamics of, let alone predicting significant social change. Social movement and historical scholarship frequently demonstrate that significant shifts in habits of mind originate in the liminal spaces on the social, cultural or geographical margins (Alvarez *et al.* 1998, Stephens 1998, Kenney 2002). The problem has been, and remains, identifying the marginal vectors with transformatory potential within the prevailing set of material circumstances and conflicts. In terms of the themes we have engaged with, there is no consensus over these conditions but some key elements are arguably clear. Amongst these, the significance of networks and the primacy of mobilities, encounters and knowledge practices in a global age stand out as key examples (Castells 1996, Melucci 1996a, Hardt and Negri 2000, Urry 2000, 2003).

As we have shown (Chapter 2, Chesters and Welsh 2005) these accounts typically share an analytical focus upon the rise of computer-based communications, the transition to knowledge economies and the significance of 'sign values' (see Lash and Urry 1994). Hardt and Negri argue for the increasing importance of 'immaterial labour' producing services, 'cultural product, knowledge or communication' (2000: 290). Their analysis emphasises that such 'affective labour' is a *collective* production of 'social networks, forms of community' (2000: 293). Our interrogation of plateaux suggests that this resonates with the *production* of a cultural politics rather than a political culture and the creation of a 'new type of resistance' such as that envisaged by Hardt and Negri (2000, 2004). Just as cultural forms have suffused products and brands (Klein 2000) they are affecting the 'political' by rendering visible and declaring global stakes – namely that 'what is at stake is life itself' (Hardt and Negri 2000: 313). Inverting this we could also say that the AGM has rediscovered the project of political life to be immanent to the style in which one lives (Bogue 2004: 9–26, Deleuze and Parnet 2002: 127–128). In this sense there is an articulation of the need to 'live in truth' at a global level recognising that the threat to life posed by Hardt and Negri includes *both* the material conditions of physical existence *and* the anatomy of the human subject in an age of genetic modification (Habermas 2003).

We broadly agree with Hardt (2002) that one of the central tensions within GCS lies between those advocating a renaissance of the nation state as a political bastion against capitalist globalisation and the antagonistic orientation to challenge all forms of capitalism and centralised political representation. However, our conception of this dynamic differs in a crucial respect with significant methodological implications. By approaching protest events as plateaux, rather than one of many 'nodes in its indefinitely expansive network' (Hardt 2002: 118), we are preserving the integrity and centrality of rhizomatic forms. Network analyses sometimes reproduce a cartographic form of engagement within social science that seeks to map networks, measure densities and so on. Networks are depicted *as if* they are bounded conduits connecting discrete actors with specific grievances and aims intersecting within equally bounded 'nodes'. This approach faces the cartographic contradiction dating from Aristotle namely that it is impossible to draw a map of the world on the world.

The rhizome metaphor does not just stand for non-hierarchical forms but also reflects the multi-layered diffuse and interactional nature of the processes through which rhizomes constitute and shape 'forceful bodies' – the 'particular force arrangements of chemical, biological and social bodies' (Protevi 2001: 3). When understood radically this distinction allows us to move beyond the reductive aspect of network analyses, which are prone to emphasise connectivity over the capacities for material self-ordering arising from such connectivity and the force arrangements that emerge from these processes. This is consistent with the argument advanced by Deleuze and Guattari and articulated by Protevi (2001, Bonta and Protevi 2004), who suggests that 'questions of human freedom are only explicable when we address emergence above and below the level of the subject' (Bonta and Protevi 2004: 35). These are theoretical postulates consistent with Bateson's emphasis upon systemic aspects of communication. The increasing potential for 'free acts' (Eve *et al.* 1997: XV) requires attention to the experiential degrees of freedom through which individuals subjectively experience, recognise, modulate and replicate liberatory repertoires of self. This might include anything from exercising constraint upon the autonomic nervous system through to perturbating social, cultural or institutional constraints inhibiting emergence. In this way, the extensive creation of a rhizomatic movement through plateaux is an experiment, in the pre-subjective, subjective and collective invocation of singularities co-operating to express difference.

Whilst mapping the networks is analytically useful, it is important not to equate such maps with 'the movement' as this merely reproduces the reification the term social movement has been accused of. As Hardt's own account of a WSF meeting attests, it was 'unknowable, chaotic, dispersive' due to the huge penumbra of 'weak' actors and their sprawling networks. In terms of our data, the notion of 'serendipitous entrants' (Welsh 2002) and the mapping of the impact of one such entrant upon the framing and force arrangements occurring within the Prague plateaux (Chapter 3) is an empirical illustration of this phenomenon and an example of a methodology designed to address it.

Collective identity, identity politics, identization

Many commentators have remarked upon the 'unity in diversity' that is characteristic of the AGM, most celebrated in the 'Teamsters and Turtles' united in Seattle (Berg 2002). Behind such formalisations lies the interactive 'reality' through which a constellation of contingent factors are configured as unity through an iterative negotiation and intercession. This can only be revealed through rigorous empirical and analytical work of a genealogical nature. The potential for unified collective action constructed by a diverse range of social actors is, of course, implicated in analytical formulations of the term social movement (Melucci 1980, 1981, Diani 1992: 13). However, as Melucci (1996a: 187) notes, the tendency to conflate the concept of a movement and the discursive category of 'identity politics' is widespread. This, as Melucci (1996a: 187–188) argues, is why the concept of collective identity should be separated for analytical purposes from the idea of 'identity politics' and underpins our questioning of the very basis of collective identity formulations.

The rise of interest in collective identity formation paralleled the decline in interest in Hegelian/Marxist conceptions of social change as the capital/labour axis began to be regarded as less important in understanding social dynamics in 'post-industrial' (Bell 1973), 'programmed' (Touraine 1971) 'information' (Castells 1996) or 'complex' societies (Melucci 1996a). This was reinforced by the claims and actions of those who had previously been conceived as marginal social actors: women, students, ethnic minorities, young people, gays, lesbians, and the unemployed. This in effect constituted the modern sub-disciplinary domain of new social movement studies as a theoretical and empirical endeavour (Melucci 1996a, Diani and Della Porta 1998, Tarrow 1998, McAdam *et al.* 2001). Here, despite Touraine's (1981) attempts to construct a conception of society based upon a praxis of social conflict undertaken by movements, there was a notable decline in discussion of how diverse groups might unify to form antagonist movements at particular historical junctures.

For the purposes of clarity, we define 'identity politics' as the pursuit of political recognition for aspects of the social and cultural specificity arising from his or her particularistic identity based upon gender, sexuality, ethnicity, disability, age and so on. These are akin to what Castells (1997: 8) refers to as a 'resistance identities' generated by actors who are repressed, stigmatised or devalued by the structure of domination in a given society. Other commentators have noted how these identities are often manifest as a politics of difference and cultural hybridity (Lash and Urry 1987, 1994, Rutherford 1990, Featherstone 1991), and still others have addressed the problematic nature of theorising particularistic identities (Hooks 1981, Haraway 1989, Appiah 1992, Butler and Scott 1992).

We have shown how network movements consist of a number of analytically distinct social practices and forms of action, which connect deterritorialised elements of the social field in a given historical and political context. Thus, 'identity politics' can be an integral aspect of the social practice of a movement, without the movement being reducible to it. Melucci (1996: 70) defines collective identity as the process of constructing an action system. This identity is neither static nor fixed, but remains continuously in motion, requiring active identity-work even where it crystallises into semi-permanent institutional forms. Melucci calls this process 'identization' (1996a: 77) to delineate the orientation towards solidarity over solidity and the iterative process of renegotiation that occurs in social movement networks. Therefore, the Meluccian concept of collective identity *presumes* the self-reflexive capacity of social actors to recognise themselves and the field of opportunities and constraints (environment) in which they are situated. This book reveals something of the complexity underlying the operation of this presumption as process. However, the term 'identity politics' is often used as a discursive means of describing a set of empirical actors for whom the analytical distinction between political engagement and identity has been attenuated. Melucci (1996a: 187–188) suggests that this is because political engagement with established institutional actors requires a reduction of the multi-dimensionality of the issue at stake, a process which foregrounds substantive demands and grievances subordinating identity issues (Welsh 2000: 226). This frustrates the potential of the associated identity claims increasing the potential for movement dis-unity as 'identity wars' break out inside the movement milieu. This paradox is not easily resolved within the narrow means of political engagement with institutional frameworks:

> The issues they raise are inextricable from the problem of how difference can be accommodated in a differentiated society, in which both of the two horns of the dilemma must necessarily be kept together: a differentiated society can function only based on the acknowledgement and valuation of differences, but, at the same time, the increased differentiation of the system calls for a proportionate intensification of its mechanisms for integration.
>
> (Melucci 1996a: 188)

Consequently, in institutionalised politics, differing marginalised and oppressed groups are forced to compete for political mediation and representation by seeking the extension of integrative mechanisms within representative democracy to realise minority claims. However, particularistic identities can also find parallel means of expression through extra-institutional forms manifest in a range of social and cultural realms simultaneously coexistent with and constitutive of social movement networks, some of which leads to antagonistic collective action. This is an important distinction precisely because such actions can hasten the process of 'becoming-minor' in the Deleuzian sense (Deleuze and Guattari 2002: 104–106). The process of unfolding culturally sedimented potential as political action by accentuating the gap between subjectivity and normative order intersects with the 'paranoid' dynamic of capital towards reterritorialisation of 'minority' claims within institutional frameworks, reducing them to 'special interests' or niche markets based upon a fixed concept of identity.

This dispersed, hybridised culture of diffuse engagement along cultural and political fault lines could lead one to reject the possibility of unifying struggles which are capable of addressing Melucci's (1996a: 188) 'dilemma', struggles in which social movement organisations and networks recognise the difficulties and tensions of negotiating 'unity', yet remain able to mobilise diverse constituencies around a meta-identity or protest theme. Melucci's (1996: 40) development of a typology of social movements (Chapter 5) sensitises us to the role of 'ends', 'means' and 'environment' in structuring such social movement activity. This typology also allows us to indicate the level at which social movements threaten the internal variability of the systems they seek to challenge, defined as the limits at which a system can no longer assimilate the movement's demands or the forms of action it employs. In Melucci's (1996a) model of complex societies, these systems include the cultural sphere of the 'lifeworld', the administrative and organisational systems, the political system, and the system of production, distribution and exchange of crucial social resources (capitalism).

Theoretically, then, Melucci (1996a) illustrates how 'identity politics' as a form of social practice within social movements may discursively invest and perturbate a variety of different systems, often paradoxically through the development of a mutable concept of identity. Such social practices might cause legislative changes, facilitate cultural experimentation and result in a host of differing outcomes for their participants. Despite the centrality of such forms of expression to social movement activity, this does not mean that the potential of social movement networks are reducible to it. The crucial question for Melucci remains:

> Are contemporary movements capable of bringing about social and political change or are they simply reducing collective action to expressive and 'narcissistic' celebration of the particularism of identities?
>
> (1996a: 185)

This is also a rhetorical question framed by Melucci to retain a focus upon the orientation of movements and the systemic levels they address/ articulate/effect – perturbate. Despite its rhetorical formulation this question remains critical because it is frequently deployed at the political level as an argument for forging collective identity via party mechanisms and at the theoretical level as a riposte to those broadly perceived to be within the postmodernist cannon, including Deleuze and Guattari (2002). However, this charge misses Deleuze and Guattari's distinction between minor, minority and minoritarian (2002: 104–106), which informs our understanding of the emergence of social force within the AGM through the process of 'becoming-minor' effected by the circulation of struggles in plateaux:

> The notion of *minority* is very complex, with musical, literary, linguistic, juridical and political, references. The opposition between minority and majority is not simply quantitative. Majority implies a constant, of expression or content, serving as a standard measure by which to

evaluate it...A determination different from that of the constant will therefore be considered minoritarian, by nature and regardless of number, in other words, a subsystem or an outsystem...That is why we must distinguish between: the majoritarian as a constant and homogenous system, minorities as subsystems; and the minoritarian as a potential, creative and created, becoming.

(Deleuze and Guattari 2002: 105–106)

This becoming is immanent to plateaux where the artisanal 'under-labourers' cultural work – deliberation, negotiation, symbolic exchange, identity construction and affectivity supersedes the hylomorphism of prescriptive party organisations and is processualised through weak ties and spaces of encounter, multiplying the possibility of combinatory forces. Both Melucci (1996a) and Deleuze and Guattari (2002) recognise that the multiplicity of possible modes of engagement within the differing systems of complex society leaves open this potential and as such they distance themselves from the assumption which contends that a politics of difference and cultural hybridity (Lash and Urry 1987, 1994, Rutherford 1990, Featherstone 1991) marks an end to political projects that are expressed antagonistically. Rather, as we have shown, political projects that emerge in social movements do not have to be built upon particularistic identities, although they may contain characteristics that can be expressed by the term 'identity politics'. Equally, transgressive identities that rest upon cultural practices are not only performative and expressive (Hetherington 1998), they may also contain within them orientations that are antithetical to the prevailing system of production, distribution and exchange and therefore produce/reconfigure the phase space of mobilisation re-introducing valency with other antagonist actors (Chapter 5). Consequently, Melucci's typology of social movements (1996a: 34–35), combined with the detailed empirical exposition of the formation of an antagonist orientation in social movement networks, sensitises us to the possibility of philosophically coherent, unified and 'minoritarian' political projects emerging from amongst the empirically observable diversity of global social movement networks.[2]

Lines of flight and force

The word flight is often abused and at any rate carries dangerous connotations. Flight does not mean necessarily an escape into some mythical outside free from social conditioning. It is rather a moment of active creation of autonomous spaces within the existing order. Flight enables you to try and elude the status quo which subjects individuals to its political power and thereby defines their spatial movement.

(Viano and Binetti 1996: 252)

There is no need to fear or hope, but only to look for new weapons.

(Deleuze 1995: 178)

The parallelogram of forces constituted by the AGM and the play of those forces within movement plateaux leads to resultant force combinations that can become sources of the symbolic power noted by Goffman (1974, see Chapter 1). Examples of this process include challenging the legitimacy of the global institutional nexus (WTO/IMF/World Bank) and the global anti-war demonstrations on 15 February 2003, initially proposed at the Florence European Social Forum meeting in 2002. This returns us to the question of what model of social change emerges from the concept of global movement as a parallelogram of forces and consideration of agency and organisation in complex systems. This requires us to examine differing vectors, the resultant force-combinations and emergent properties that are manifest in protest events and symbolic challenges in specific space-times and the lines of flight represented by experiments in the creation of autonomous spaces, cultural production and radical subjectivities best described by the Deleuzian concept of 'becoming-minor'. If Deleuze has been central to recent theoretical attempts to meld insights from the complexity sciences with empirically informed social theory (Delanda 1997, 2002, Protevi 2001, Massumi 2002) it is because his and Guattari's (1995, 2000) work enables consideration of the properties of material self-ordering within complex systems whilst retaining a pragmatic emphasis upon intervention, upon agency as immanent structuring and ethics as a means of experimentation within a 'body-politic'. Unsurprisingly then, a Deleuzian formulation is also useful here, particularly the delineation of a relationship between the self, knowledge practices and power deployed in his exposition of Foucault's work.

As Bogue has shown, Deleuze systemises Foucault's thought by 'establishing the relationship between the archaeological strata of knowledge, the genealogical domain of power and the ethical folds of the self' (2004: 53). Deleuze's project here it seems is to locate the ethical self as a locus of resistance to the systematicity of knowledge–power processes in ways that enable the interstices in those systems to be exploited and the reproduction of control to be traversed or subverted. Moreover, it is to situate those ethics in a broader process of becoming-minor that has relevance for contemporary resistances expressed by the AGM.

In Foucault's genealogies of disciplinary control (1975, 1977, 1979), his 'histories of the present', he describes a system of power that becomes ever more complete through the extension of disciplinary institutions and discursive, linguistic and symbolic formations that regulate and order life. Deleuze (1992) takes this further in his 'postscript on societies of control' arguing that the pervasive character of technology and disciplinary logic allows for the dispersal of control mechanisms throughout society, so that we are now subject to continuous monitoring through the modulation and extension of formerly spatially bounded institutional logics. The socio-spatial discipline provided by schools, factories, hospitals and prisons are replaced by technologically mediated and 'virtual' enclosures – 'life-long' learning, corporatisation, risk assessment, 'performance' management and the universalised panopticon of the 'invisible', immaterial prisons constructed by CCTV, electronic tagging, bio-metric identity cards and house arrest. These forms of control find local and global expressions and have developed in parallel to the extension of systems of governance to the global level, the integration of financial systems and the liberalisation of capital flows to form what Guattari (2000: 47) calls 'integrated world capitalism' and what Hardt and Negri (2000) describe as 'Empire'.

Against this, Deleuze sees in Foucault's ethical studies the possibility of 'the self as a locus of resistance, a point at which thought itself can become a political force' (Bogue 2004: 53). Resistance is located in the rejection of 'habits of mind' (see Chapter 1) associated with the 'common sense' constructed through the dispersed logics of control and the formulation through encounter of an ethics of invention and intensity rather than a moral politics. Deleuze suggests that the entropic tendency of force towards dispersion and disorganisation can be accelerated through minoritarian becomings leading to the deterritorialisation of key elements of the social and political field. This is not then, a personal ethics, but a knowledge practice based upon what Massumi (2002: 255) calls 'symbiosis tending' the bringing together of diverse elements in a way which allows them to escape the plane of organisation. The 'schizophrenic' tendency of capitalism identified by Deleuze and Guattari (2002) ensures ever-greater differentiation and the subsequent elevation of difference as the generative dynamic behind informationalised production – new styles, objects, modes of exchange – create both opportunities and pitfalls for further experimentation. In this context, plateaux allow lines of flight constructed locally in the spatio-temporal dynamics of protests and sub-cultural experiments to be multiplied globally resulting in force-combinations that act against specific sites and manifestations of the neo-liberal axiomatic through the ethics and practices of a 'coming-together' (Massumi 2002: 255) which valorises affectivity, deliberation and consensus. Examples of which include the use of street parties as protest repertoire (Jordan 1998), carnival as a cultural analytic, and the symbolic multiplier effect of participatory practices, from participatory budgeting in Porto Alegre (Bruce 2004) to deliberative decision-making in the Zapatista 'Caracoles'. These experiments transcend the local and are diffused globally as both force and flight, they are increasingly the *exodus* of those who 'flee but whilst fleeing seize a weapon' (Deleuze and Parnet 2002: 136).

Thought as weapon and attractor: intellectual deterritorialisation

So far we have argued that the parallelogram of forces is composed of material, symbolic and discursive aspects which allow for the emergence of molecular lines of flight and force combinations that are catalysed by the

AGM's capacity to access virtualities present in GCS. If as Bogue (2004) suggests, Deleuze's reading of Foucault posits the self and thought as a locus of resistance then we must also ask the question of how this resistance maps between the individual and the collective and in what contexts and through what knowledge-practices this resistance becomes more or less likely. We have already demonstrated the importance of overcoming the majoritarian 'habits of mind' that Bateson (1973) identified and the 'dogmatic' image of thought criticised by Deleuze for its purely representational perspective (see Patton 2000: 18–23). However, we must also clarify the scope of what Deleuze means by 'thought' and reconsider how this relates to individual agency and collective action in the light of CMC, proliferating 'weak ties' and the emergence of complex global movements. To live and think differently is intensely difficult and as Deleuze admits, minoritarian becomings are rarely individual. However, the possibilities for connecting to others through new patterns of communication, interaction and mobility have never been greater. These new topologies of social relations increase the range and space for thinking together and enable the circulation and iteration of minoritarian ideas and perspectives, affirming the possibility of lines of flight from orthodox understandings and generating emergent knowledge-practices based upon collective reflection, iteration and critique. This encourages intellectual deterritorialisations, the appearance of new concepts (attractors) and subsequent reterritorialisations, as these attractors become practices (see Chapter 2). A collective process and a *thinking-through* action that has given rise to creative concepts, some of which are systemised as a means of temporarily stabilising debate and reflection. Consequently, knowledge-practices serve constitutive and explanatory ends within movements providing suggested trajectories and enabling forms of feedback that can multiply expressions of either force or flight. The most obvious examples here are those of 'Empire' and 'Multitude' proposed by Hardt and Negri (2000, 2004); however, there are other theoretical constructs that emerge from similar traditions that are also worthy of further examination because of their sensitivity to the rhizomatic, informationalised and cultural politics of the AGM.

For example, one way of envisaging the potential of flight and force combinations explored by the AGM is through the concept of exodus originally developed by the Italian 'workerist' movement (*Operaismo*) and subsequently articulated by Virno (1996, 2004). This concept provides a powerful metaphor through which to describe the lines of flight that can actualise the immanent qualities of the virtual field created by new forms of material and cultural production. As we go on to argue there is a need to redress the over-emphasis upon labour processes and the deduction of a 'subject' of revolution from economic and class analysis in the work of both Hardt and Negri. Whilst Virno's analysis shares many of the same 'workerist' tendencies, the symbolic power of exodus is its capacity to communicate the seemingly paradoxical idea of *flight and/as force*. Exodus recalls the refusal of work thesis that has found expression from Mario Tronti's 'Strategy of Refusal' (Tronti 1966, Wright 2002) to the Situationist exhortation: '*Ne travaillez jamais*', it evokes the nomadic resonances of asignifying movements familiar in Melucci (1996a) and echoes the Deleuzian concept of 'absolute deterritorialisation', wherein a system is moved past a critical threshold allowing new bifurcators and attractors to emerge through the accleration of intensity enabled by the 'connection of flows' (Deleuze and Guattari 2002: 220). For Virno (1996: 196) exodus requires the 'institution of a non-State public sphere' (GCS) through a cultural politics that develops the 'publicness of intellect' in opposition to the capitalist axiomatic.

Workerism in the Italian tradition has then, somewhat heretically given other Marxist traditions, sought to avoid the reduction of life to work, and instead valorises the creative capacities of labour for self-organisation *against* capitalist production processes rather than *within* them. The extension of this current to include the 'new social subjects' in the late 1960s and the re-thinking of the centrality of the proletariat within Marxist class analysis by prominent young intellectuals such as Sergio Bologna, Mario Tronti, and Toni Negri (Lotringer and Marazzi 1980, Wright 2002) led to the replacement of *Operaismo* by the broader movement of *Autonomia*, a movement that shook the cultural, economic and political foundations of Italian society in the mid-1970s (Wright 2002). The rhizomatic organisational forms that characterised Autonomia and the active participation of women, students and the unemployed combined with a strong bias towards social and cultural activity provided a vivid experimental context in which to explore afresh the dynamics of social struggle. This brought together Italian autonomists and radical French philosophers in the mid-70s including Negri and Deleuze initiating the intellectual trajectory resulting in Hardt and Negri's work (2000, 2004), and stimulating an avid interest in a previously marginal and still 'minor' intellectual and revolutionary tradition.

This tradition provides an interesting lens through which to examine some suppositions and differentiations in conceptual attractors that are animating the AGM, specifically the contemporary salience of Hardt and Negri's (via Spinoza's) category of Multitude (2000, 2005). Virno draws attention to Hardt and Negri's rejection of the 'hybrid thesis', the idea that capitalism can be as simultaneously creative as labour, rather he argues in a similar vein to Deleuze and Guattari (2002) that capital is mutable, inventive and creative as well as destructive. Lotringer (2004) thus argues that Virno is presenting a description of combat, 'a cartography of virtualities made possible by post-Fordism' where one is 'meant to strengthen some forces present in capital and join them with other forces to form a new communist ensemble' (2004: 16–17).

Opposed to this is the tendency to reconstruct Multitude as both the sustaining and productive force of Empire *and* the source of its ultimate demise which as Lotringer notes, places Hardt and Negri's telos before Multitude. The intellectual line of flight taken by Virno's conception of multitude (2004) and the political theory of Exodus (1996) is more Deleuzian and more sociological. Whilst it is full of pragmatic considerations, including points of intervention in and sensibility to the subjective and collective insecurities, hopes and fears created by informationalised capitalism, it also embraces the subsequent projection of self and community into a continuous relationship to the other. In this context, Virno suggests the crumbling concept of a people secure behind the walls of community and representing the unified subject of the state, can be contrasted with the sense of 'not feeling at home' that results from transverse lines of communication, interaction and affect experienced by the Multitude. Whilst the generalisation to the public sphere of this feeling is a precursor of multitude, it also creates space for 'molar' reterritorialisations (Deleuze and Guattari 2002: 40, 335), the return of vectors tracing themes of terror, racism and war, to which multitude must respond.

Virno's (1996) political theory of Exodus provides a framework for examining the establishment of this context and a prescription for how the Multitude might respond. He demonstrates how lines of flight traverse movement milieu connecting practices of resistance to the broader dynamics of social and economic systems, including the post-Fordist reorganisation of production and the centrality of communication and 'performance' within an informationalised global economy. Virno argues that 'post-Fordist' methods of production result in the absorption by the labour process of the key attributes of political action. Therefore novelty, unpredictability, creativity, communicative networks, and linguistic 'performances', all become characteristics of information-orientated production that assumes 'actionist' traits.[3] Virno (1996) argues that work has colonised the sphere of the 'general intellect', using 'general social knowledge' to service an economy that is reliant upon the production and processing of knowledge and information:

> In any case, what other meaning can we give to the capitalist slogan of 'total quality' if not the attempt to set to work all those aspects that traditionally it has shut out of work – in other words the ability to communicate and the taste for action?
>
> (Virno 1996: 193)

This position is not unlike the position taken by proponents of the 'reflexive modernization' thesis (Beck *et al.* 1994), whose central claim is that 'post-Fordist' structures of production require the progressive freeing of agency from structure (*Freisetzung*). Scott Lash explains this as follows:

> Knowledge-intensivity necessarily involves reflexivity. It entails self-reflexivity in that heteronomous monitoring of workers by rules is displaced by self-monitoring. It involves (and entails) 'structural reflexivity' in that the rules and resources (the latter includes the means of production) of the shop floor, no longer controlling workers, become

the object of reflection for agency. That is, agents can reformulate and use such rules and resources in a variety of combinations in order chronically to innovate.

(Lash in Beck *et al.* 1994: 119)

Neither Virno (1996) nor Lash (1994) suggest that this 'reflexivity', this resort to and promotion of a 'general intellect', are homogenous processes, instead they acknowledge the anomalous and paradoxical patterns of 'freisetzung' which produces 'reflexivity winners' and 'losers'.[4]

In his theoretical explorations of structure and agency in complex societies, Virno recovers Marx's conception of *virtuosic performance*, meaning intellectual labour without a recognisable product, a process exemplified by 'performing artists', but which also covers teachers, doctors, priests, barristers and, contemporarily, counsellors, advisors, therapists, direct action trainers and movement facilitators. From Marx's perspective, these virtuosi are special and problematic categories, which are eventually equated with service work, due to their 'non-productive' nature. For Virno (1996), this category has subsequently come to represent much of the 'post-Fordist' organisation of production, where the function of labour:

> consists no longer in the carrying out of a single particular objective, but in the modulating (as well as the varying and intensifying) of social cooperation; whereby the process of production mimics the experience of activism (poiesis and praxis) through variations on a theme he describes as a 'parody of self-realization'... [which] represents the true acme of subjugation.
>
> (1996: 193)

This leads Virno (1996) to theorise the possibility of collective action that is subversive to capitalist relations of production, through the annexation of a 'general intellect', defined in the broadest sense as a 'public resource' (faculty of language, ability to learn, abstract, correlate and reflect in an information-orientated context) to a political community, in a non-State public sphere. When unpacked, this is taken to mean that in order for collective action to assume an antagonist orientation, one would expect the precursors of the manifestation of that action to be a politicised, reflexive community of activists acting within global civil society. This is precisely the context in which the AGM has emerged over the past ten to fifteen years.

Thus, Virno defines exodus as ultimately involving 'defection from the state, the alliance between general intellect and political action, and a movement towards the public sphere of intellect' (Virno 1996: 197). Intemperance, for Virno (1996), is the cardinal virtue of exodus; as it represents a *nonservile virtuosity* that transforms civil disobedience – 'the sine qua non of political action' (1996: 197) – from a liberal construct premised upon the assumption of obedience to the state, to a radical position of fundamental opposition to state forms. A refrain that is echoed amongst social movement networks is:

> Is taking direct action our way of being heard by, and asking favours from, the policy makers because we are not represented properly in parliament? Is this what we're doing? Or is direct action an attempt to form communities of resistance in a global anti-capitalist struggle: to create a world fit for our desires – one free of hierarchy, exploitation and oppressions? If direct action is about anything at all, it's about taking power away from the politicians and bureaucrats and seizing control of our own lives.
>
> (Anonymous 1998 *Do or Die*, 7: 143)

This *intemperance* resonates with Melucci's notion of *antagonism* and indeed, they are both process-orientated analytical categories denoting 'a complex ensemble of positive actions' (Virno 1996: 198) and involving 'a magma of empirical components' (Melucci 1996a: 38). According to Virno (1996), intemperance leads exactly to the position portrayed in the quote above. Where capital is progressively freed from spatial–temporal constraints, representative democracy is equated with the restriction of democracy *per se*:

> The States of the developed West are today characterized by a political non-representability of the post-Fordist workforce. In fact they gain strength from it, drawing from it a paradoxical legitimation for their authoritarian restructuring.
>
> (Virno 1996: 202)

Whilst informational modes of production produce a degree of autonomy that creates ambivalence in the operation and diffusion of power through normative systems of control:

> Capitalist power in its post-Fordist stage discovers that it must control a set of organizational dynamics that progressively eludes its grasp. The introduction of psycho-social techniques of intervention in interpersonal relationships and the management's growing interest in analysis of organizational systems reveal within the organization a set of relationships governed by autonomous mechanisms and resistant to immediate sub-ordination to dominant interests.
>
> (Melucci 1996a: 253)

Consequently, the spaces for collective action are those in which autonomy, defection, and disobedience become repertoires of agency, using the virtuosic skills of activism (poiesis and praxis). Importantly these are spaces in which 'nomads' normatively associated with other 'spaces' increasingly participate blurring the boundaries between formal political culture and cultural politics.

Virno also describes what he terms a 'right to resistance'; this, once again, has similarities with Melucci's (1996a: 48, 73) evocation of the important role that recognition of adversaries plays in the process of identization. Melucci emphasises that if collective action is to avoid atrophying into ritual and banal equivocation *an* enemy must be located amongst seemingly inchoate inter-locutors and that enemy's orchestration of power must be 'revealed' if the collective movement actor is to remain credible within the movement milieu and wider public sphere. Virno argues that exodus involves a reorientation of the 'geometry of hostility' (1996: 204) where engagements between activists, the state and capital are seen as taking place at numerous points of intersec-tion in both cultural and political spheres involving a line of flight. Seen in these terms, conflict is 'asymmetrical', with activists 'evacuating' predictable positions such as the 'sedentary' positions that became the norm after the upheavals of the 1960s. Established protest repertoires effectively became demonstrations of powerlessness from this perspective (Camatte 1973). Thus Virno (1996: 205) argues that effective antagonistic action involves a war opened on many fronts; social movements and contentious collective actors need to flee from engagements defined by their opposition, reappearing on terrain they have chosen, to confuse and blind their 'enemy'.[5]

Conclusion: Exodus as cultural politics?

The theory of Exodus reminds us of the folding of agency, theory and philosophy in knowledge-practices that are *thought-through* action within social movement networks. It hopes to frame and explain possibilities imma-nent to informationalised capitalism and the subsequent post-Fordist reorgan-isation of the labour process and it describes the efficacy of the war machine constituted by the AGM as a means of deterritorialising important elements of the social and political field. It is both of and about the process of 'becoming-revolutionary' and as such, it illustrates the recursive structuration in complex social systems by positive feedback mechanisms. It also exhibits the impor-tance of concepts in the creation of new ways of looking, in new ways of seek-ing correspondences between the potential theorised and the artisanal process of discovering singularities through practice. In this spirit, we would seek to emphasise in accordance with other movement participants the importance of a cultural politics that gets beyond political cultures (Osterweil 2004b).

We have described how the AGM exerts a deterritorialising force that traverses along lines of flight, over-coding what Deleuze and Guattari call (2002: 40, 335–336) 'molar' lines of segmentarity (economic, social and political norms) wherein power produces and imposes order. However, the creation of a Deleuzian 'war machine' capable of opening the 'war on many fronts' envisaged by Virno (1996: 205) is also a task of discovery and artistic intervention that locates and synthesises forces immanent to global practices of resistance, refusal and escape. Contextually then, what emerges is a fractal movement space, akin to the patterning of self-similarity in complex systems, where modes of symbolic contestation, discursive democracy and antagonistic conflict overflow borders and are iterated through various scales from the local to the global.

This leads us to suggest that the AGM derives as much of its antagonistic quality from its capacity for cultural intervention and experimentation as it does from its acts of political and economic contestation many of which are already culturally rendered through laying siege to the signs of information-alised capital flows, wherein the capitalist axiomatic of free markets; corporate power; brand identities and so forth is creatively disrupted, re-presented and re-appropriated by a 'hacker class' (Wark 2004) of activists. Their ability to conjugate the virtual singularities inhering in communications technologies and the desire for co-presence creates new categories and uses for interactive domains – Indymedia, wikis, pod-casts etc. In this and many other ways the AGM works with the raw material of subjectivity and symbol, preferring poetic utterances to political rhetoric and deploying carnival rather than collectivism as its modus operandi, in celebration of the (eternal) return of forceful bodies-politic (Protevi 2001: 3):

> In carnival the body is always changing, constantly becoming, eternally unfinished. Inseparable from nature and fused to other bodies around it, the body remembers that it is not a detached, atomised being, as it allows its erotic impulse to jump from body to body, sound to sound, mask to mask, to swirl across the streets, filling every nook and cranny, every fold of flesh. During carnival the body with its pleasures and desires, can be found everywhere, luxuriating in its freedom and inverting the everyday.
>
> (*Notes From Nowhere* 2003: 175–176)

The self-conscious adoption by the AGM of artistic modes of expression, seeking space for ritornellos of the subject, movement refrains and 'rhythms of resistance',[6] helps constitute a complex ontology of signification (Chapter 3). Therefore, as we have repeatedly argued it remains inaccessible to social movement models of political exchange that operate within the conceptual confines of the nation state and frame analyses focussing on collective identity as a mechanism of expressing political claims or grievances. This dwelling in the cultural and the manipulation of codes and behaviours is a well-worn line of flight for network actors in social movement networks, it marks an exodus from the 'political', from institutionalised assimilation and mechanisms of capture and reaffirms the importance of factors otherwise downplayed in 'politics as usual' (Stephens 1998).

The AGM thus proceeds through a cultural politics (Jordan and Weedon 1995, Osterweil 2004b) that questions the reification of the political as the preserve of structures, institutions and frameworks that are separate from, or exclude the everyday. This is a familiar trajectory in the 'south' where Alvarez argues 'all social movements enact a cultural politics' (Alvarez *et al.* 1998: 6), thus supporting De Sousa Santos (2003) who suggests that plateaux such as the WSF, constitute an 'epistemology of the south' simultaneously averse to the techno-scientific rationality of western modernity but conducive to a 'sociology of emergences'.

Complimenting this 'southern epistemology' is the return in the 'north' of the aesthetic and the affective through multiple repertoires of creative action and autonomous cultural production. Such an aesthetic has deep roots in radical art practices, such as Dada, the surrealists and the Situationist International (SI 2003, Jappe 1999) and was a strong feature of the 1960s movements. Jerry Rubin, a US activist/author of that period described it in the following terms, 'Life is a theatre and we are the guerrillas attacking the shrines of authority … The street is the stage. You are the star of the show and everything we're taught is up for grabs' (cited in Stephens 1998: 97). The end of post Second World War bi-polar geo-politics has been accompanied by a resurgence in the performative appropriation of public spaces for the enactment of critical messages. Such repertoires were part of the transition to globalisation. Poland's 'Orange Alternative', a colour distinct from both socialist red and Papal yellow, engaged in an extended communal party deploying street theatre and iconic acts such as banner drops. Orange Alternative became a focal point of conversation across Poland. In Wroclaw there were no factory occupations mirroring Solidarity actions because 'We had the streets, so we didn't need to strike'. (Kenny 2002: 224). These forms of action erupted across Europe, the Americas and Australia as the global south burned GM crops, resisted deforestation and occupied factories and; the AGM is the network of networks capable of holding these vectors in tension as a parallelogram of forces.

Elsewhere as we described earlier (Chapter 3), Tactical Frivolity (TF), radical cheerleaders, the Yes Men, the Laboratory of Insurrectionary Imagination and countless other imaginative, aesthetic, affective and self-organising groups have proliferated. The apparently marginal, defiantly subversive and profoundly internationalist character of such practices enables them to escape easy assimilation. Consequently, the play of these lines as vectors of force and flight allows questions about the boundaries of art, politics and culture under neo-liberal globalisation to be re-thought and reframed. The planeterisation of these tendencies, the epistemology of *thinking-through* action and the return of a radical aesthetic within the AGM expressed through the parallelogram of forces marks a return to desire as becoming, to the affective, to rhythms of speech, music, and modes of movement as important political terrain. This extends movement repertoires of connectivity into new assemblages that strive to maintain open boundary conditions and thus continue to find different and other registers of antagonistic expression leading the Zapatistas to argue that:

> The revolution in general is no longer imagined according to socialist patterns of realism, that is, as men and women stoically marching behind a red, waving flag towards a luminous future: rather it has become a sort of carnival.
>
> (Subcommandante Marcos cited in Rachenburg E. and Heau-Lambert C. 1998)

If as Marcos suggests the fusion of north and south in this 'open' and 'planetary' action system has led to the prevailing image of revolution *becoming-carnival*, this suggests that, the role of the AGM is crucial to defining the contemporary anatomy of revolution.

The umbrella organisation Globalise Resistance (as an offshoot of the Socialist Workers Party) repeats the refrain 'One Solution Revolution' with no systematic or programmatic anatomy of a contemporary revolutionary form. Under conditions of global complexity (Urry 2003) the Marxist–Leninist historical record is of limited utility in reading off necessary conditions, appropriate targets for revolutionary capture, or the desirability and appropriateness of representative structures and processes. However, this is not the only historical canon open to us.

Commentators, including ourselves, have noted the centrality of anarchism in the expressive form adopted by the AGM (Graeber 2002, Chesters 2003a, Welsh and Purkis 2003, Bowen and Purkis 2004). The logic of an anarchist stance is that revolution cannot be led by a vanguard party or sedimented through a revolutionary government or state as these institutional forms lead back to the establishment of old habits of mind. Instead, revolution requires the dissipative undermining of established institutional forms not their re-titling. The nineteenth century formalisation of the other road to revolution involved the self-organising expression of associative forms of productive activity. Federal associations between communes, workshops, districts, towns would dissolve national frontiers integrating societies through economic *co-operation and exchanges* with money being *a* form of exchange medium *not the form*. Bakunin's formalisation of anarchist agency within this process emphasised the role of 'invisible pilots' working not through 'overt power' but by tapping into and expressing the collective ethical stakes declared by 'all our allies':

> Without tricks, without official titles, without official rights, and therefore all the more powerful, as it does not carry the trappings of power.
> (Dolgof 1972: 180–181)

This revolutionary coalition based on autonomy was essential because as Bakunin wrote in a passage with significant contemporary relevance:

> Never was international reaction in Europe so formidably organised against any movement of the people. Repression has become a new science systematically taught in the military schools of all countries.
> (1972: 344, see also Chapter 4)

This anarchist sensibility has continued its trajectory as a historical force for greater autonomy and freedom of self-organisation, becoming amplified again through the parallelogram of forces constituted by the AGM. This coincides with a Deleuzian pragmatics that is sensitive to the possibilities of complex societies and which calls for creative intervention in every stratum, material, emotional and cognitive. So that the pursuit of intensities that are subversive to the controlling characteristics of aggregations of norms might be resisted, and the virtual singularities immanent to such intensities might be discovered and actualised. Thus, both antecedents and virtual futures merge in the parallelogram of forces, which maps the emergent phase space of the AGM as strange attractor.

8 The map is not the territory

To conclude we would like to locate our account of complexity and global social movement within some of the wider theoretical stakes associated with complexity theory, having demonstrated that the AGM is a social expression of complexity. As such, we build on David Byrne's concluding conclusion that whilst complex-based social science can inform social action such rational knowledge cannot be determinate due to agency. His hope that the agency in question be that of 'free-citizens' acting as a 'perturbative force which chooses the future' (1998: 167) is embodied within the AGM. As we have argued the commitment to open processes within the AGM maximises the operation of weak ties, a key step in socially 'engineering' plateaux optimising the potential for 'free-acts'. Taken together the totality of such free acts constitutes the AGM as a particularly dense strange attractor enunciating the other worlds that are possible.

This commitment to the maintenance of open boundary conditions is a necessary condition for emergence. The resultant fluidity of network forms associated with the AGM enables the declaration of collective stakes and their symbolic coding and deployment as free-floating signs and embodied forms of expression in the ecology of action. These associative forms combine multiple identities and force relations spanning North and South to constitute a parallelogram of forces enabling the pursuit of common antagonistic objectives and multiple pro-active ways of becoming and intervening. The meld here includes peasant, socialist, anarchist, feminist, radical liberal and environmentalist sensibilities. These constitute innovative margins where the aesthetics and ethics underlying the pursuit of knowledge are driven by intensities of feeling far removed from the dangerous 'habits of mind' identified by Bateson.

Both the technical expression and social relations associated with these processes depart widely from those central to the prevailing neo-liberal axiomatic conceived as the antagonistic other. The apparent marginality of these actors and their projects can make them appear insignificant compared to the 'cutting edge' developments within supra-state scientific and technical projects and corporate product development systems. However, as technical innovations are vitally dependent upon socially negotiated rules and are therefore contingent upon cultural norms, these rules include rates of return, amortisation periods, forms of ownership, liability and so on. These are the social constructs shaping market formation and the currently exploitative relations associated with 'turbo-capitalism', which are consolidated within legal traditions where the sanctity of private property represents the axiomatic orchestrating the entire assemblage. The exploitative intensity associated with these constructs increases with distance from the centres of modernity but the underlying anatomy of priorities remains the same.

It is worth noting that profit before people and planet and innovation within existing supply chains are habits of mind that produce incremental refinement of established technologies and techniques consolidated in the nineteenth century. These habits and relations were formalised in relation to the production of material products but extend now to an era where immaterial labour has become an increasingly important phenomenon and immaterial products increasingly problematise these constructs. Compare buying a pressed vinyl record to downloading a digital signal through peer-2-peer file sharing and one arrives at the situation where Sony takes its consumers to court. Commodified platforms (e.g. MP3 players) and immaterial exchange (P2P Networks) have thus perturbed the relations governing the exchange of the product of immaterial labour (e.g. music). The hacking, replication and assimilation of immaterial product is in its infancy but is growing precisely because the manipulation of information (electronic, genetic etc.) remains embedded within established commercial relations underpinned by the notion of an abstract self-interest maximising individual.

Established habits of mind typically incorporate innovations within the familiar resulting in inappropriate initial applications, an area where computing stands out as a particularly clear example (Levy 1984), with sustainable energy production being another. For instance, market-led wind turbine development requires that generators are aligned to central grid provision under rates of return requiring turbine location in prominent windy positions, thereby fuelling controversy over the damage done to the aesthetics of wilderness. Wind farms are perceived commercially as broad equivalents to power stations, whilst dispersed generating approaches remain the preserve of entrepreneurial margins hampered by prevailing social constructs. Until recently, reverse metering (selling surplus domestically generated electricity back to the grid) was not permitted and technically difficult. The advent of micro-wind generator systems suitable for rooftop mounting offers the prospect of households generating significant amounts of electricity reducing demand on centralised generating systems, whilst free fuel removes a key step in prevailing supply chain, commodity, and exchange relations. A shift in cultural orientation towards dispersed networks and autonomous production coupled to the availability of non-proprietary technologies, as is already taking place around broadband wireless technologies could quickly tip the balance with regard to patterns of ownership and control.

Urry (2000) has noted that sociology has had a parasitic relationship with social movements ascribing progress to 'rational' processes originating within modernity when the impetus for such change has lain within the liminal movement milieu. We close by situating the AGM within the context of such intellectual stakes through the notion of a bifurcated modernity that features prominently in the work of Beck (1992) and Touraine (1995). We would suggest that the tension between community and society formalised by Tonnies and state centric rationalities and 'affect' expressed through Weber represent significant sub-texts to these formalisations. As the appropriation of the future becomes a moral trajectory (Giddens 1991) societal/state actors have focussed on scientific and economic progress and prospects as a key means of displacing contemporary critiques through promissory futures. We have argued here that the AGM's prioritisation of becoming represents the rejection of justifying the present by reference to temporally distant ends. As the Argentinean activist and research collective 'Colectivo Situaciones'[1] put it: 'The future has stopped being the key of the present.'

In the rush to complete the promise of modernity ascribed in the discourses of science, progress and development the 'rational' forces of modernity have progressed the pursuit of increasingly global aspirations over and above locally sedimented traditions and aspirations. Meaning that defence of the local in the face of scientific and technical progress harnessed to the enhanced realisation of profit continues to be dismissed as irrational. This bi-polar reduction of choice to the local or global, between a scaled, socially liberating and environmentally appropriate use of technology or the continuation of 'giganticism', exploitation and degradation of the organic realm – both human and environmental is now confronted within changed circumstances.

In this context, the AGM represents a strange attractor with the potential to impact on the default resolution of this bi-polar tension. Eve *et al.* (1997) are clear that scientific theorising is a product of attempts at sense making confronted by the white noise of complexity. We are suggesting that rather than seeking to impose old moral sensibilities the AGM is, as Offe argued in relation to environmental movements of the 1970s and 1980s, in pursuit of a selective modernisation of modernity's values (Offe 1985).

There is here the continuation of a historically persistent critique of modernity based in the exploitation of external (environment) and internal (human) nature. Such disaffection is commonplace within contemporary democracies where membership of environmental and humanitarian organisations significantly exceeds political party affiliations. As Maffesoli (1996) notes, publics are disengaged from politics and investing in new forms of sociality more congruent with their immediate and local needs. The AGM represents a massive experiment in the global expression of such sociality, self-organised as a complex, adaptive system. CMC and enhanced freedom of movement facilitate the co-ordinated expression of this network of networks rendering the multitude of global locales as a worldwide social force. Continuing to approach social movements as actors operating within discrete societies ignores the complex interactions which complexity theory offers a useful and useable means of engagement.

Postmodernism and neo-materialism

Postmodernism, the pessimistic epilogue of modernity, has become a catch-all term with a dominant discursive representation as heralding the death of science and rationality as the foundation stones of now defunct meta-narratives. Postmodernism has taken many forms ranging from the linguistic relativism of Derridean deconstruction, that is apt to see the material world as inert and amorphous and as such defined purely through linguistically expressed cultural conventions, through to the more materially orientated philosophical positions taken by such as Lyotard (1988). His stance is material in the sense that it is underpinned by the presumed extinction of humankind as the ultimate end against which the individual has to pursue a life. Given this end, the postulated singular ontological positioning belief in any over-arching meta-narrative is ultimately pointless as all lead to the same terminal end point when the Sun goes super-nova.

Deleuze is often presumed to fall within the postmodernist canon although his philosophical stance is profoundly realist and materialist, accepting as it does the existence of actual and virtual forms and theorising the morphogenetic processes through which the complex interplay between the actual and virtual occurs. Deleuze, as we have shown, is a philosopher who is adept at utilising the full force of contemporary physics and biology to analyse and articulate flows of difference and complexity. From the biological foundation of the body through the embryonic folding and stretching, dividing and augmentation of cellular layers to the realisation of infinite microscopic differences that constitute us as singularities composed of singularities, and the translation of the resultant ontological isolation into the basis of solidarity through recognition, respect for and ease with difference. In this way, the potential for re-forging new meta-narratives becomes a possibility, meta-narratives which transcend the particularism of nationalisms or wider geo-political and ideological identities. The Deleuzian influence in Hardt and Negri's meta-narrative of Empire (2000) and Multitude (2004) is particularly apparent, as we have noted previously. This is one of the reasons why Deleuze (and Guattari's) work resonates with the range of nomadisms noted in the introduction. Enhanced mobility is part of the postmodern condition bringing with it shifts in the ontological positioning of these nomads who begin to reframe the project of life as immanent to life, thus allowing possibilities to multiply in the face of a seemingly futile future of species extinction.

Marx suggested humankind is the ultimate zoon politicon – a political animal as well as a force of nature. By recognising and acting upon the signals of growing planetary imbalances, elements of the AGM declare global collective stakes within a philosophy based on the recognition of difference as generative and creative, and expressed simply through the slogan 'unity in diversity', where diversity is the becoming of a plane of immanence, catalysed by difference:

> Difference is not diversity. Diversity is given, but difference is that by which the given is given, that by which the given is given as diverse.
>
> (Deleuze 1994: 280)

Conceptually then the slogan 'unity in diversity' resonates with the concept of the multitude defined by Negri (2004 http://www.makeworlds.org/comment/reply/104) as a 'whole of singularities'; an outcome and effect of the interplay of difference within open systems that are maintained by the dynamic iteration of practices, procedures and structures devised to facilitate consensual outcomes through encounter and deliberation. As Žižek (2004) points out, iteration is correlative with a Deleuzian emphasis upon *becoming* thus highlighting the 'proper' Deleuzian paradox that 'something truly new can only emerge through repetition' (Žižek 2004: 12).

Melucci (1989, 1996a) makes similar points about the 'epistemological limitation' of both sides in the debate about the 'novelty' of the 'new' social movements where contemporary movement phenomena are perceived as 'unified empirical objects' – 'living characters moving and acting upon a stage of history', rather than as combinatory effects of forms of action impacting upon different levels of a social system, containing diverse goals and belonging to different phases of the development of particular historical systems (1989: 43). In both instances process comes to the fore, allowing us to pay attention to the diachronic and synchronic elements of movements and to acknowledge how the process of iteration can re-configure the relationship between the virtual (as the quality of potential immanent to an event) and the actual (as the degree to which that potential was realised). Therefore, as Žižek argues, 'what repetition repeats is the not the way the past "effectively was" but the virtuality inherent to the past and betrayed by its past actualisation' (2004: 12).

The iteration amongst movement milieu of practices that ostensibly reside within the 'cultural', affective gestures, performances, encounters with and articulations of difference indicate a cultural politics here which decisively breaks the limits of the system of 'politics' opening up multiple lines of f(l)ight for all parties. In emphasising these multiple lines of f(l)ight we depart from Hardt and Hegri's emphasis upon the use of smooth space to strike directly at Empire. We have characterised these differences graphically in terms of the institutional anatomy of the prevailing global axiomatic, key power relations and avenues through which cultural perturbation is constituted through reflexive framing, plateaux and resultant parallelograms of force (see Figures 8.1 and 8.2).

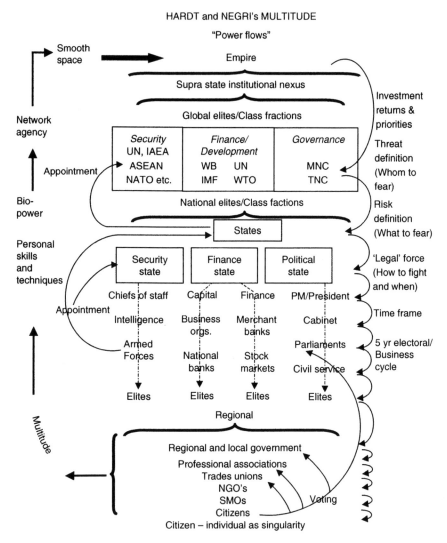

Figure 8.1 Power flows, empire and smooth space.

We make no claims whatsoever to being able to project the trajectories of the resultant parallelogram(s) of forces but we have endeavoured to depict some of the main vectors and forces, the relationships between them and the anatomy of, what are probably, the opening skirmishes between nomad war machines and the assemblage of empire(s) constituting the neo-liberal axiomatic. The profound challenge here is to set aside the established habits of mind identified by Bateson and to look for signs and patterns in counter-intuitive places. If complexity theory has anything to say about how things

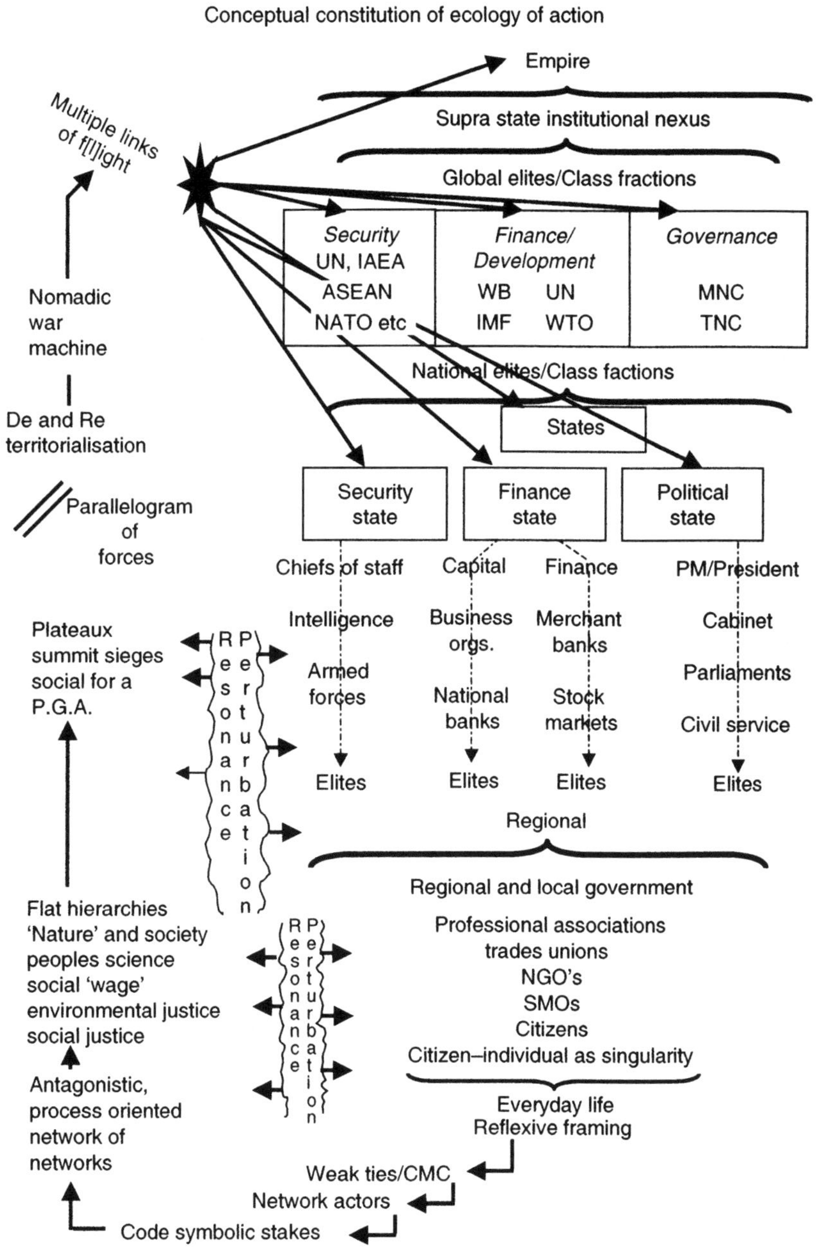

Conceptual constitution of ecology of action

Figure 8.2 Parallelograms of force, empire multitude lines of f(l)ight.

might be done differently, then this is surely the central maxim – perturbation, bifurcation and emergence often come from micro changes in marginal locations such as the interface between the laminar global flows of meaning. We have argued that the free radicals discussed here are identifiable individuals with elements of this sense and ontological stance – individuals sensitised to aspects of planetary and social fates which are perceived as intimately linked – in our terms free radicals are observable change agents in a planetary action system. We emphasise that there are equivalents of our free radicals in the multiple social universes constituting the postmodern condition. As the advocates of this cultural politics engage systemically with the various elements of the fractured states preoccupied with maintenance of old habits of mind, as their incumbents suture global flows in an attempt to maintain discursive coherence, the resultant perturbations lay siege to other signs, symbols and moral frameworks.

One domain where this is clearly visible is in the proliferating and intensifying contest between 'mainstream' and emergent sciences. As 'Royal' science (Deleuze and Guattari 2002: 369) pursues a return to old 'Big' sciences such as nuclear power, 'minor' or 'nomad' science (Deleuze and Guattari 2002: 361) articulates techniques with profound implications for what it is to be human and how long it might be possible to remain human. Fledgling techniques with the potential to combine in assemblages that permit human existence beyond a solar collapse are discernable today. The fascination with and pursuit of frontiers that has fuelled space exploration has assumed a military orientation that is about to be transformed by the commercialisation of space as space tourism becomes an entrepreneurial niche. Whilst the details of these developments cannot be addressed here, they highlight a key tension for the environmental and social justice movements within which varying degrees of antipathy towards technoscience exist: for example, Lyotard's problematic means that a complete rejection of technology would ultimately guarantee species extinction, if it became a norm.

The challenge is not pro- or anti-science but the social shaping of science and technology towards collectively prioritised objectives executed in ways which do not subordinate these social goals to profit maximisation within corporate structures. In terms of the fragmented state, the single most important factor here is a massive reduction in the military research and development burdens dedicated to detecting and killing human beings and imposing 'collateral' damage. There is sufficient extant science to go on perfecting the practical barbarism associated with nation state democratic systems for at least another 50 years without spending another Euro or dollar on more research. Whilst there are some comparatively minor civilian benefits from the trickle-down effect of this expenditure, they represent a tiny fraction of the gains which could be achieved if these were the primary objective of R and D efforts.

These challenges are unfolding as complexity theory impacts upon the natural sciences accentuating historic disciplinary tensions and methodological disputes. Whilst the mathematical modelling central to physics colonised the biological sciences, the resultant emphasis on clearly defined chains of causality sits uneasily with biological concerns around system effects outside the controlled environment required by the experimental method. In terms of genetics, the result is a dualistic declaratory posture emphasising both causality and complex indeterminacy (Wynne 2005). McFadden argues that systems biology uses mathematics to address 'the system properties of the entire network' approaching genes not as causal nodes but 'more diffuse entities whose functional reality may be spread across hundreds of interacting DNA segments' (2005). The model of genetic change advanced by McFadden mirrors the model of social change advanced here. Rather than causal genes (organised political actors) particular traits 'represent a network perturbation generated by small, almost imperceptible changes in lots of genes' (2005) (the apparently irrelevant free acts of free radicals' perturbating countless individual perceptions and practices). This emphasis on infinitesimal differences is consistent with the philosophical importance attached to difference by Deleuze. Royal science's quest to isolate causal genes to produce targeted therapies in an attempt to realise the commercial promise associated with the new genetics from the early 1980s onwards seems set to be confounded by nomad science's embrace of disciplinary difference via interactivity and networking. In this contest the ability to perceive open system architectures becomes a key condition of competence which a nomad ontology and epistemology is peculiarly adapted to. For Deleuze and Guattari nomad science starts from the premise that 'everything is situated in an objective zone of fluctuation that is coextensive with reality itself' (2002: 373).

Cultural politics – forms and expressions

In his later work, Melucci (1996) adopted increasingly liberal stances as he sought to accommodate criticisms of his work. Three of these accommodations are of particular importance to this work given that we claim Melucci as a complexity theorist standing in a minoritarian lineage. First, Melucci asserts the imperative that his nomads of 1989 *must* be listened to (see McKechnie and Welsh 2002), second, he accepts that his new social movements must adopt durable forms broadly associated with grievance and interest representation, and third, he approaches direct action as a strategy tending to result in dissolution through violence (see Welsh 2000).

The process of emergence and operation of the AGM as a strange attractor allows us to move beyond these concessions to resource mobilisation theory and political opportunity structure approaches through the genealogical data we have presented. We have demonstrated that there is no imperative to listen (Chapter 3), that the majoritarian use of violence by the state and corporate actors far exceeds that of demonstrators (Chapter 4), and we have proposed an open system of networks as a model vital to the order on the edge of chaos necessary to avoid the replication of habits of mind. How then can this cultural politics achieve the kinds of systemic impacts that Melucci was seeking in his accommodations? Our short answer is: by remaining cultural in order to impact upon the political and the Political.

The network of networks we have engaged with here has not assumed that it must be listened to but started instead from the position that the movement of movements *must* make itself heard. By embracing direct action as a preferred *modus operandi* rather than a tactic of desperation and last resort, key elements of the movement entered a nomadic war of manoeuvre. By engaging in successive sieges, high profile global summits were effectively driven from prominent public venues into walled citadels. Analytically there are significant differences between movements that seek to violently overthrow a social system and movements that seek to challenge a social system using direct action. The AGM falls firmly within the latter category something that explains continuing levels of public support for and adoption of direct action stances *despite* the attempt to demonise protestors. In order to be heard a 'radical flank' is sometimes necessary.

Despite a massive asymmetry in discursive resources, the AGM has been central to the placing of question marks over the neo-liberal axiomatic at the global level in a way that resonates with the experience of people(s) worldwide. As we have shown, in contemporary fractured states it is elements of the finance state and advocates of turbo-capitalism who have most rapidly recognised the challenges posed by this movement(s) whilst the security state has reacted along predictable lines, frequently leading to an increase in public support for direct action. The liminality of network actors is necessary for the cultural and political creativity that enables the declaration of stakes that is crucial to the prophetic role of movement identified by Melucci. Permanence, grievance and interest representation are the concerns of Social Movement Organisations and NGOs and must not be conflated with social movement. In our view, any organisation with a pension fund is not a social movement. Greenpeace, Friends of the Earth, Oxfam, WWF and so on are *not* social movements. They are however, Social Movement Organisations, which now have somewhere to turn when their limit for manoeuvre within the formal systems of interest representation is reached. This is the arena of cultural politics that declares and defines stakes and implicitly sets thresholds of ethical and moral acceptability.

As Halliday (1998) argues ethical and moral issues now extend to the sphere of international relations. This leaves the actions of national leaders on world stages open to moral judgement and the incremental extension of international law at a time when images of immoral acts such as those from inside detention camps in Iraq achieve rapid prominence. A Western journalist embedded with a front line unit in the assault on Iraq relates the experience of one platoon member during US Survival, Evasion, Resistance and Escape training. The Texan in question was forced to wear a Ku Klux Klan hood for several days whilst pulling an African American Marine around on a leash 'treating him as a slave' (Wright 2005: 24). The same artefacts and relations of subservience were subsequently used in the field as part of the increasingly normalised control and constraint repertoires of democratic states. Insulating national politics from the cultural impacts of such acts is ultimately a futile task.

It is worth recalling the comparison of social movements and tectonic plates within the complexity literature. Political ruptures occur when tensions accumulate as an old order seeks to replicate itself bureaucratically in the context of consumer individualism and social activism within knowledge economies. To many the ruptured institutional trust that became a prominent feature of the 2005 UK General Election campaign was sedimented in February 2003 with the massive street presence demonstrating against military action in Iraq, between one and two million people having participated in becoming links in complex webs of communication and meaning throughout the United Kingdom.

The subsequent exercise of autonomous executive power by Tony Blair in aligning the United Kingdom with a US action headed by key members of the Project for a New American Century could only be taken in the full knowledge that such moves have become culturally contested and Politically dangerous. Cultural politics defines the tides within which politicians must swim: treading water whilst chanting mantras of 'traditional values' is not a viable option when a global rip tide is running. A further example is the referendum defeats on the European Constitution suffered by the French and Dutch political elites in 2005. The desire for 'another Europe' articulated by ATTAC and la Confédération paysanne striking a deeper cord than a bureaucratic exercise in harmonisation of structures and processes within the context of a neo-liberal axiomatic.

For us the desire for permanence underlying the third of Melucci's 'accommodations' stems from the need for standing forms of cultural politics not the institutionalisation of particular movement actors. We are arguing that the AGM has the *potential* to become one of the first global expressions of such a standing form with implications for the constituent empires aligned with the prevailing neo-liberal axiomatic. Whilst the institutional networks constituting the current Imperium remain dominated by habits of mind consolidated throughout the nineteenth and twentieth centuries the threat to life will intensify. Capital can continue to realise profit even during its own demise and so long as interest representation continues to be expressed in terms of a price, this will remain the case.

The environmental and the human individual represents the impact points of these multiple acts of profit maximisation rendering us all singularities and underpinning the relationship between personal and planetary 'health' introduced by Melucci (1996a,b). We regard Melucci's notion of a 'planetary action system' as an initial attempt to incorporate the complexity inherent in the person planet relationship within *both* social theory and new social movement studies. As such it can be thought of as a discursively constructed outer layer of meaning (and value) against which the operation of the neo-liberal axiomatic can be assessed (see Figure 8.3). The ecology of action advanced here is our contribution to making the constitution of such a planetary action system a tangible in terms of social process.

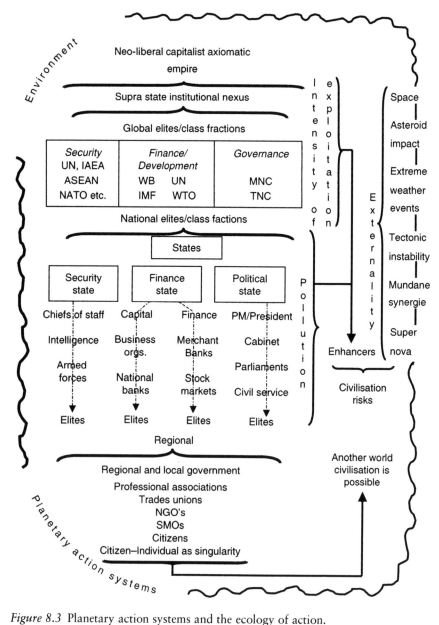

Figure 8.3 Planetary action systems and the ecology of action.

In terms of historical iteration, we are suggesting that two persistent themes are melded within the AGM that suggest it can become a standing form of cultural politics. These are the pursuit of socio-economic and environmental justice. Within organised capitalist societies like the United Kingdom, these are historically persistent themes (Hardy 1979, Gould 1988, Wall 1994) around which considerable social force has been exercised. The Marxist historian E.P. Thompson's account of such force provides a useful summary of themes relevant to this task. Thompson draws a distinction between the 'mob' and forms of 'direct action' arising under 'specific conditions', being 'highly organized' and under the protection of 'the local community' (1978: 67). The impetus for such action in both rural and urban contexts was a 'consumer-consciousness' and the attempt to 'reimpose the older moral economy…against the economy of the free market' around issues of price[2] and quality of food stuffs[3] (1978: 70–73). Thompson is clear that such expressive forms pre-figured organised concerns over control of the labour process and political representation.[4] As Žižek (2004) commentary on Karatani (2003) notes 'If workers can become subjects at all, it is only as consumers' who actively complete the process of circulation by purchasing the product of abstract labour (Žižek 2004: 124). Without this final act of consumption, the production of a commodity merely results in a product with the potential to realise value.[5]

Excursus: citizen states and market maker democracies

In the opening chapter, we rejected the idea that the AGM lacked the capacity for strategic, programmatic change. In returning to this claim, it is important to reflect upon Thompson's argument that class-consciousness emerged as much from the sphere of consumption as from within the sphere of production. What is central here is the manner in which the prevailing neo-liberal axiomatic places the consumer and consumer rights at the heart of its preferred civil sphere. Whilst the consumer in mind is a consumer of products, the consumer consciousness engendered by this discourse migrates to *both* the material products of immaterial labour *and* the consumption of services provided by political elites. The 2005 UK general election demonstrated that previous assumptions about self-interested rational actors entering a polling booth and voting in their calculated self-interest are now challenged by a growing number of morally engaged actors. Tactical voting delivered an election result in which the public resonance with anti-war protests represented a significant electoral social force. History's first third term Labour administration came to office with the smallest share of the available overall vote of any administration for over one hundred years. In part, this was a response to the autocratic exercise of Political power in the face of significant demonstrations of public doubt over the moral legitimacy of the arguments for use of military force advanced by the prime minister's office. This moral judgement in the realm of international relations where the legitimate use of state violence is an expression of the body politic became a deterritorialising force as voters asserted their integrity and autonomy in the face of appeals to party discipline and the threat of returning a Conservative government by default. In the UK case the re-election of Labour Party rebels prepared to vote against the Iraq war, identity cards and a range of other issues leaves Labour in office but arguably not in power.

Whilst 'e-government' has progressively been enlarged and is claimed as an arena for transparency and communication, this is not e-democracy. The formal democratic participation of the citizen has not changed for centuries – requiring a cross on a ballot. The knowledge economy produces informed voters who are then asked to abrogate all decisional power to politicians and grant the rights to take at least 20% of their taxable income for the next five years. Polling data regularly shows that the moral politics of the contemporary UK elector prioritises health and education as their main concerns. E-democracy holds the potential to permit both instantly counted votes and a more sophisticated set of rights consistent with individual moral choices. The right to vire one's taxes towards areas of public policy regarded as priorities and withhold them from areas considered morally unacceptable would begin to make the Political reflect the cultural political sphere.

Death and taxes

The idea that death and taxes are the only certainties in life has been a central axiom of democratic theory. Whilst campaigns to withhold the proportion of tax directed towards military budgets have been part of 'peace movement' tactics for some time, a proactive allocation initiative would be a far more effective way for 'consumers' of political 'services' to express their desires. Rather than attempting to attract participation by making access to the established system easier such a scheme would offer voters the incentive of 'up stream' influence. Permitting all voters to allocate a proportion of their taxes between budgetary headings, perhaps 20% in the first instance, and aggregating these individual choices would effectively yield a 'peoples budget' reflecting electoral preferences. If this allocation reflected UK issue priorities then health and education would be beneficiaries. The resultant 'people's budget' would be a barometer against which overall state expenditure could be assessed. By limiting the percentage of individual's tax take which could be vired, established core budgets relating to long-term commitments would remain protected during a period when voters learned the implications of participation. Such a move would begin to invert political trust relations within an increasingly participatory democracy with Politicians trusting publics to shape overall expenditure programmes. The resultant dialogical exchanges would shape the development of such extended democratic rights with governments having to justify the need for core areas of expenditure not prominently supported by expressions of popular will via the 'people's budget'. It is highly likely that military R and D would be an area where such exchanges would become critical.

In order to claim to represent the people, governments would have to strive to make their overall state expenditure reflect the distributive spread of the people's budget. In the longer term, the introduction of such a scheme would reconfigure the anatomy of political parties by breaking the historic mould of class forces from previous centuries. Representative democratic government would be required to implement the spending preferences of the people and compete on the basis of their ability to achieve maximum value. The social learning associated with the distribution of responsibility would require a phased approach and some attention to ring fenced core requirements relating to historic commitments (such as military pensions for example) in the first instance.

The desire for ever more participatory mechanisms is evident throughout the network of networks we have engaged with here. The anatomy of the UK General Election outlined above shows how the mass classes of the twentieth century have fragmented as difference becomes dominant. Claims to represent everyone whilst in office by one party simply lack credibility in the face of difference and become derisory caricatures in the context of a worldwide war on the poor which commenced in 1976 and has been continuing ever since. In the United Kingdom, an individual coming of age in a year when there is a general election can make a cross on a ballot 13 times by the time they are 68 years of age assuming a general election every 4 years. For knowledge economy workers in an informationally complex society this is hardly an expression of informed choices. Politicians are a professional elite whose upper echelons are prone to 'autonomous' acts of executive authority. Vired voting would begin to redress this asymmetrical relationship translating individual choices into tangible expressions of collective will with material implications.

Conclusion: intellectual destratification

> Staying stratified is not the worst thing that can happen; the worst that can happen is if you throw the strata into demented or suicidal collapse, which brings them back down on us heavier than ever. This is how it should be done: Lodge yourself on a stratum, experiment with the opportunities it offers, find an advantageous place on it, find potential movements of deterritorialisation, possible lines of flight, experience them, produce flow conjunctions here and there, try out continuums of intensities segment by segment, have a small plot of new land at all times.
>
> (Deleuze and Guattari 2002: 161)

In our brief excursus on the (revolutionary) reforms offered by ideas of participatory budgeting through vired voting we have sought to give a concrete example of how the desire for participation and autonomy might translate into practices that are consistent with yet undermining to the neo-liberal contractualisation of everyday life and the rise of a concomitant consumer consciousness. We do not advance this as either platform or policy, but rather in the spirit of experimentation that Deleuze and Guattari exhort, as a means of illustrating how comparatively minor changes might transform relations of power and governance. For, if Thompson and Žižek are correct in closely associating class consciousness and class action with the sphere of consumption as well as production then the neo-liberal axiomatic has unwittingly given prominence to the milieu that is *most likely* to reconfigure the anatomy of force-relations during what Foucault hoped tongue-in-cheek might eventually be a Deleuzian century.

Theoretical debates on class within the AGM have been entered into around competing notions of a continuing teleology of class (Callinicos 2004[6]) and the renewed search for a 'subject' of revolution leading to the theoretical construction of a singular yet highly differentiated Multitude engaging with a singular yet dispersed Empire by Hardt and Negri (2000, 2004). In a debate between Callinicos and Negri at the European Social Forum in Paris in 2003 however, Negri argued that the multiplicity represented by multitude stood alongside and augmented traditional class concepts, whilst Hardt has also suggested that:

> For us, economic analysis, class analysis, analysis of the forms of labor and new forms of cooperation – those are what give the possibility to new notions of democracy.[7]

For us, however, this suggests certain habits of mind that are yet to be overcome. Habits that are ultimately reductive of complexity despite their best intentions. Notwithstanding the work of Hardt and Negri in emphasising the multitude as a locus of generative and creative action they nevertheless return to a telos that precedes multitude,[8] in order to re-pose a bi-polar struggle between opposing actors, albeit one in which their 'new proletariat' is somewhat more inclusive that the industrial working class. This marks the eternal return to the centrality of one's (class) location in the process of production as the barometer of revolutionary potential and is combined with the desire to call into being a revolutionary subject from one's own thought. Part of this is as a result of their desire to bring into being that which they believe to be immanent to the political and economic relations of Empire (a project which we have a good deal of empathy with) and part of it is evidently born of frustration; as Hardt suggests 'all of this political theorizing about democracy remains wishful thinking unless there's a subject that can fill it'.[9]

We are not suggesting that analysis of productive relations is unimportant, rather the opposite in fact (see Chapter 7), we are suggesting it is essential to complete the circle, to understand how co-operation might extend from production to consumption, enabling the forging of autonomous non-marketised relations of distribution and exchange. Our fear is that the understandable desire for a subject to fill the contingent spaces of complexity and multiplicity carries with it a map, a map that elides the space between the analytical, the virtual and the actual and as we know the map cannot be the territory. If we are to look for the virtual singularities, the points of bifurcation and the strange attractors, we must be certain that our analytical constructs remain open to the feedback of the empirical without ever being reduced to it and that our teleologies are merely aide memoires to the importance of contingency.

In the final section of *language, counter-memory and practice* (Foucault 1977a) there is a discussion between Foucault and Deleuze on intellectuals and power. In it, Deleuze speculates on an emergent new relationship between theory and practice where practice becomes 'a set of relays from one theoretical point to another'. As a theory encounters a wall marking its limit as a guide to practice, it is practice which provides the means of piercing the wall (Foucault 1977a: 206) and such practice can only be exercised by 'those directly concerned...in a practical way on their own behalf' (207). If we are to heed this message then proximity to movements for social change is everything, for theory cannot heed that which it remains distant from and the emergence of the AGM as an antagonistic attractor within a global civil society represents a protean cultural politics with the potential to reconfigure not only social theory, but the other worlds we would wish to make possible.

Notes

1 Introducing global movements

1 G.W. Bush's assertion of the sanctity of 'the American way of life' and 'America's economic interest' as grounds for not ratifying the Kyoto climate change protocols stands out as one particularly clear example of a decision embodying this 'habit of mind'. The need to avoid such mindsets within contemporary environmental education is particularly important (see Orr 1994).
2 This is redolent of the notion of a 'self' and a 'Self' introduced by the deep green philosopher Arnie Naess (1973, 1989) and performs similar work by positing a human capacity to perceive both social and natural domains whilst recognising the inescapable interdependence of these realms.
3 Advances in the natural sciences have subsequently highlighted the importance of mitochondria in generating electrical impulses within organisms as they interact with the prevailing environment. Rhythm and cadence are important elements of musical performance in terms of energising an audience and shape pattern recognition and valency in-utero representing perhaps the earliest form of socialisation. Here the mother's heart beat represent a primal metronome – a feature of human evolution which would be removed should synthetic reproduction become a norm.
4 Bateson's approach to framing thus extended to a societal level through a consideration acts of communication achieving forms of consciousness. By contrast Goffman asserts his intention not to address social processes and structural domains by applying frame analysis to the individual and regarding it as a ubiquitous practice within social interaction.
5 This distinction is analogous to the one drawn by Touraine between an individual and an actor (Touraine 1995).
6 This is particularly important as a redress to the very strong claims that have been made within the social movement literature based entirely on the analysis of newspaper clippings as if this represents the entirety of the movement domain.
7 These elements of Bateson's work represent particularly coherent expressions of themes that later become formalised through Lyotard's notion of the different (Lyotard 1983), the increasing importance of autopoiesis argued by Luhman, and the importance of aesthetics in relation to reflexive modernisation (Jowers 1994, Lash 1994, Welsh 2000).
8 Kropotkin's emphasis on co-operation as an important evolutionary trait represents an early 'scientific' formalisation of such thinking.
9 The work of the late Murray Edeleman is another significant example with his focus on the symbolic uses of politics (1971) and the place of symbolic expression within political language (1977). Neo-Marxist attempts to incorporate these

dimensions within work on political consciousness is evidenced by the presence of both Foucault and Edelman in the footnotes to Poulantzas's (1973) *Political Power and Social Classes.*

10 According to Granovetter 'the strength of a tie is a (probably linear) combination of the amount of time, the emotional intensity, the intimacy (mutual confiding), and the reciprocal services which characterise the tie' (Granovetter 1973: 1361). This is immediately redolent of the affective domain we are seeking to include within our approach to framing.

11 Deleuze and Guattari emphasise the importance of a 'method' for the construction of plateau as multiplicities and reject 'mimetic procedures' (p. 22) as a means to achieve such ends. They thus question the capacity for the mimetic construction of other aesthetic prioritisations central to the work of the Frankfurt School and formalised by Adorno and Horkheimer and the subsequent use of this by Scott Lash to argue for 'another' modernity (Beck *et al.* 1994).

2 Prefiguration and emergence

1 In the natural sciences a free radical is an ultimately destructive agent, this is not the sense in which we adopt the term. Whilst we are arguing that free radicals are central to the deconstruction of dominant discourses associated with the neo-liberal capitalist axiomatic these acts of deconstruction are the basis for the proactive re-construction of counter discourses with libratory potential.

2 See Chapters 3 and 4 for detailed examples of these processes in operation.

3 Reflexive framing: identities, protest dynamics and technology

1 For a discussion of the historic and symbolic significance of Prague, and Wenceslas Square in particular, see Holy (1996, 34 et seq.).

2 See: http://www.nadir.org/nadir/initiativ/agp/en/

3 See *The Guardian*, 23 September 2000, p. 19. This term had been previously used to signify the UK direct action movement's emergent affinity with carnival as a cultural analytic (see Chesters 2000).

4 *The Prague Post*, 27 September–3 October 2000, p. A11.

5 *The Guardian*, 23 September 2000, p. 15.

6 Within Prague the appropriation of prominent corner locations by banks and financial services institutions and the associated escalation of rental values is a prominent theme in locals efforts to 'live in neo-liberal truth'. The targetting of banks in actions dominated by 'locals'reflected this particular dwelling perspective.

7 This data was gathered as part of an ESRC small grant (R000223486) project which focussed on pre-event, event and post-event frames of participants. Respondents were selected from within hubs key to the event including KSCM, INPEG, and the third element, London RTS, Tactical Frivolity, and OPH legal rights monitors. Wider points relating to global movement networks draw upon research on leadership (British Academy: LRG: 33561) within social movements conducted by Dr Graeme Chesters and Alan Johnson.

8 In Prague this was a protracted processes which teetered on the verge of collapse. Multiple interview accounts emphasise the centrality of the 'third element' in ultimately securing a space. In one account the deadlocked negotiations were resolved in minutes following one phone call from a third element actor.

9 See *The Guardian*, 27 September 2000, p. 18.

10 Ibid.

11 See extensive media coverage of the 'WOMBLES' (White Overall Movement Building Liberation Through Effective Struggle) prior to and post the Mayday protests in London during 2001.

12 Ya Basta's! subsequent standing within Prague was also portrayed negatively by the third element in terms of their failure to pay for accommodation where small local enterprises suffered loss of income.

13 The experience of the BBC following its coverage of the so-called Iraq War conducted by an axis of weevils against an axis of evil testifies to the on-going nature of both institutional media crises and the struggle over signification and discourse.

14 The affiliations of the founders include ORA-Solidarita, Ulice Lidem (Reclaim the Streets) and the Czech Anarchist Federation. Users include Feminist Group 8 March, Earth First!, Car Busters, IMC Prague and FoodnotBombs.

15 The research team involved in the ESRC project under which the Prague data was gathered was inter-disciplinary and we thank Andrew Tickle and Fiona Donson for their contributions to this process and regret their resignations from the academic community. We continue to discuss and debate many of the issues addressed here within activist circles and acknowledge the invaluable role these interactions play in our academic work.

4 From carnival against capitalism to death at high noon: states fight back

1 Marx and Engels noted capitalism's capacity to incorporate even the most 'barbarian' civilisations by force in *The Communist Manifesto*. The reflex recourse to force becomes the hallmark of advanced barbarism associated with a fresh cycle of 'primitive' accumulation (Habermas 1990).

2 The British Government is reportedly considering introducing another new criminal offence of 'economic sabotage' whilst increasing penalties for minor offences deemed part of a 'vicious campaign'. The move followed Aegis Defence Systems estimates that 16 billion of inward investment could be lost per year unless the government acted to protect companies (*The Guardian* 13.01.05, p. 13). In the interim existing legislation has been used to achieve similar ends (see fn 18).

3 In 2005, the McDonald too won their case in the European Court of Human Rights which found in favour of their claim that legal aid should be available to citizens in libel cases involving corporate litigants. The court ruled that the lack of legal representation had in effect infringed the defendants' human rights and awarded damages to the plaintiffs (*The Guardian* 16.02.05, p. 1).

4 A 1980 *Sociological Review* article by S.K. Ratcliffe (1,4,373–375) 'Aspects of the Social Movement in India' details how establishment approaches sought to weaken popular movements by dismissing nationalist claims. Here we argue that the global claims of the AGM are also subject to a range of discursive sanctions focusing upon deviance frames.

5 A prominent example being the Project for the New American Century (PNAC). Their 'Statement of Principles' dated 3 June 1997 argued for significant increases in US defense expenditure, challenging hostile regimes, and accepting America's 'unique' role in spreading international order 'friendly to our security, our prosperity and our principles'. Prominent PNAC members include Jeb Bush, Dick Cheney, Francis Fukuyama, Dan Quale, Donald Rumsfeld and Paul Wolfowitz. See www.newamericancentury.org/statementorprinciples.htm accessed 21.04.2004.

6 Tony Blair, *The Guardian*, 2/5/00

7 See Martinez (2000) for one account of the alienated experience of black and minority ethnic groups within convergence centre dynamics and attempts to participate within Direct Action Network (DAN). (Martinez, E.B. 2000 'Where Was the Color in Seattle? Looking for Reasons Why the Great Battle was So White', *Monthly Review*, 52, 3, 141–148.)

8 Oregon has a significant number of 'primitivist' anarchists noted for their rejection of modern technology and science. This concentration is largely accounted for by the presence of prominent exponents of this stance within the state.

9 The tacit denial of any significant political crisis is interesting given the recognition of crisis arising from the stakes declared by the AGM within the World Bank and International Monetary Fund nexus. Whilst the entrenched 'habits of mind' operating within the political domain offer one explanation, we would suggest that reflex recourse to policing the crisis reflects deeper tensions as the role of the representative bourgeois state as the perfect vehicle for capitalism is attenuated by global accumulation strategies.

10 Police authorities responsible for areas with particularly high levels of movement activity represented a 'front line' in the interpretation and application of new laws. Thames Valley, London Metropolitan Police Force, and Gloucestershire were significant forces in this respect. Certain police authorities used legislation to intervene in the daily life of the movement milieu in pursuit of relatively trivial ends. Gloucestershire Police continued committing significant resources to stop and search operations subjecting festival traffic passing through their patch on the M4 to searches aimed at seizing small amounts of reclassified recreational drugs in the summer of 2004. Precisely how this contributed to a policing strategy for Gloucestershire is unclear though the expenditure was a continuation of a policy of active harassment.

11 Activist repertoires of action hibridised to include tree sitting and tunnelling. Intense debates over the ethics of working for these authorities developed within national climbing and caving communities illustrating the way in which diverse communities became involved in the associated issues.

12 The publication of photographs of individuals associated with particularly prominent acts of property damage alongside appeals to turn them in carried an implicit assumption of guilt with wider implications in terms of social standing, personal relationships and security of employment. To some activists such acts of public denunciation reinforce the importance of concealing their identity through the use of bandanas. On 2 May 2000, *The Daily Mail* printed pictures of protesters under the title 'Do you recognise any of the rioters?' The following day *The Independent*, led with 'PM asks families to name May Day rioters' (*The Independent* 3.05.00, p. 1).

13 In London Speakers Corner is another space subject to special policing measures (see Roberts J. 2003)

14 One RTS respondent indicated that Trafalgar Square was the last place the event was intended to end up in as it was a site in which the British state historically used force against protestors.

15 Previous cases yielding iconic images of destruction involving the Metropolitan Police Force such as a burning police vehicle on Euston Road are also accompanied by eye-witness accounts of police abandoning vehicles in locations with good surveillance video capture. These include accounts from 'embedded academic researchers'.

16 Reclaim the Streets leaflet Guerrilla Gardening 2000.

17 The irony of this Orwellian term was not lost on Congressman Barney Frank who commented: 'As we read the First Amendment to the Constitution, the United States is a "free speech zone!" ', – www.house.gov/frank/scprotester2003.html

18 A high court ruling deemed that laws drafted to protect celebrities and citizens against 'stalkers' could be used to establish an 'exclusion zone' around the Brighton premises of weapons system design firm Edo MBM Technology pending the outcome of legal action against campaigners for 'unlawful harassment' *The Guardian* 30.04.05, p. 12).

19 This practice has been noted since the Rio Earth Summit in 1992 when street children were removed from view. Another example was the removal of rickshaws from Bangkok as they were considered archaic compared to modern (polluting) taxis.

20 During the G8 meeting at Evian in 2003 an international was seriously injured when traffic police cut a rope that was suspending two activists on either side of a bridge, in order to maintain the flow of vehicles.

21 We acknowledge the incorporation of key externalities through a variety of market mechanisms, notably climate change related emission trading schemes, these are however, far weaker than the 'economic instruments' initially envisaged as a means of creating a level playing field. Given the time frames associated with climate change such delayed and diluted measures represent the substantive failure of Margaret Thatcher's 1980s initiative to put global warming at the centre of global politics.

5 Ecologies of action within global civil society

1 Argentina is a recent example of this tendency (Jordan and Whitney 2002; *Notes from Nowhere* 2003).

2 Patrick Taylor, 'A New Power in the Streets', *The New York Times*, 2 February, 2003.

3 By 'inverted totalitarianism' Wolin is describing the integration of corporate capitalism with political power to promote 'generalized fear'. He considers it inverted because of its reliance upon promoting 'a sense of weakness and collective futility' amongst people in comparison to the Nazi regime, which he argues, was dependent upon a sense of collective power and strength.

4 The concept of a digital commons is closely associated with the free software movement, however it is used here in a broader sense to include the patterns of information/knowledge exchange within activist milieu that are mediated by digital technologies.

5 This is a description proffered to the author by a Dutch activist from People's Global Action.

6 Shadow realm: beyond resistance to global nexus

1 Shiller (2000) describes how, in 1996, a seemingly innocuous question by the Chairman of the Federal Reserve Alan Greenspan in a dinner speech: 'how do we know when irrational exuberance has unduly escalated asset values, which then become subject to unexpected and prolonged contractions as they have in Japan over the past decade?' was sufficient to knock 3% off the Tokyo stock market, 4% off the London stock market and 2% off the US stock market. The question referred to the impact of the emotional and 'irrational' characteristics of asset markets, which subsequently became a self-fulfilling prophecy given that it would seem to make little sense for markets to react globally to a question in the middle of a dinner speech.

2 See Elliot, L. and White, M. 'Brown's Marshall Plan for World Poor', *The Guardian*, 7 January 2005.

3 http://www.cetri.be/

4 Porto Alegre is a stronghold of the Brazilian Worker's Party (Partido dos Trabalhadores) and achieved renown through its implementation of participatory community budgeting.

5 By periphery we do not necessarily mean outside the event. 'Life After Capitalism' organised by Z-Magazine during the 2003 WSF was wholly within the organised process, as a forum within a forum. Yet due to perceptions of its

critical standpoint relative to the WSF and the machinations of administrative and political processes it became a 'marginal' space on the peripheries, both figurative and geographical of the forum.

6 The peasant forum at the Mumbai WSF was partially initiated by the Indian KRRS, one of the originators of PGA.

7 Peripheral in the geographical sense of existing at the edges, rather than as peripheral to the substantive debates of the forum or the impossibility of describing a periphery within a 'n' dimensional state space such as GCS.

8 See in particular the Choike portal – www.choike.org

9 Members of the IC of the WSF proposed the 'Porto Alegre Consensus' at the end of the 5 WSF in 2005, a statement of proposals and demands that amounts to a 'synthesis of what the WSF is proposing globally'. However, this statement was also roundly critiqued by other members of the IC including the Brazilian committee member Cândido Grzybowski who argued that 'What kills this proposal is the method with which it was created and presented. It goes against the very spirit of the Forum. Here, all proposals are equally important and not only that of a group of intellectuals, even when they are very significant persons' (Choike Portal: http://www.choike.org/nuevo_eng/informes/2622.html).

10 In Latin America this includes the PT (Partido dos Trabalhadores) and the Movement of the Fifth Republic in Venezuela. In Europe, this would include the Ligue Communiste Révolutionnaire in France, Rifondazione Communista in Italy and the Socialist Workers Party in Britain.

7 The death of collective identity? Global movement as a parallelogram of forces

1 The public relations use of this strategy is evidenced by the US suggestion that the anti-debt campaigner and rock star Bono be made Head of the World Bank, see Borger, J. 'Bono's Next No 1 Might be at World Bank' *The Guardian*, 7 March 2005. This appears to have been part of a PR 'spin' to pre-empt/distract from the appointment of a key US neo-conservative – Paul Wolfowitz – to this post as US Defence Secretary Wolfowitz was one of the architects of the war against Iraq in 2003.

2 There are similarities here to Castells' (1997: 8) identification of 'project identities' in the 'network society', which he defines as coming into being when 'social actors, on the basis of whichever cultural materials are available to them, build a new identity that redefines their position in society and, by doing so, seek the transformation of overall social structure.'

3 This is an inversion of Hannah Arendt's (1958) claim that Marxist conceptions of social change have been predicated upon forms of social organisation that rely upon the concept of work, as synonymous with a process of making a product. Thus, Arendt (1958) claimed that notions of political activity came to be seen as having a 'product' – history, the state, the party and so forth.

4 This leads Lash to ask the rhetorical question 'just how much freedom from the "necessity of structure" and structural poverty does (a) ghetto mother have to self-construct her own "life narratives"?' (1995: 120).

5 A similar analysis has emerged in the work of Arquilla and Rondfelt (1993, 1996a,b) who have been working for the RAND Corporation on theorising the strategic implications for the US government, of what they have termed 'social netwar' – the capacity of civil society to mobilise solidarity networks, to take collective action and to facilitate their organisation through communications technology.

6 Rhythms of Resistance is the name of a international collective of musicians and dancers that play during anti-capitalist protests – www.RhythmsofResistance. co.uk. Frequently referred to as a 'Samba Band' their roots are 'closer to the

Afro Bloc parading drum bands that emerged in the mid 70s in Salvadore, Bahia in Brazil'. The outcome of such rhythmic interventions is to introduce an affective and ambiguous dimension to the space of protest, which marks the becoming-Carnivalesque of that space. The use of musical metaphors – 'ritornellos', 'refrains' etc. as a means of illustrating the complex and dynamical interplay between action, agency, affect and sensation is prominent in Deleuze (1994) and Deleuze and Guattari (2002). See also Buchanan and Swiboda (2004).

8 The map is not the territory

1 http://www.situaciones.org/
2 The use of direct action by 'fuel protestors' in the United Kingdom in 2000 revolved centrally around the price of fuel suggesting that such consumer sensibilities persist and are significantly enabled by modern communication techniques.
3 Public responses to GMO food crops throughout Europe and the developing world have been significantly influenced by concerns over food safety, environmental impacts and maintaining established property right systems.
4 The Chartists use of direct action in pursuit of more representative democratic institutions and structures is a good example of an insurrection which is subsequently re-appropriated as the origin of true democracy featuring prominently in Newport's bid for city status more than a hundred years after the 'last rising' (Jones 1999).
5 Corporate sensitivity to the uptake of genetically modified (GM) crops illustrates this point. According to an academic biotech researcher in Iowa 'I think that what we need to watch very very closely is what the consumer continually communicates around the world. The consumer is King...we have elevated the consumer to a high pedestal. The consumer doesn't have to be right. The consumer doesn't have to be knowledgeable. The consumer makes a choice and we do what the consumer wants...Consumers are aware that the greatest change is occurring in the history – probably – of the human family on the globe in their foodstuffs and no processor no seller of food products wants to ever be caught selling something the consumer does not want' (BBC Radio 4, Seeds of Trouble, Pt II, 14.01.03).
6 http://multitudes.samizdat.net/auteur.php3?id_auteur=796
7 http://www.theminnesotareview.org/ns61/hardt.htm
8 'Since great collective means must be mobilized for this mutation, the telos must be configured as a collective telos. It has to become real as a site of encounter among subjects and a mechanism of the constitution of the multitude' (Hardt and Negri, 2000: 405). We are not alone in making this observation, Sylvere Lotringer in the preface to Virno's 'Grammar of the Multitude' suggests that for Hardt and Negri: 'The telos...precedes the multitude, and for the most part replaces it' (Virno 2004:15).
9 Continues from the interview at: http://www.theminnesotareview.org/ns61/hardt.htm

Bibliography

Albert, M. (2001) 'What Are We For?' *Znet*, Online. Available: <http://www.globalpolicy.org/globaliz/econ/2001/0906gbz.htm> (accessed 10 January 2005).

Alvarez, S. (2000) 'Translating the Global: Effects of Transnational Organizing on Latin American Feminist Discourses and Practices' *Meridians: A Journal of Feminisms, Race, Transnationalism*, 1, 1: 29–67.

Alvarez, S.E., Dagnino, E. and Escobar, A. (eds) (1998) *Cultures of Politics, Politics of Cultures: Re-visioning Latin American Social Movements*, Boulder: Westview Press.

Anderson, B. (1989) *Imagined Communities*, London: Verso.

Andrle, V. (2003) 'Czech Dissidents: A Classically Modern Community', in Humphrey, R., Miller, R. and Zdravomyslova, E. (eds) *Biographical Research in Eastern Europe: Altered Lives and Broken Biographies*, London: Ashgate.

Appadurai, A. (1990) 'Disjuncture and Difference in the Global Cultural Economy', *Public Culture*, 2, 2: 1–23.

Appiah, K.A. (1992) *In My Father's House*, Oxford: Oxford University Press.

Arato, A. (1995) 'Ascensão, Declínio e Reconstrução do Conceito de Sociedade Civil: Orientações para Novas Pesquisas' *Revista Brasileira de Ciências Sociais*, 10, 27: 18–27.

Arendt, H. (1958) *The Human Condition*, Chicago, IL: University of Chicago Press.

Arquilla, J. and Ronfeldt, D. (1993) 'Cyberwar Is Coming!', *Comparative Strategy*, 12, 2: 141–165.

Arquilla, J. and Ronfeldt, D. (1996a) 'Information, Power, and Grand Strategy: In Athena's Camp,' in Schwartzstein, S. (ed.) *The Information Revolution and National Security: Dimensions and Directions*, Washington, DC: Center for International and Strategic Studies.

Arquilla, J. and Ronfeldt, D. (1996b) *The Advent of Netwar*, Santa Monica, CA: RAND.

Atton, C. (2002) *Alternative Media*, London: Sage.

Bak, P. and Chen, K. (1991) 'Self-Organized Criticality', *Scientific American*, 264: 46–53.

Baker, S. and Welsh I. (2000) 'Differentiating Western Influences on Transition Societies in Eastern Europe: A Preliminary Exploration', *Journal of European Area Studies*, 8, 1: 79–103.

Barabasi, A.-L. (2002) *Linked: The New Science of Networks*, Cambridge, MA: Perseus.

Barabasi, A.-L. and Albert, R. (1999) 'Emergence of Scaling in Random Networks', *Science*, 286: 509–512.

Barker, C., Johnson, A. and Lavalette, M. (2001) *Leadership and Social Movements*, Manchester, NH: Manchester University Press.

Bateson, G. (1973) *Steps to an Ecology of Mind*, London: Paladin.

Bauman, Z. (1993) *Post-Modern Ethics*, Oxford: Blackwell.

Bauman, Z. (1995) *Life in Fragments: Essays in Post-modern Morality*, Cambridge, Oxford University Press.

Bauman, Z. (2000) *Liquid Modernity*, Cambridge: Polity Press.

Beck, U. (1992) *Risk Society*, London: Sage.

Beck, U., Giddens, A. and Lash, S. (1994) *Reflexive Modernization: Politics, Tradition and Aesthetics in the Modern Social Order*, Cambridge: Polity Press.

Bell, D. (1973) *The Coming of Post-Industrial Society*, New York: Basic Books.

Benhabib, S. (ed.) (1996) *Democracy and Difference*, Princeton, NJ: Princeton University Press.

Benjamin, M. (2000) 'The Debate Over Tactics' in Dannaher, K. and Burbach, R. *Globalize This!*, Monroe, Maine: Common Courage Press.

Berg, J.C. (ed.) (2002) *Teamsters and Turtles: U.S. Progressive Political Movements in the 21st Century*, Boulder, CO: Rowman and Littlefield.

Bogue, R. (2004) *Deleuze's Wake: Tributes and Tributaries*, New York: State University of New York Press.

Bohman J. and Rehg, W. (eds) (1997) *Deliberative Democracy: Essays on Reason and Politics*, Cambridge, MA: MIT Press.

Bonta, M. and Protevi, J. (2004) *Deleuze and Geophilosophy*, Edinburgh: Edinburgh University Press.

Bouchard, D.F. (ed.) (1977) *Language Counter-memory and Practice: Selected Essays and Interviews by Michel Foucault*, Ithaca, NY: Cornell University Press.

Bowring, F. (2003) *Science, Seeds and Cyborgs: Biotechnology and the Appropriation of Life*, London: Verso.

Brecher, J., Costello, T. and Smith, B. (2000) *Globalization From Below*, Cambridge, MA: South End Press.

Bruce, I. (ed.) (2004) *The Porto Alegre Alternative: Direct Democracy in Action*, London: Pluto Press.

Buchanan, I. and Swiboda, M. (2004) *Deleuze and Music*, Edinburgh: Edinburgh University Press.

Buchanan, M. (2002) *Small World: Uncovering Nature's Hidden Networks*, London: Wedenfeld Nicholson.

Burawoy, M. (ed.) (2000) *Global Ethnography: Forces, Connections and Imaginations in a Postmodern World*, Berkeley, CA: University of California Press.

Butler, J. and Scott, J. (eds) (1992) *Feminists Theorize the Political*, New York: Routledge.

Byrne, D. (1998) *Complexity Theory and the Social Sciences: An Introduction*, London: Routledge.

Callinicos, A. (2003) *Regroupment, Realignment and the Revolutionary Left*, Online. Available: <http://www.istendency.net/pdf/Regroupment.pdf> (accessed 1 August 2004).

Camatte, J. (1973) *Against Domestication* (pamphlet), Ontario: Falling Sky Books.

Castells, M. (1996) *The Rise of the Network Society, Vol. 1, The Information Age: Economy, Society and Culture*, Oxford: Blackwell.

Castells, M. (1997) *The Power of Identity, Vol. 2, The Information Age: Economy, Society and Culture*, Oxford: Blackwell.

Castells, M. (2000) 'Information Technology and Global Capitalism,' in Hutton, W. and Giddens, A. (eds) *Global Capitalism*, New York: The New Press, pp. 52–74.

Chesters, G. (1999) 'Resist to Exist? Radical Environmentalism at the End of the Millennium', *ECOS*, 20, 2: 19–25.

Chesters, G. (2000) 'The New Intemperance: Protest, Imagination and Carnival', *ECOS* 21, 1: 2–9.

Chesters, G. (2003a) 'Shapeshifting: Civil Society, Complexity and Social Movements', *Anarchist Studies* 11, 1: 42–65.

Chesters, G. (2003b) 'New Modes of Struggle in the Alternative Globalization Movement', in Johns, S. and Thompson, S. (eds), *New Activism and The Corporate Response*, London: Palgrave, pp. 227–239.

Chesters, G. (2004a) 'Complexity Theory', in Ritzer, G. (ed.) *Encyclopedia of Social Theory*, London: Sage, pp. 125–127.

Chesters, G. (2004b) 'Global Complexity and Global Civil Society', *Voluntas: The International Journal of Voluntary and Non-Profit Organizations*, 15, 4: 323–342.

Chesters, G. and Welsh, I. (2002) 'Reflexive Framing: An Ecology of Action' *Research Committee 24: Globalization and the Environment*, XV World Congress of Sociology, July 6–13, at the University of Brisbane, Queensland, Australia. Online. Available: <http://www.shiftingground.freeuk.com/isapaper.htm> (accessed 15 June 2005).

Chesters, G. and Welsh I. (2004) 'Rebel colours: "Framing" in Global Social Movements', *Sociological Review*, 53, 3: 314–335.

Chesters, G. and Welsh, I. (2005) 'Complexity and Social Movement: Process and Emergence in Planetary Action Systems', *Theory, Culture and Society* 22, 5: 187–212.

Cilliers, P. (1998) *Complexity and Postmodernism*, London: Routledge.

Clark, I. (2003) 'Legitimacy in a Global Order', *Review of International Studies* 29 (Special Supplement 1): 75–95.

Cleaver, H. (1998) 'The Zapatistas and the Electronic Fabric of Struggle', in Holloway, J. and Pelaez, E. (eds) *Zapatista! Reinventing Revolution in Mexico*, London: Pluto Press, pp. 81–103.

Cockburn, A., St Clair, J. and Sekula, A. (2000) *5 Days That Shook the World*, London: Verso.

Cohen, S. (1972) *Folk Devils and Moral Panics: The Creation of the Mods and Rockers*, Oxford: Martin Robertson.

Cottle, S. (1999) 'TV News, Lay Voices and the Visualisation of Environmental Risks' in Allan, S., Adam, B. and Carter, C. (eds) *Environmental Risks and the Media*. London: Routledge.

Crosland, C.A.R. (1974) *Socialism Now*, London: Jonathan Cape.

Dannaher, K. and Burbach, R. (eds) (2000) *Globalize This!*, Maine: Common Courage Press.

Delanda, M. (1997) *A Thousand Years of Nonlinear History*, New York: Swerve.

Delanda, M. (2002) *Intensive Science and Virtual Philosophy*, London: Continuum.

Deleuze, G. (1992) 'Postscript on the Societies of Control' *October*, 59: 3–7. Online. Available: <http://www.n5m.org/n5m2/media/texts/deleuze.htm> (accessed 7 February 2005).

Deleuze, G. (1994) *Difference and Repetition*, New York: Columbia University Press.

Deleuze, G. (1995) *Negotiations*, New York: Columbia University Press.

Deleuze, G. and Guattari, F. (2002) *A Thousand Plateaus*, 4th edn, London: Continuum.

Deleuze, G. and Parnet, C. (2002) *Dialogues II*, 2nd edn, London: Athlone.

De Sousa Santos, B. (2003) 'The World Social Forum Towards a Counter Hegemonic Globalization' Presented at the XXIV International Congress of the Latin American Studies Association, Dallas, 27–27 March. Online. Available: <http://www.duke.edu/%7Ewmignolo/publications/pubboa.html> (accessed 25 March 2005).

Diani, M. (1992) 'The Concept of Social Movement', *Sociological Review*, 40, 1: 1–25.

Diani, M. (2000) 'The Relational Deficit of Ideologically Structured Action', *Moblization*, 5, 1: 17–24.

Diani, M. and Della Porta, D. (1998) *Social Movements: An Introduction*, Blackwell: Oxford.

Doherty, B. (2002) *Ideas and Actions in the Green Movement*, London: Routledge.

Dolgof, S. (1972) *Bakunin on Anarchy*, New York: Random House.

Donson, F. (2000) *Legal Intimidation*, London: Free Association Books.

Donson, F., Chesters, G., Tickle, A. and Welsh, I. (2004) 'Rebels with a Cause, Folk Devils without a Panic: Press Jingoism, Policing Tactics and Anti-Capitalist Protest in London and Prague', *Internet Journal of Criminology*, Online. Available: <http://www.internetjournalofcriminology.com/Donson%20et%20al%20-%20Folkdevils.pdf> (accessed 25 October 2005).

Dryzek, J. (1990) *Discursive Democracy: Politics, Policy and Political Science*, Cambridge: Cambridge University Press.

Dunleavy, P., Margetts, H. and Weir, S. (2001) 'Worst Ever Turnout', *The Guardian*, 12 June 2001.

Dwyer, P. and Seddon, D (2002) 'The New Wave? A Global Perspective on Popular Protest', Paper presented at the 8th International Conference on Alternative Futures and Popular Protest, 2 April–4 2002, Manchester Metropolitan University.

Eco, U. (1986) *Faith in Fakes*, London: Secker & Warburg.

Edelman, M. (1971) *Politics as Symbolic Action: Mass Arousal and Quiescence*, Chicago, IL: Markham.

Edelman, M. (1997) *Political Language: Words that Succeed, Politics that Fail*, New York: Academic Press.

Edelman, M. (2001) 'Social movements: Changing Paradigms and Forms of Politics', *Annual Review of Anthropology*, 30: 285–317.

Elster, J. (ed.) (1998) *Deliberative Democracy*, Cambridge: Cambridge University Press.

Elster, J. (1998) 'Emotions and Economic Theory', *Journal of Economic Literature*, 36, 1: 47–74.

Elster, J., Offe, C. and Preuss, U.K. (1998) *Institutional Design in Post-communist Societies: Rebuilding the Ship at Sea*, Cambridge: Cambridge University Press.

Enloe, C. (1989) *Bananas, Beaches & Bases: Making Feminist Sense of International Politics*, Berkley, CA: University of California Press.

Eschle, C. and Stammers, N. (2004) 'Taking Part: Social Movements, INGOs and Global Change', *Alternatives* 29, 3: 333–372.

Etzioni, A. (1993) *The Spirit of Community: Rights, Responsibilities and the Communitarian Agenda*, New York: Crown.

Eve, R.A., Horsfall, S. and Lee, M.E. (1997) *Chaos, Complexity & Sociology: Myths, Models and Theories*, London: Sage.

Fagin, A. (1999) 'The Development of Civil Society in the Czech Republic: The Environmental Sector as a Measure of Associational Activity', *Journal Of European Area Studies*, 7, 1: 91–108.

Fairclough, N. (2000) *New Labour, New Language?*, London: Routledge.

Farrer, L. (2004) 'World Forum Movement: Abandon or Contaminate' in Sen, J., Anand, A., Escobar, E. and Waterman, P. (eds) *World Social Forum: Challenging Empires*, New Delhi: The Viveka Foundation.

Featherstone, M. (1991) *Consumer Culture and Postmodernism*, London: Sage.

Fischer, K. (1997) 'Locating Frames in the Discursive Universe', *Sociological Research on Line*, 3,3. Online. Available: <http://www.socresonline.org.uk/socresonline/2/3/4/.html> (accessed 15 June 2005).

Fisher, W.F. and Ponniah, T. (eds) (2003) *Another World Is Possible: Popular Alternatives to Globalization at the World Social Forum*, London: Zed.

Foster, J. (2001) 'Knowing ourselves: A brief history of emerging global civil society', presented to the 4th *CIVICUS* World Assembly, August, Vancouver, B.C., Canada.

Foucault, M. (1975) *Birth of the Clinic*, London: Tavistock.

Foucault, M. (1977a) *Discipline and Punish*, London: Penguin.

Foucault, M. (1977b) *Language, Counter-memory and Practice*: Selected Essays and Interviews, edited by Bouchard, D.F., Ithaca, NY: Cornell University Press.

Foucault, M. (1979) *The History of Sexuality*, London: Penguin.

Foweraker, N. (1995) *Theorizing Social Movements*, London: Pluto.

Fox-Piven, F. (1979) *Poor Peoples' Movements: Why they succeed, How they fail*, New York: Random House.

Freeman, J. (1970). *Tyranny of Structurelessness*, Online. Available: <http://flag.blackened.net/revolt/hist_texts/structurelessness.html> (accessed 14 June 2005).

Freidman, T. (1999) *The Lexus and the Olive Tree*, New York: Farrar, Straus and Giroux.

Fukyama, F. (1989) 'The End of History?', *The National Interest* (summer) 16, 3–18.

Fukuyama, F. (1992) *The End of History and the Last Man*, New York: The Free Press.

Functowicz, S. and Ravetz, J. (1994) 'Emergent Complex Systems', *Futures*, 26, 6: 568–582.

Gamson, W.A. (1995) 'Constructing Social Protest' in Johnston, H. and Klandermans, B. (eds) *Social Movements and Culture*, London: UCL Press.

Giddens, A. (1987) *The Nation State and Violence*, Oxford: Polity.

Giddens, A. (1990) *The Consequences of Modernity*, Oxford: Polity.

Giddens, A. (1991) *Modernity and Self Identity*, Oxford: Polity.

Gillham, P.F. and Marx, G.T. (2003) 'Irony in Protest and Policing: The World Trade Organisation in Seattle', in Opel, A. and Pompper, D. (eds) *Representing Resistance: Media, Civil Disobedience and the Global Justice Movement*, New York: Prager.

Goffman, E. (1974/1986) *Frame Analysis: An Essay on the Organization of Experience*, Boston: Northeastern Press.

Goode, E. and Ben-Yehuda, N. (1994) *Moral Panics: The Social Construction of Deviance*, Oxford: Blackwell

Gorz, A. (1999) *Reclaiming Work: Beyond the Wage-Based Society*, Oxford: Polity.

Gould, P.C. (1988) *Early Green Politics: Back to Nature, Back to the Land, and Socialism in Britain 1880–1900*, Brighton: Harvester.

Graeber, D. (2002) 'The New Anarchists' *New Left Review*, 13: 61–73.

Gramsci, A. (1976) *Selections from the Prison Notebooks*, London: Lawrence & Wishart.

Granovetter, M.S. (1973) 'The Strength of Weak Ties' *American Journal of Sociology* 78, 6: 1360–1380.

Greenpeace (2001) *Breaking Down the Walls*, London: Greenpeace.

Grubacic, A. (2003) 'Life After Social Forums: New Radicalism and the Question of Attitudes Towards Social Forums' *Znet*. Online. Available: <http://www.zmag.org/content/showarticle.cfm?SectionID=41&ItemID=3010> (accessed 25 October 2005).

Guattari, F. (1995) *Chaosmosis: An Ethico-Aesthetic Paradigm*, Bloomington and Indianapolis, IN: Indiana University Press.

Guattari, F. (2000) *The Three Ecologies*, London: Athlone Press.

Habermas, J. (1976) *Legitimation Crisis*, London: Heinemann.

Habermas, J. (1985) 'Civil Disobedience: The Litmus Test for the Democratic Constitutional State', *Berkeley Journal of Sociology* 30: 95–116.

Habermas, J. (1990) *Moral Consciousness and Communicative Action*, Cambridge, Mass: MIT Press.

Habermas, J. (2003) *The Future of Human Nature*, Oxford: Polity.

Halivais, A. (2000) 'National Borders on the World Wide Web', *New Media and Society*, 2, 1: 7–28.

Hall, S. (1980) 'Encoding/Decoding', in Halls S., Hobson, D. Lowe A. and Willis P. (eds) *Culture, Media Language*, London: Hutchinson.

Halliday, F. (1998) 'Morality in International Affairs: a Case for Robust Universalism', in B. McSweeney (ed.) *Moral Issues in International Affairs: Problems of European Integration*, London: MacMillan Press.

Haraway, D. (1989) *Primate Visions*, New York: Routledge.

Haraway, D. (1999) 'A Cyborg Manifesto: Science Technology and Socialist Feminism in the Late Twentieth Century', in Hopkins, P.D. (ed.) *Sex/Machine: Readings in Culture, Gender and Technology*, Bloomington, IN: Indiana University Press.

Hardt-Landsberg, M. (2000) 'After Seattle: Strategic Thinking About Movement Building', *Monthly Review*, 52, 3: 103–126.

Hardt, M. (1995) 'The Withering of Civil Society', *Social Text*, 45: 27–44.

Hardt, M. (2002) 'Today's Bandung?,' *New Left Review*, 14: 112–118.

Hardt, M. and Negri, A. (2000) *Empire*, Cambridge, MA: Harvard University Press.

Hardt, M. and Negri, A. (2003) 'Forward', in Fisher, W.F. and Ponniah, T. (eds) *Another World Is Possible: Popular Alternatives to Globalization at the World Social Forum*, London: Zed, pp. xvi–xix.

Hardt, M. and Negri, A. (2004) *Multitude: War and Democracy in the Age of Empire*, New York: Penguin.

Hardy, D. (1979) *Nineteenth Century Alternative Communes*, Harlow: Longman.

Harvey, D. (1996) *Justice, Nature and the Geography of Distance*, Blackwell: Oxford.

Havel, V. (1989) *Living in Truth*, London: Faber & Faber.

Havel, V. (1990) *Disturbing the Peace*, London: Faber & Faber.

Hecht, S. (1989) 'Chico Mendes: Chronicle of a Death Foretold', *New Left Review*, 173: 47–55.

Held, D. (ed.) (2000) *A Globalizing World?* London: Routledge.

Held, D. and McGrew, A. (eds) (2000) *The Global Transformations Reader*, Cambridge: Polity Press.

Hetherington, K. (1998) *Expressions of Identity: Space, Performance, Politics*, London: Sage.

Holloway, J. (2002) *Change the World Without Taking Power*, London: Pluto Press.

Holloway, J. and Pelaez, E. (1998) (eds) *Zapatista! Reinventing Revolution in Mexico*, London: Pluto Press.

Holy, L. (1996) *The Little Czech and the Great Czech Nation: National Identity and the post-communist Trausformation Society*, Cambridge: Cambridge University Press.

Hooks, B. (1981) *Ain't I a Woman*, Boston, MA: South End Press.

Hopkins, N. Kelso, P., Wilson, J. and Vasagar, J. (2002) 'Peace in Paris, Skirmishes on the Streets of London', *The Guardian*, 2 May 2002, p. 1.

Houtart, F. and Polet, F. (eds) (2001) *The Other Davos: The Globalization of Resistance to the World Economic System*, London: Zed.

Humphrey, R., Miller, R. and Zdravomyslova, E. (2003) *Biographical Research in Eastern Europe: Altered lives and broken biographies*, Aldershot: Ashgate.

Hutton, W. (2002) *The World We're In*, London: Little Brown.

Hutton, W. and Giddens, A. (eds.) (2000) *Global Capitalism*, New York: The New Press.

Inoguchi, T., Keane, J. and Newman, E. (1998) *The Changing Nature of Democracy*, Tokyo: United Nations University Press.

Jappe, A. (1999) *Guy Debord* 3rd edn., Berkeley and Los Angeles, CA: University of California Press.

Jervis, R. (1997) *System Effects: Complexity in Political and Social Life*, Princeton, NJ: Princeton University Press.

Jones, D.V.J. (1999) *The Last Rising: The Newport Chartist Insurrection of 1839*, Cardiff: University Of Wales Press.

Jordan, G. and Weedon, C. (1995) *Cultural Politics, Class Gender, Race and the Postmodern World*, London: Blackwell.

Jordan, J. (1998) 'The Art of Necessity: The Subversive Imagination of Anti-road Protest and Reclaim the Streets', in McKay, G. (ed.) *DIY Culture: Parties and Protest in Nineties Britain*, London: Verso.

Jordan, J. and Whitney, D. (2002) *Que Se Vayan Todos: Argentina's Popular Rebellion. An eyewitness account of the financial meltdown and ongoing grassroots rebellion*, London: Notes from Nowhere, Online. Available: <http: www. chiapasnews.ukgateway.net> (accessed 14 June 2005).

Jowers, P. (1994) 'Towards the Politics of the "Lesser Evil": Jean-Francois Lyotard's Reworking of the Kantian Sublime', in Weeks, J. (ed.) *The Lesser Evil and the Greater Good*, London: Rivers Oram.

Kaldor, M. (2003) *Global Civil Society: An Answer to War?*, London: Polity Press.

Karatani, K. (2003) *Transcritique. On Kant and Marx*, Cambridge MA: Harvard University Press.

Katsiaficas, G. (1997) *European Autonomous Social Movements and the Decolonization of Everyday Life*, New Jersey: Humanities Press International.

Keane, J. (2003) *Global Civil Society?*, Cambridge: Cambridge University Press.

Kenney, P. (2002) *A Carnival of Revolution*, Oxford and Princeton, NJ: Princeton University Press.

Kettle, M. (2004) 'A whole new class of victim', *The Guardian*, 10.08.04.

Klein, K. (2003) 'More Democracy – Not More Political Strongmen', *Znet*. Online. Available: <http://www.zmag.org/content/showarticle.cfm?SectionID=41& ItemID=2946>

Klein, N. (2000) *No Logo*, London: Flamingo.

Kuhn, T. (1962/1996) *The Structure of Scientific Revolutions*, London: University of Chicago Press.

Lacan, J. (1979) *The Four Fundamental Concepts of Psychoanalysis*, Harmondsworth: Peguin.

Lash, S. (1990) 'Learning from Leipzig', *Theory Culture and Society*, 7, 4: 145–158.

Lash, S. (1994) 'Reflexivity and its Doubles: Structure, Aesthetics, Community', in Beck, U., Giddens, A. and Lash, S. (eds) *Reflexive Modernization: Politics, Tradition and Aesthetics in the Modern Social Order*, Cambridge: Polity Press.

Lash, S. (2002) *Critique of Information*, London: Sage.
Lash, S. and Urry, J. (1987) *The End of Organised Capitalism*, Cambridge: Polity.
Lash, S. and Urry, J. (1994) *Economies of Signs and Space*, London: Sage.
Latour, B. (1996) *Aramis, or the Love of Technology*, Trans. Catherine Porter., Cambridge, MA and London: Harvard University Press.
Latour, B. (1999) *Pandora's Hope: Essays on the Reality of Science Studies*, Cambridge: Harvard University Press.
Latour, B. (2004) *Politics of Nature: How to Bring the Sciences into Democracy*, Cambridge: Harvard University Press.
Law, J. and Hassard, J. (1999) *Actor Network Theory and After*, Oxford: Blackwell and Sociological Review.
Lawson, G. (2005) *Negotiated Revolutions: The Czech Republic, South Africa & Chile*, Aldershot: Ashgate.
Levy, S. (1984) *Hackers: Heroes of the Computer Revolution*, New York: Dell.
Lewis, M. (2004) 'At the service of politicians', *The Guardian*, 04.08.04.
Lotringer, S. (2004) 'Foreward', in Virno, P. (ed.) *A Grammar of the Multitude*, New York/Los Angeles: Semiotext(e).
Lotringer, S. and Marazzi, M. (1980) *Italy: Autonomia: Post-Political Politics*, New York: Semiotext(e).
Lyotard, J.-F. (1983) *Le différend*, Paris: Editions de Minuit.
Lyotard, J.-F. (1988) *The Inhuman*, Oxford: Polity.
Lyotard, J.-F. (2004) *Libidinal Economy*, London: Continuum.
McAdam, D., McCarthy J.D. and Zald, M.N. (eds.) (1996) *Comparative Perspectives on Social Movements: Political Opportunities, Mobilizing Structures, and Cultural Framings*, Cambridge: Cambridge University Press.
McAdam, D., Tarrow, S. and Tilly, C. (2001) *Dynamics of Contention*, Cambridge: Cambridge University Press.
McCormack (1991) 'The Price of Influence: The Political Economy of Japanese Leisure', *New Left Review*, 188: 121–134.
McDonald, K. (2002) 'From Solidarity to Fluidity: Social Movements Beyond "Collective Identity" – The Case of Globalization Conflicts', *Social Movement Studies* 1, 2: 109–128.
McFadden, J. (2005) 'The unselfish gene', *The Guardian*, 6 May 2005, p. 25.
McKay, G. (1996) *Senseless Acts of Beauty: Cultures of Resistance since the Sixties*, London: Verso.
McKay G. (1998) *DiY Culture: Party & Protest in Nineties Britain*, London: Verso.
McKechnie, R and Welsh, I. (2002) 'When the Global Meets the Local: Critical Reflections on Reflexive Modernisation' in Buttel, F., Dickens, P., Dunlap, R. and Gijswijt A. (eds) *Sociological Theory and the Environment: Classical Foundations, Contemporary Insights*, Boulder, CO: Rowan and Littlefield.
McRobbie, A. (1994) 'The Moral Panic in the Age of the Postmodern Mass Media', in McRobbie, A. (ed.) *Postmodernism and Popular Culture*, London: Routledge.
Maffesoli, M. (1996) *The Time of the Tribes*, London: Sage.
Marcos, Subcommandante (2001) *Our Word is Our Weapon*, New York: Seven Stories Press.
Martin, G. (2002) 'Conceptualizing Cultural Politics in Subcultural and Social Movement Studies', *Social Movement Studies*, 2, 1: 73–88.
Martinez, E.B. (2000) 'Where Was the Color in Seattle? Looking for Reasons Why the Great Battle was So White', *Monthly Review*, 52, 3: 141–148.

Massumi, B. (1992) *A User's Guide to Capitalism and Schizophrenia*, Cambridge, MA: MIT Press.

Massumi, B. (2002) *Parables for the Virtual: Movement, Affect, Sensation*, Durham, NC and London: Duke University Press.

Melucci, A. (1980) 'The New Social Movements: A Theoretical Approach', *Social Science Information*, 19, 2: 199–226.

Melucci, A. (1981) 'Ten Hypothesis for the Analysis of New Movements', in Pinto, D. (ed.) *Contemporary Italian Sociology*, New York: Cambridge University Press.

Melucci, A. (1985) 'The Symbolic Challenge of Contemporary Movements', *Social Research*, 52, 4: 789–816.

Melucci, A. (1989) *Nomads of the Present*, London: Radius Hutchinson.

Melucci, A. (1996a) *Challenging Codes: Collective Action in the Information Age*, Cambridge: Cambridge University Press.

Melucci, A (1996b) *The Playing Self: Person and Meaning in the Planetary Society*, Cambridge: Cambridge University Press.

Mendes, C. (1989/1992) *Fight for the Forest: Chico Mendes in his own words*, London: LAB.

Mertes, T. (ed.) (2004) *A Movement of Movements: Is Another World Really Possible*, London: Verso.

Middlemas, K. (1979) *Politics in Industrial Society*, London: Andre Deutch.

Mies, M. and Shiva, V. (1993) *Ecofeminism*, London: Routledge.

Mirrabelle Productions (2000) *Tactical Frivolity . . . protesting against the IMF and World Bank in Prague, 26 September 2000*, Video available via The Basement@ purpleturtle.com

Monbiot, G. (2004) *The Age of Consent*, London: Perennial.

Mueller, T. (2003) 'Empowering Anarchy: Power, Hegemony and Anarchist Strategy', *Anarchist Studies* 11, 2: 122–149.

Munck, R. (2004) 'Global Civil Society: Myths and Prospects', in Taylor, R. (ed.) *Creating a Better World: Interpreting Global Civil Society*, Bloomfield, CT: Kumarian Press, pp. 13–26.

Naess, Arne. (1973) 'The Shallow and the Deep, Long-Range Ecology Movements: A Summary,' *Inquiry* 16, 95–100.

Naess, A. (1989) *Ecology, Community and Lifestyle*, Cambridge: Cambridge University Press.

Neale, J. (2002) *You Are G8, We Are 6 Billion: The Truth Behind the Genoa Protests*, London: Vision.

Norberg, J. (2003) 'Why We Should Fight Anti-Globalists', *The Wall Street Journal Europe*, 27 October 2003.

Notes from Nowhere (eds) (2003) *We Are Everywhere: The Irresistible Rise of Global Anticapitalism*, London: Verso.

Obando-Rojas, B. Welsh, I. Bloor, M. Lane, T. Badigannavar and V Maguire, M. (2004) 'The Political Economy of Fraud in a Globalised Industry: The Case of Seafarers' Certifications', *Sociological Review*, 52, 3: 314–336.

Offe, C. (1985) 'New Social Movements: Changing Boundaries of the Political', *Social Research*, 52: 817–868.

O'Neill, J. (2001) 'Representing People, Representing Nature, Representing the World', *Environmental Planning C: Government and Policy* 19: 483–500.

O'Neill, J. (2002) 'Deliberative Democracy and Environmental Policy', in Minteer, B. and Pepperman-Taylor, B. (eds) *Democracy and the Claims of Nature*, Oxford: Rowman and Littlefield, pp. 257–275.

On Fire (2001) *On Fire: The battle of Genoa and the anti-capitalist movement*, Edinburgh: One-Off Press.

Orr, D.W. (1994). *Earth in mind: On Education, Environment, and the Human Prospect*, Washington, DC: Island Press.

Osterweil, M. (2004a) 'De-centring the Forum: Is Another Critique of the Forum Possible?', in Sen, J., Anand, A., Escobar, E. and Waterman, P. (eds) *World Social Forum: Challenging Empires*, New Delhi: The Viveka Foundation, pp. 183–190.

Osterweil, M. (2004b) 'A Cultural-Political Approach to Reinventing the Political', *International Social Science Journal*, 56, 182: 495–506.

Patton, P. (2000) *Deleuze and the Political*, London: Routledge.

Pearson, K.A. (1997) *Deleuze and Philosophy: the Difference Engineer*, London: Routledge.

Pfohl, S. (1992) *Death at the Parasite Café: Social Science Fiction and the Postmodern*, London: Macmillan.

Porter, A. (2001) 'It was like this before', in *On Fire*, Edinburgh: One-Off Press, 75–79.

Poulantzas, N. (1973) *Political Power and Social Classes*, London: Verso.

Protevi, J. (2001) *Political Physics*, London: Athlone Press.

Purdue, D.A. (2000) *Anti-GenetiX: The Emergence of the Anti-GM Movement*, London: Ashgate.

Purkis, J. and Bowen, J. (eds) (2004) *Changing Anarchism: Anarchist Theory & Praxis in a Global Age*, Manchester: Manchester University Press.

Puttnam, R. (1995) 'Bowling Alone: America's Declining Social Capital', *Journal of Democracy*, 1, 1: 65–78.

Rajchenburg, E. and Héau-Lambert, C. (1998) 'History and Symbolism in the Zapatista Movement', in Holloway, J. and Peleáz, E. (eds) *Zapatista: Reinventing Revolution in Mexico*, London: Pluto Press.

Revkin, A. (1990) *The Burning Season: The Murder of Chico Mendes and the Fight for the Amazon Rain Forest*, London: Island Press.

Roberts, J.M. (2003) *The Aesthetics of Free Speech: Rethinking the Public Sphere*, Basingstoke: Palgrave.

Rootes, C. (1992) 'The New Politics and the New Social Movements: Accounting for British Exceptionalism', *European Journal of Political Research*, 22, 171–191.

Roseneil, S. (1995) *Disarming Patriarchy: Feminism and Political Action at Greenham*, Buckingham: Open University Press.

Routledge, P. (2004) 'Convergence of Commons: Process Geographies of People's Global Action', *The Commoner*, 8. Online. Available: <http://www.commoner.org.uk/previous_issues.htm#n8> (accessed 15 June 2005).

Rutherford, J. (ed.) (1990) *Identity, Community, Culture, Difference*, London: Lawrence and Wishart.

St Clair, J. (1999) 'Seattle Diary: It's a Gas, Gas, Gas', *New Left Review*, 238: 81–96.

Scholte, J.A. (1999) *Global Civil Society: Changing the World?* Warwick: University of Warwick Centre for the Study of Globalisation and Regionalisation (CSGR).

Scholte, J.A., Schnabel, A. and Crockett, A. (eds) (2002) *Civil Society and Global Finance*, London: Routledge.

Schöpflin, G. (1993) *Politics in Eastern Europe*, Oxford: Blackwell.

Sen, J. (2003) 'The WSF as logo, the WSF as commons: Take a moment to reflect on what is happening in the World Social Forum', *Choike*, Online.

Available: <http://www.choike.org/documentos/Jai_Sen_wsf2004_as_logo.pdf> (accessed 25 October 2005).

Sen, J., Anand, A., Escobar, E. and Waterman, P. (eds) (2004) *World Social Forum: Challenging Empires*, New Delhi: The Viveka Foundation.

Shabi, R. and Hooper, J. (2005) 'Now the Reckoning', *The Guardian*, 22 January 2005.

Shaw, M. (1996) *Civil Society and Media in Global Crises*, London: Continuum.

Shaw, M. (1999) 'Civil Society' in Kurtz, L. (ed.), *Encyclopaedia of Violence, Peace and Armed Conflict*, San Diego, CA: Academic Press, pp. 269–278.

Shiller, R. (2000) *Irrational Exhuberence*, Princeton, NJ: Princeton University Press.

Shiva, V. (1992) 'The Greening of Global Reach', *The Ecologist*, 22, 6, 358–359.

Shiva, V. (1999) 'Diversity and Democracy: Resisting the Global Economy', *Global Dialogue*, 1, 1: 19–30.

Simmel, G. (1955) *Conflict and the Web of Group Affiliations*, New York: Free Press.

Singer, D. (2000) '1968 Revisited: "Be Realistic, Ask for the Impossible" ', *New Politics*, VIII, 1: 133–140.

Singer, P. (1979) *Practical Ethics*, Cambridge: Cambridge University.

Situationist International (2003) *The Real Split in the International*, London: Pluto Press.

Snow, D. Rochford, B., Worden, S. and Benford, R. (1986) 'Frame Alignment processes Micromobilization and Movement Participation', *American Sociology Review*, 51: 464–481.

Solomon, W.S. (2000) 'More Form than Substance: Press Coverage of the WTO Protests in Seattle', *Monthly Review*, 52, 1: 12–20.

Stallings, R.A. (1973) 'Patterns of Belief in Social Movement', *Sociological Quarterly*, 14, 4: 165–180.

Starr, A. (2000) *Naming The Enemy: Anti-Corporate Movements Confront Globalization*, London: Zed Books.

Stebbing, S. (1937/1944) *Philosophy and the Pysicists*, Harmondsworth: Penguin.

Stephens, J. (1998) *Sixties Radicalism and Postmodernism*, Cambridge: Cambridge University Press.

Stiglitz, J. (2002) *Globalization and its Discontents*, New York: Norton.

Strange, S. (1996) *The Retreat of the State: The Diffusion of Power in the World Economy*, Cambridge: Cambridge University Press.

Sullivan, S. (2004) 'We are heartbroken and furious! Violence and the (anti-) globalisation movement(s).' *Working Paper 133/04*, Warwick: Warwick University Centre for the Study of Globalisation and Regionalisation.

Tabb, W.K. (2000) 'Turtles, Teamsters and Capital's Designs', *Monthly Review*, 52,3: 28–45.

Tarrow, S. (1998) *Power in Movement: Social Movements and Contentious Politics*, Cambridge: Cambridge University Press.

Tarrow, S. (2004) *The Dualities of Transnational Contention: 'Two Activist Solitudes' or a New World Altogether?* Online. Available: <http://falcon.arts.cornell.edu/sgt2/contention/documents/mobanniv.fnl.sept%207.pdf> (accessed 15 June 2005).

Taylor, R. (2004a) 'Interpreting Global Civil Society', in Taylor, R. (ed.) *Creating a Better World: Interpreting Global Civil Society*, Bloomfield, CT: Kumarian Press, pp. 1–12.

Taylor, R. (ed.) (2004b) *Creating a Better World: Interpreting Global Civil Society*, Bloomfield, CT: Kumarian Press.

Tesh, S.N. (2000) *Uncertain Hazards: Environmental Activists and Scientific Proof*, Ithaca, NY and London: Cornell University Press.

Thompson, E.P. (1978) *The Making of the English Working Class*, Harmondsworth: Penguin.
Thompson, J.B. (1995) *The Media and Modernity*, Oxford: Polity.
Thrift, N. (1999) 'The Place of Complexity', *Theory Culture and Society*, 16, 3: 31–69.
Tickle, A. and Welsh, I. (eds) (1998) *Environment and Society in Eastern Europe*, Harlow: Longman.
Tormey, S. (2004) *Anti-capitalism: A Beginners Guide*, Oxford: One World Press.
Touraine, A. (1981) *The Voice and the Eye*, Cambridge: Cambridge University Press.
Touraine, A. (1983) *Anti-nuclear Protest: the Opposition to Nuclear Energy in France*, Cambridge: Cambridge University Press.
Touraine, A. (1995) *Critique of Modernity*, Cambridge: Cambridge University Press.
Touraine, T. (1971) *The Post-Industrial Society*, London: Wildwood House.
Tronti, M. (1966) *Operai e Capitale* ('Workers and Capital'), Turin: Einaudi.
Turner, B.S. (2001) 'The Erosion of Citizenship', *British Journal of Sociology*, 52: 189–209.
Urry, J. (1981) *The Anatomy of Capitalist Societies*, London: Macmillan.
Urry, J. (2000) *Sociology Beyond Societies: Mobilities for the Twenty-First Century*, London: Routledge.
Urry, J. (2003) *Global Complexity*, London: Routledge.
Urry, J. (2004) 'Small Worlds and the New "Social Physics" ', *Global Networks*, 4, 2: 109–130.
Urry, J. and Wakeford, J. (eds) (1973) *Power in Britain*, Heinemann: London.
Vanderford, A. (2003) 'Ya Basta! A Mountain of Bodies that Advances, Seeking the Least Harm Possible to Itself', in Opel, A. and Pompper, D. (eds) *Representing Resistance: Media, Civil Disobedience and the Global Justice Movement*, New York: Prager.
Viano, M. and Binetti, V. (1996) 'What Is to Be Done? Marxism and Academia', in Makalisi, S. *et al.* (eds), *Marxism Beyond Marxism*, New York: Routledge.
Vidal J. and Branigan T. (2001) 'Backlash Against May Day Zero Tolerance', *The Guardian*, 30 April 2001.
Virno, P. (1996) 'Virtuosity and Revolution: The Political Theory of Exodus', in Virno, P. and Hardt, M. (eds) *Radical Thought in Italy: a Potential Politics*, Minneapolis, MN: University of Minnesota Press.
Virno, P. (2004) *A Grammar of the Multitude*, New York/Los Angeles: Semiotext(e).
Waddington, P.A.J. (1994) *Liberty and Order*, London: UCL Press.
Waddington, P.A.J. (1999) *Policing Citizens*, London: UCL Press.
Wahl-Jorgensen, K. (2003) 'Speaking Out Against the Incitement to Silence: The British Press and the 2001 May Day Protests', in Opel, A. and Pompper, D. (eds) *Representing Resistance: Media, Civil Disobedience and the Global Justice Movement*, New York: Prager.
Wainwright, H. (2003) *Reclaim The State: Adventures in Popular Democracy*, London: Verso.
Wall, D. (1994) *Green History: A Reader in Environmental History, Philosophy and Politics*, London: Routledge.
Wall, D. (1999) *Earth First! and the Anti-Roads Movement: Radical Environmentalism and Comparative Social Movements*, London: Routledge.
Wark, M. (2004) *Hacker Manifesto*, Cambridge, MA: Harvard University Press.
Waterman, P. (2003) *First Reflections on The 3rd World Social Forum*. Online. Available: <http://www.nadir.org/nadir/initiativ/agp/free/wsf/waterman_poa.htm>

Waters, S. (2004) 'Mobilising Against Globalisation: Attac and the French Intellectuals' *Western European Politics*, 27, 5: 854–874.

Watts, D.J. and Strogatz, S.H. (1998) 'Collective Dynamics of "Small World" Networks', *Nature* 393: 440–442.

Webster, A. (2002) 'The Environmental Lawyer', in Bennet, J. (ed.) *Facing The Future: Listening to the Past*, Upper Basildon: United Kingdom Environmental Law Association.

Welsh, I. (2000a) *Mobilising Modernity: the Nuclear Moment*, London: Routledge.

Welsh, I. (2000b) 'Desiring Risk: Nuclear Myths and the Social Selection of Risk', in Adam, B. Beck, U. and Vanloon, J. (eds) *The Risk Society and Beyond: Critical Issues for Social Theory*, London: Sage.

Welsh, I. (2001) 'Anti Nuclear Movements: Failed Projects or Heralds of a Direct Action Milieu? 'Sociological Research online, 6, 3, <http://www.socresonline.org. uk/6/3/welsh.html>

Welsh, I. (2002) 'Where do Movement Frames Come From? Insights from S26 and Global "Anti-capitalist" Mobilisations', in *Proceedings of the 8th Alternative Futures and Popular Protest Conference*, Vol. 2, April 2–4, Manchester, NH: Manchester Metropolitan University.

Welsh, I. (2004) 'Network Movement in the Czech Republic: Peturbating Prague', *Journal of European Area Studies*, 12, 3: 321–337.

Welsh, I. (2005) 'Values, Science and the EU: Bio-technology & Transatlantic Relations', in Manners, I. and Lucarelli, S. (eds) *Peace and War: Values and Principles in EU Foreign Policy*, London: Routledge.

Welsh, I. and McLeish, P. (1996) 'The European Road to Nowhere: Anarchism and Direct Action against the UK Roads Programme', *Anarchist Studies*, 4, 1: 27–44.

Welsh, I. and Purkis, J. (2003) 'Redefining Anarchism for the Twenty-First Century: Some Modest Beginnings', *Anarchist Studies*, 11, 1: 5–12.

Welsh, I., Evans, R. and Plows A. (2005) 'Another Science for Another World?: Science and Genomics at the London European Social Forum', Cardiff School of Social Sciences, Working paper series, No. 70.

Wittel, A. (2001) 'Towards a Network Sociality', *Theory, Culture and Society* 18: 31–50.

Wolfe, A. (1989). *Whose Keeper?* Berkeley, CA: University of California Press.

Wolin, S. (2003) 'Inverted Totalitarianism', *The Nation*, 1 May 2003.

Wright, E. (2005) Generation Kill, London: Corgi.

Wright, S. (2002) *Storming Heaven: Class Composition and Struggle in Italian Autonomist Marxism*, London: Pluto Press.

Wynne, B. (1982) *Rationality & Ritual: The Windscale Inquiry and Nuclear Decisions in Britain*, Chalfont St. Giles: BSHS.

Wynne, B. (2005) 'Reflexing Complexity: Post-Genomics Knowledge and Reductionist Returns in Public Science', *Theory Culture & Society*, 22, 5: 67–94.

Yuen, E. Burton Rose, D. and Katsiaficas, G. (2001) *The Battle of Seattle: The New Challenge to Capitalist Globalization*, New York: Soft Skull Press.

Zald, M.N. (2000) 'Ideologically Structured Action: An Enlarged Agenda for Social Movement Research', *Moblization*, 5, 1: 1–16.

Zirakzadeh, C.E. (2000) 'Some Quotidian Meanings of "Frame" and "Framing" and Some Non-democratic Tendencies in Social Movement Theory', in *proceedings of the Alternative Futures and Popular Protest Conference*, April 25–27 2000, Manchester, NH: Metropolitan University.

Žižek, S. (2004) 'The Parallax View', *New Left Review*, 25: 121–134.

Index

Note: Page numbers in italics indicates figures.